The Collaborative Analysis of Student Learning

The Collaborative Analysis of Student Learning

*Professional Learning
that Promotes Success for All*

Amy Colton

Georgea Langer

Loretta Goff

*Foreword by
Delores B. Lindsey and Randall B. Lindsey*

A Joint Publication

FOR INFORMATION:

Corwin
A SAGE Company
2455 Teller Road
Thousand Oaks, California 91320
(800) 233-9936
www.corwin.com

SAGE Publications Ltd.
1 Oliver's Yard
55 City Road
London EC1Y 1SP
United Kingdom

SAGE Publications India Pvt. Ltd.
B 1/I 1 Mohan Cooperative Industrial Area
Mathura Road, New Delhi 110 044
India

SAGE Publications Asia-Pacific Pte. Ltd.
3 Church Street
#10-04 Samsung Hub
Singapore 049483

Acquisitions Editor: Dan Alpert
Associate Editor: Kimberly Greenberg
Editorial Assistant: Cesar Reyes
Production Editor: Amy Joy Schroller
Copy Editor: Allan Harper
Typesetter: C&M Digitals (P) Ltd.
Proofreader: Dennis W. Webb
Indexer: Judy Hunt
Cover Designer: Anupama Krishnan
Marketing Manager: Amy Vader

Printed in the United States of America

ISBN 978-1-4833-5817-8

This book is printed on acid-free paper.

15 16 17 18 19 10 9 8 7 6 5 4 3 2 1

Contents

Visit the companion website at
http://resources.corwin.com/Collaborativeanalysis
for additional resources.

Foreword

Delores B. Lindsey and
Randall B. Lindsey

This is a critically important book. This book is important for the manner in which the complexity of teaching and learning is intertwined with a refreshing straightforwardness in what is possible and achievable. The complexity tackled in this book is a generations-old struggle, namely, the education of all students in our diverse society. The major value of this book is the authors' approachable manner in which they straightforwardly pose three implicit and pivotal questions: *What* structures do we need to develop in order to effectively educate our students? *How* do we develop support systems for facilitating student learning? *Why* are my assumptions and deeply held habits of practice with regard to our students important to the development of trust with colleagues and basic to transformative changes that benefit our students?

As educators and authors, we, Delores and Randy, have been engaged in equity-based work for over four decades and have observed slow progress in schools shifting from deep-seated resistance to a burgeoning support for equitable educational practices. Active and passive resistance are still expressed in comments such as, *"Given the circumstances these students come from, we can't expect too much."* Or, *"They are doing the best they can for who they are."* The "circumstances" and "who they are" are too often focused on students' race, ethnicity, gender, or social class not being aligned with white middle-class norms and experiences. Increasingly we are witnessing educators and schools, albeit unevenly across the country and with pockets of deep antagonism, embracing the notion that all students can learn to high levels. When progress is evident, schools reject the cultural deficit model and regard students' cultures as assets on which to build their (and our) educational experiences.

In the educational history of the United States, systemic awareness of racial, ethnic, gender, and socioeconomic academic achievement gaps is a fairly modern concept. Reading and mathematics achievement gaps were first ushered onto the consciousness of educators with the initial National Assessment of Educational Progress (NAEP) report in 1971. That ground-breaking report documented the gender and racial achievement gap for 9, 13, and 17-year-old students in reading (Perie, Moran, & Lutkus, 2005). It was followed in 1973 by the NAEP report on mathematics that described gender and racial achievement gaps. NAEP has continued to issue reports every odd-numbered year since then and has provided the reports to school districts and related agencies across the United States. Unfortunately, those reports were rarely embraced or studied by mainstream educators and too often were remanded to those involved with Title I or school desegregation programs. President George W. Bush revealed the achievement gap to all educators and the general public with the signing of No Child Left Behind Act (NCLB) in 2002. What had been the province of equity advocates became public and set forth a veritable tsunami of finger pointing, ill-conceived accountability measures, and consternation among educators who were content to avoid equity issues. However, for equity advocates, NCLB provided a "silver lining" by removing systemic excuses of blaming students for their under-education, and rightfully, holding us, educators and our schools/districts, accountable for identifying and closing achievement gaps.

A myriad of programs and approaches to addressing "achievement gap issues" were rolled out by commercial enterprises and think tanks in response to NCLB and related state level actions. A common characteristic of most programs is that they provided educators with detailed processes for the *What* and *How* of educational reform and change. The downside of such efforts has been programs, strategies, and accountability movements that promote mechanistic, top-down approaches but do little to engage teachers and administrators in substantive dialogue about curriculum or pedagogy. Such approaches have rarely involved educators in understanding how student engagement is hindered or facilitated by uncovering the assumptions embedded in curriculum and instruction. In marked contrast, Colton and her colleagues contend that the professional learning of educators is a key ingredient to accessing and narrowing achievement disparities. In presenting professional learning as the central activity in their Framework: Teacher as Collaborative Inquirer, the value of *Why* is coupled with the *What* and *How* in fostering personal, professional, and institutional changes required in transforming assumptions about teaching, learning, and leading (Sinek, 2009). This approach is what sets this book apart from others.

This book demonstrates that the inquiry approach is important at two levels: (1) guiding educators to understand the manner in which their assumptions and beliefs about student cultures influence how they interact with students and (2) engaging educators with colleagues in ways to facilitate student learning. The Collaborative Analysis of Student Learning (CASL) engages educators, teachers, and administrators as co-learners. This book is a substantive rewrite and update of their successful 2003 ASCD publication. This new edition is recognition by these reflective authors that they, too, continue to learn. In doing so, this volume holds cultural diversity and the transformative power of educators as a central organizing theme in recognition that the question pivots away from asking *if* students can learn to asking what is it that we educators need to learn in order to be effective teachers and school leaders. In doing so, this becomes a critically important book. The authors provide a source of hope for today's educators. The hope is found in the authors' clearly defined framework. The Framework: Teacher as Collaborative Inquirer defines the knowledge, skills, and dispositions possessed by teachers who successfully pursue, discover, and apply responsive approaches for learning so that each and every student reaches standards of excellence. This approach translates hope into practice and reality for educators and the students they serve.

We close as we began this essay: this is a critically important book. The authors demonstrate that we have the capacity to learn what it takes to teach all students to higher levels than ever before.

Acknowledgments

We thank the hundreds of teachers and administrators who worked with us over many years to develop our understanding of teachers' professional learning, growth, and reflective practice. We especially acknowledge teachers and administrators from the following schools and districts for helping us refine the CASL professional learning design:

- Reading Apprenticeship Teachers, Washtenaw Intermediate School District, and Livingston Education Service Agency, Michigan
- Forest Hills Public Schools, Grand Rapids, Michigan
- Ann Arbor Public Schools, Ann Arbor, Michigan
- University Preparatory Academy, Detroit, Michigan
- All elementary and secondary schools, George County, Mississippi
- Rawsonville Elementary School, Van Buren Public Schools, Michigan
- Kettering Elementary School, Wayne-Westland School District, Michigan
- Kosciusko Middle School, Hamtramck School District, Michigan

Finally, many thanks to Jennifer Rosenberg for her valuable insights and inputs. We also wish to thank the Corwin staff for their guidance throughout the writing and publishing process, with special appreciation for Dan Alpert for believing in the power of CASL and inviting us to share what we have learned with other educators.

PUBLISHER'S ACKNOWLEDGMENTS

Corwin gratefully acknowledges the contributions of the following reviewers:

Gustava Cooper-Baker
Principal
Kansas City School District
Kansas City, MO

Barb Keating
Educational Consultant

Lois B. Easton
Consultant and Author, LBE Learning
Learning Forward
Oxford, OH

About the Authors

As executive director of Learning Forward Michigan and senior consultant for Learning Forward, **Amy Colton** works tirelessly with educators to build their capacity to design, facilitate, and evaluate quality professional learning so that all students are successful in school and in life. Amy's work is influenced by years as a special education teacher and district professional learning consultant. While serving as a teacher-in-residence of the National Board for Professional Teaching Standards, she played an active role in coordinating the development of the Board's first teaching certificates. Dr. Colton is best known for her professional learning designs that create learning communities and tasks that support professional and student learning for excellence with equity. She holds a doctorate in teacher education from the University of Michigan. Her work appears in publications including *Journal of Teacher Education*, *Educational Leadership*, *National Comprehensive Center for Teacher Quality's Research and Policy Brief*, and *The Journal of Staff Development*.

Georgea Langer became intrigued with teacher growth and expertise when she taught middle-school foreign language. To pursue this interest, she completed her PhD in Educational Psychology at Stanford University. As a professor of teacher education at Eastern Michigan University, Langer won three teaching awards and published extensively in professional journals. She has co-authored five books for both beginning and experienced teachers. She lives happily in Michigan and Florida with her husband, Peter, and their cat, Murphy.

 **Loretta Goff** worked as a K–12 teacher, guidance counselor, adjunct professor for two universities, assistant principal, principal, director of instruction, and assistant superintendent in charge of an attendance area of five schools, K–12. Loretta retired from her work in public schools after 27 years and served 9 years as a consultant for JBHM Education Group, which later became Generation Ready. With experience at all levels in public education, she was able to provide teachers and administrators guidance and support in many areas; but she is especially proud of her collaborative work with teachers to implement struggling-learner initiatives in many schools throughout Arkansas. Loretta received her doctorate from the University of Southern Mississippi and has co-published with the Association of Supervision and Curriculum Development and in the *Journal of Staff Development*.

This book would not have been possible without the constant encouragement and support from my family, friends, and colleagues. I wish to thank my husband Ken, who has tolerated piles of papers and books in every nook and cranny of our house for years, and whose unconditional love and support gave me the courage to put pen to paper. I am grateful for my precious sons, Andy, Josh, and Zach, who have always believed in me and are excited about my accomplishments. My admiration and appreciation go out in loving memory of my mother, who was my first editor, and my father who was my mentor. If it wasn't for Georgea, I would never have found my voice and believed that I could be a writer. Her willingness and patience to tease out the kernels of my abstract thoughts is uncanny. Finally, I wish to extend a special thank you to Victoria Duff, who helps me reach my greatest potential; Joellen Killion, who continues to support my professional learning; Margie Fellinger, a strong advocate for CASL, and my go-to person when exploring the potential of new ideas; and Virginia Winters, who has given me the strength and knowledge to stay the course toward building my own cultural proficiency.
—Amy B. Colton

◆◆◆

First, I must thank my mother, who inspired my interest in education by insisting that my elementary school get the best teachers possible—and they did! Second, I am so very grateful to my husband, Peter, for his steadfast encouragement as I spent many long days and nights in trying to understand and promote teachers' best professional learning. Finally, thank you to my friend, Amy, for sharing this journey with me. Her creativity, intelligence, and caring helped us to develop and refine CASL, and then to bring this book to you. We hope it is of service to you and your students.
—Georgea M. Langer

◆◆◆

To my loving husband, Jerry; my four daughters, Stacy, Erin, Rachael, and Emily; and in loving memory of my mother and father, Lois and "Chopper," for their unconditional love, commitment, and support for every endeavor.
—Loretta S. Goff

Introduction

Thousands of our nation's students are failing or dropping out of school every year. For a host of reasons, school is not working for them. What if, instead of such devastating outcomes, we heard students telling their parents and friends about how much they love school and their teachers? Imagine, if at the end of the school year, students were heard telling their friends what Nika told his:

> You are going to want to take American History from Mrs. Baker. She is awesome. I thought I was going to flunk out of her class back in the fall. I was getting failing grades on most of my tests and papers. She really criticized everything I did. But something changed mid-year when we were studying westward expansion. Mrs. Baker started treating me differently. She was much more patient with me and talked to me more about my interests, family background, and experiences. It was like she wanted to get to know me as a person. She even talked to the class about how the White man treated Native Americans during this time in history. No other teacher ever took time to talk about my own people this way. She even invited my dad in to share what he had learned from my great grandfather. I really felt like I belonged in that class. I think she really cared about me and wanted me to be successful. And I was. I passed the class with a really good grade. I can't wait to take history again.

We attribute Nika's success in American History to Sue Baker's year-long participation with her colleagues in the Collaborative Analysis of Student Learning (CASL). During that time, Sue was challenged to examine her beliefs about Nika, his Native American heritage, her own white middle-class upbringing and values, and her practice. She shared this reflection during the end-of-year celebration:

I chose to study Nika because he represented other students in my class who struggled to organize their thinking in writing. I also wanted to learn ways to be more responsive to my Native American students. Over the many years I have been in this school, I never have felt totally successful in establishing relationships with the Native American students in my classroom. They always seemed to be a bit standoffish with me, and I wondered why. I am glad I chose this focus, because mid-year I had a major breakthrough that changed not only how I thought about my Native American students, but my students of color in general, and how I teach history.

My success was a shining example of how helpful my participation in my CASL study group was for me. Not only did Nika's writing and his interactions with me greatly improve, so too did those of most of my other students. Only a few still struggle, and that has raised additional questions, which I hope to address in my inquiry next year.

We believe scenarios like the one with Nika and Sue are possible when teachers engage in facilitated and structured collaborative inquiry that not only enriches their existing professional knowledge base but also heightens their awareness of how their beliefs and values about their students drive their practice. Such transformative learning supports teachers in their persistent pursuit of responsive learning approaches that support each and every student's success in reaching standards of excellence.

What kind of professional learning experience resulted in such transformative learning for the teacher? This book will help you understand how you and your colleagues can implement the Collaborative Analysis of Student Learning in your school and district.

THE ESSENTIAL FEATURES OF CASL

The Collaborative Analysis of Student Learning (referred to by teachers as "castle") is a professional learning design in which teacher groups analyze student work samples and assessments to learn how to effectively support students' learning of complex academic standards. Teachers' engagement in the process is driven by their relentless pursuit to discover and apply responsive approaches for learning so that each and every student reaches standards of excellence. This inquiry extends over a period of months "because deep learning rarely results from a single experience, and teachers need time to conduct longitudinal studies in which they test and reconstruct their current theories of what works" (Putnam & Borko, 2000).

Through collaborative inquiry, teachers move away from using uniform "best practices" toward tailoring culturally and linguistically responsive approaches that meet the needs of each and every student.

Teacher self-awareness is an important part of developing culturally responsive approaches and positive attitudes about teaching and learning. Through the structured and facilitated CASL processes, teachers examine their beliefs and practices about teaching and learning. During the study group sessions, teachers actively move beyond "polite" conversations of simply sharing practices toward more in-depth conversations, known as dialogue, about students whom teachers feel challenged to reach and teach (Little, Gearhart, Curry, & Kafka, 1999).

In the process, assumptions that may be limiting teachers' capacity to give full attention to the needs of each of their students are revealed. Potential solutions are identified, tested, analyzed, and refined through a systematic inquiry process. Consequently, CASL allows teachers to find equitable ways for all students in the present and future to reach standards of excellence.

THE BENEFITS OF CASL

Several research studies (see Chapter 1) support CASL's positive influence on students' learning of complex curriculum standards. To promote this growth, CASL teachers enhance their professional knowledge of content, curriculum alignment, student development and learning, responsive instruction, assessment design and interpretation, and contextual factors. CASL teachers also demonstrate confidence in their ability to promote student learning and the commitment to do so. Finally, teachers demonstrate cultural competence, collaborative inquiry skills, and the ability to self-assess their professional learning needs. Schools and districts benefit from curriculum alignment within and across grade levels and institutional norms of collaboration and inquiry are established.

WHY THE IMPLEMENTATION OF CASL IS SO TIMELY

Why did we write this book? What makes this book so important right now? CASL is the result of over two decades of our efforts to help teachers become more reflective about their practice and, therefore, more intentional and effective in promoting student learning. Early on, we noticed that many professional learning designs taught strategies but did not promote the analytical decision-making required to figure out what strategy to use with which student under what conditions. At the same time, the student demographics in our nation's schools were becoming more and more diverse. Teachers were, and still are, faced with the challenge of meeting the learning needs of students whose race, socioeconomic status, and cultural background are very different than the teacher's own. Furthermore, few professional learning designs have helped teachers inquire into or understand how students from diverse backgrounds learn—a key piece in becoming a more effective and responsible teacher.

Since we wrote the 2003 ASCD bestseller, *The Collaborative Analysis of Student Work: Improving Teaching and Learning,* we have used and refined CASL with several hundred teachers in scores of schools and districts. As we have conducted research and reflected upon our experiences, we have made an exciting discovery: *Facilitated structured collaborative inquiry into how students learn complex academic standards helps teachers relentlessly and effectively pursue, discover, and apply responsive approaches for learning so that each and every student, regardless of students' backgrounds or interests, reaches standards of excellence.*

This new book differs from the previous one in two significant ways. First, we focus the CASL inquiry more specifically on those very students for whom equity is often not in place. We explain how CASL is structured to help study group members develop the knowledge, skills, and dispositions to provide every student access to a rigorous curriculum, high content standards, quality instruction, and appropriate assessments. Second, we provide many more tools and directions for how to facilitate CASL's collaborative skills and inquiry processes.

Six primary developments have prompted our decision to substantively rewrite our 2003 book:

1. The *cultural and linguistic diversity* of students is growing at an unprecedented rate, which compounds the challenges of successfully preparing all students to be college- and career-ready, and responsible and active citizens. CASL study groups develop the knowledge, skills, and moral purposes that are required to provide every student equal access to a rigorous curriculum, including high content standards and quality instruction.

2. The *Common Core State Standards* have introduced a new level of rigor and specificity into teachers' daily work. The standards focus on students' application of knowledge in authentic situations and on the construction of new knowledge. To be successful, teachers will need to use and be supported to understand and employ instructional strategies that facilitate critical and creative thinking, collaboration, problem solving, research and inquiry skills, and presentation or demonstration skills. The CASL inquiry process supports accomplishment of both goals.

3. *Research studies* suggest that higher levels of student achievement are more likely to be exhibited in schools where the professional learning is "primarily school or classroom based and is integrated into the workday, consisting of teachers assessing and finding solutions for authentic and immediate problems of practice as a part of a cycle of continuous improvement" (Croft, Coggshall, Dolan, & Powers, 2010, p. 2). Such job-embedded professional learning moves teachers away from isolation and toward sustained collaborative study teams (Darling-Hammond, Wei, Adree, Richardson, & Orphanos, 2009; Blank & de las Alas, 2009; Desimone, Porter, Garet, Yoon, & Birman, 2002; Garet, Porter, Desimone, Birman, & Yoon, 2001). The CASL design is one type of job-embedded professional learning that aligns closely with the qualities of professional learning supported by the research.

4. *Transformative teacher learning* raises teachers' awareness of the influence that their beliefs and assumptions have on how they interact with their students. When teachers assume that their own values are the norm, they may unconsciously be privileging students from the teachers' same cultural background and disadvantaging those different than them. "Research reveals that for lasting changes in behavior to occur, beliefs and assumptions must be brought to consciousness and the deep structures supporting behaviors must be addressed (Yero, 2002; Bocchino, 1993)" (Guerra & Nelson, 2009, p. 354). Through CASL, teachers not only add skills to their existing repertoire (additive professional learning); they also engage in *transformative learning*, defined as the "process by which we transform our taken-for-granted frames of reference to make them more inclusive, discriminating, open, emotionally capable of change, and reflective so that they may generate beliefs and opinions that will prove more true or justified to guide action" (Mezirow, 2000, pp. 7–8). Transformative learning is particularly critical in contexts in which teachers' cultural values and beliefs are different from those of their students.

5. Collaborative inquiry groups, while promising for professional learning, have often faltered due to inadequate *facilitation and leadership support*. Facilitated collaborative inquiry moves teachers toward more in-depth conversations about how they can facilitate the learning of students whom they feel challenged to reach and teach. Where rich dialogue is facilitated, we have found teachers come to believe—through concrete evidence of success—that they can have a significant impact on all of their students' learning (Loyd, 2006). After 15 years of experience, we offer several tools to maximize the effectiveness of CASL groups.

6. State and district leaders across the country are working diligently to implement more effective *teacher-evaluation systems.* These systems describe the knowledge, skills, and dispositions that teachers are expected to exhibit in their classrooms. The Framework: Teacher as Collaborative Inquirer provides both the theoretical underpinnings of the CASL professional learning design and the teacher learning outcomes for CASL. These outcomes are highly aligned with many of the teaching standards and frameworks used to measure teachers' effectiveness (e.g., Danielson, 2011; Marzano, 2011; National Board for Professional Teaching Standards, 1987). Teachers engaged in CASL are continuously asked to reflect on their own professional growth in terms of the outcomes in the framework.

THE ORGANIZATION OF THE BOOK

We recommend that you read the chapters in the order in which they are presented. In this way, you will have a clear understanding and appreciation for what CASL is intended to accomplish and how the essential features of this professional learning design are organized and implemented to lead to such outcomes.

Although we present CASL's design in a particular order, we also provide suggestions for when and how you might take a different approach based on your own context.

The book is divided into three sections which proceed from background about CASL and its outcomes, to ways to create a culture for collaborative inquiry, to specific guidelines for engaging teachers in each phase of the CASL design.

Section A. CASL Overview and Background

This first section provides an overview and background of the essential features, benefits, and outcomes of CASL.

- Chapter 1, "The Collaborative Analysis of Student Learning: Essential Features and Benefits," presents the key features of the CASL design and research on its benefits.
- Chapter 2, "Why CASL Works. The Framework: Teacher as Collaborative Inquirer," explains the conceptual underpinnings of the CASL design. This understanding is crucial for maintaining the vision of the kind of teacher CASL is intended to develop and for adapting the design to fit your needs and any challenges that may arise.

Section B. Building a Culture for Collaborative Inquiry

This section details the structures, supports, and resources necessary for creating the organizational culture that will support the effective implementation of CASL.

- Chapter 3, "Working Agreements and Communication Skills for Collaborative Inquiry," describes the kinds of positive and productive interactions that are essential in developing trust and successful inquiry among the teachers as they engage in the CASL processes.
- Chapter 4, "Leadership and Support," provides an account of the kind of support that school administrators need to provide in order to establish and maintain a school culture for collaborative inquiry.
- Chapter 5, "Facilitation of Collaborative Inquiry," details the role of the CASL facilitator in teaching, modeling, and coaching teachers as they relentlessly pursue, discover, and apply responsive approaches for learning so that each and every student reaches standards of excellence.

Section C. The Five CASL Phases

The beginning of this third section includes guidelines for conducting a workshop to introduce CASL to teachers and to begin developing the necessary skills for collaboration. Chapters 6–9 present each of the five CASL phases as follows:

- Chapter 6, "Phase I: Establishing a Focus for CASL Inquiry"
- Chapter 7, "Phase II: Defining Teachers' Professional Inquiry Goals
- Chapter 8, "Phase III: Inquiring Into Teaching for Learning
- Chapter 9, "Phase IV: Assessing Learning Progress" and "Phase V: Integrating Learning Into Teachers' Professional Practice"

CONCLUSION

Supporting Materials

- The online resources contain (a) optional activities for further professional learning, for example gaining consistency in assessment scoring, and (b) responses to the communication skills exercises presented in Section C.

AUTHORS' NOTE

The examples in this book are adaptations and composites of real situations, schools, teachers, and students. In most cases the individuals' names and identities have been altered. We are grateful to all the teachers and administrators for letting us be participant observers as they implemented and engaged in CASL.

Visit the companion website at
http://resources.corwin.com/Collaborativeanalysis
for additional resources.

SECTION A

CASL Overview and Background

We recommend that everyone who is either facilitating or engaging in the Collaborative Analysis of Student Learning (CASL) begin by reading the first two chapters of this book. The first chapter provides you with an overview of the distinct and essential features and benefits of this professional learning design. In Chapter 2, we describe the Framework: Teacher as Collaborative Inquirer. The framework defines the knowledge, skills, and dispositions possessed by teachers who successfully pursue, discover, and apply responsive approaches for learning so that each and every student reaches standards of excellence. It also explains how the CASL design develops such capacities in teachers.

Understanding the ideas presented in both of these chapters will help you maintain the vision of the kind of teacher CASL is intended to develop and to adapt the CASL design to fit your needs and any challenges that may arise.

1 The Collaborative Analysis of Student Learning

Essential Features and Benefits

Through the Collaborative Analysis of Student Learning, teachers move away from using uniform "best practices" toward the personalization of learning that is culturally and linguistically responsive so that each and every one of their students successfully reaches standards of excellence.

Let us go back to earlier in the school year, when Sue Baker is heading into her meeting with her Collaborative Analysis of Student Learning (CASL) study group. Sue has been taking Nika's work to her CASL study group for the last few months to inquire into how she might more effectively help him become a more proficient writer. She was beginning to see some real progress in Nika's expository writing when his performance started to decline during a unit on the westward expansion. Even after analyzing his work and experimenting with several strategies, his writing was still disappointing.

Sue, who is generally successful with her students, is baffled and frustrated. Most students in her class are engaged and working hard to meet her high expectations. She used to feel that she could reach most students, but now she is not so sure. In fact, she finds herself wanting to blame Nika for his lack of engagement and his sloppy, incomplete work. Many might have given up at this point and let Nika find his own way, but not Sue.

Fortunately, as a teacher committed to the success of every student, Sue refuses to let Nika fail and acknowledges that she can't meet this challenge on her own. So she brings Nika's most recent written assignment to her CASL study group.

As Sue and her colleagues analyze Nika's work sample, they talk about his most recent classroom behavior, his heritage, and his prior life experiences. As several explanations for his performance are considered, one idea in particular catches Sue's attention.

One of Sue's colleagues wonders whether Nika, who is Native American, is disengaged because he is aware of how disruptive and painful the westward expansion was for his people. The colleague suggests that, since the Native American elders often share their oral histories, Nika has probably heard such stories handed down by his grandparents. His work may reflect his anger and frustration that the textbook ignores the sacrifices of his people. In fact, it focuses only on the economic benefits of the westward expansion and on how the Native Americans actually helped the pioneers navigate across the country.

As the conversation continues, Sue and her colleagues come to understand Nika's point of view. They use these insights to consider how Sue might be more responsive to his learning needs and draw on his prior experiences as well as those of other students from diverse backgrounds.

In the process of the dialogue about Nika, Sue acknowledges that she has been presenting only the white middle-class perspective to her history students, even though she is well aware of the struggles the Native Americans and other cultural and racial groups had during the westward expansion. This makes her think long and hard about other ways she may be allowing her own cultural views to drive her instructional approach. She begins to wonder how her decisions may be creating barriers to learning for other students with cultural backgrounds different than her own.

Based on the insights gained in her study group, Sue decides to have her students read and discuss several primary sources depicting the experiences of the Native Americans and slaves during the westward expansion. She also personalizes her instruction by inviting Nika's father to share some of his people's oral history from this time. Finally, she revises the expository writing assignment to include both the positive impact on the country and the negative consequences for Native Americans and African Americans.

Sue's efforts to identify the barriers to Nika's learning and then to respond accordingly pay off. Nika's engagement in class has increased, and his final paper is very thorough and well written, as are those of Sue's African American students.

In the absence of her study group, Sue may have chosen to either lower her expectations for Nika or give up on him. Instead, by collaboratively analyzing her student's work, she increased her capacity to create an equitable learning environment not only for Nika, but for each and every one of her other students, especially her students of color, so they will become successful writers.

WHY IS THE COLLABORATIVE ANALYSIS OF STUDENT LEARNING NECESSARY?

The story of Sue and Nika illustrates how the Collaborative Analysis of Student Learning not only improves teachers' effectiveness as they diligently pursue responsive approaches for learning but also alters teachers' beliefs about their students and their own practice. We have found that such *transformative professional learning* is particularly critical in contexts in which students' cultural background is notably different than that of their teachers. Why is this important?

In our experience, as student diversity grows in schools, so too does teachers' uneasiness about successfully meeting the learning needs of all of their students. We believe, as many do, that these feelings of inadequacy can be transformed into a sense of efficacy and effectiveness when teachers use "systematic, thoughtful, and innovative . . . collaboration" to form new "visions and beliefs that guide educational practices in diverse settings" (Cooper, He, & Levin, 2011, 4–5). Such transformative learning is most likely to happen when teachers

- engage in reflection about their own cultural identities, biases, and experiences;
- explore the cultural backgrounds of their students, families, and the communities; and
- find ways to negotiate their roles as teachers and administrators to leverage students' strengths and assets to maximize learning (Cooper et al., 2011, pp. 4–5).

There are many different ways to define *culture*. We have chosen to adopt the broad definition promoted by the highly respected Lindsey, Kikanza, Robins, & Terrell (2009, pp. 11–12):

Culture is the set of practices and beliefs that is shared with members of a particular group and that distinguishes one group from others. We define *culture* broadly to include all shared characteristics of human description, including age, gender, geography, ancestry, language, history, sexual orientation, faith, and physical ability, as well as occupation and affiliations. Defined as such each person may belong to several cultural groups. An ethnic group is defined by shared history, ancestry, geography, language, and physical characteristics. Individuals may identify most strongly with their ethnic group, as well as several other groups that influence who they are.

All of our beliefs are "judgments . . . that we make up about ourselves, others, and about the world around us. Beliefs are generalizations about things such as causality or the meaning of specific actions" (Yero, 2002, p. 21). Our beliefs help us understand and respond to our world in a fairly predictable manner. Unfortunately, some of our beliefs are limiting and hinder our own success. Unless we are open to examining them, like Sue was in terms of her white middle-class beliefs, we may continue to get the same unfavorable results.

Mezirow (1995), the founder of transformative learning theory, wrote that people tend not to transform their beliefs or behaviors as long as their existing perspectives work for them. For real change to occur, individuals need to experience some dissonance between the beliefs that they hold and what they are experiencing. Thompson and Zeuli (1999) proposed that, since this kind of dissonance rarely occurs in the normal course of a teacher's day, teachers need deliberate interventions for this purpose. We found that the analysis of student learning over an extended period of time is such an intervention (Goff, Langer, & Colton, 2000; Putnam & Borko, 2000).

WHAT IS CASL?

CASL promotes such transformative professional learning by engaging small study groups of teachers in the analysis of specific students' work samples to increase their understanding of how such students construct meaning of complex content. As teachers examine their beliefs and practices about teaching and learning, they bring to the surface any assumptions or attitudes that may be limiting their capacity to effectively respond to their students' learning needs. As they dig deeper, teachers learn how their cultural perspectives may differ from those of their students and how these differences may be influencing their practice. In turn, they develop a more nuanced and multifaceted understanding of diversity (Cooper et al., 2011).

During the months of the CASL inquiry, the effectiveness of various culturally responsive approaches to learning are tested and analyzed. As discoveries are made, the teachers store this professional knowledge so that they can personalize their teaching for future students.

Consequently, the collaborative analysis of student work enables teachers to find *equitable ways* for all students in the present and future to reach *standards of excellence.*

Figure 1.1 (CASL's Theory of Change) illustrates how the CASL professional learning design develops teachers' capacities and commitment to relentlessly pursue, discover, and use responsive approaches to learning to promote learning excellence in their students. Take a moment to note the two boxes in the middle of the figure, labeled "Framework: Teacher as Collaborative Inquirer" and "Teacher Relentlessly Pursues, Discovers, and Applies Responsive Approaches for Learning." In the case of Sue, the CASL group helped her inquire into and reframe her initial impressions of Nika's behavior. She went from seeing him as a resistant problem student to understanding his frustration about the way his ancestors were portrayed in the unit's resources. Out of this new perspective, Sue could then find a way to respond to Nika's convictions. But the transformation did not end with Sue's experience with Nika. Sue also questioned how other groups in her class, specifically, the African American students, were experiencing the unit. As a result of this inquiry, she developed her capacities as a collaborative inquirer and discovered and used equitable approaches that helped all of her culturally diverse students succeed.

Figure 1.1 CASL's Theory of Change

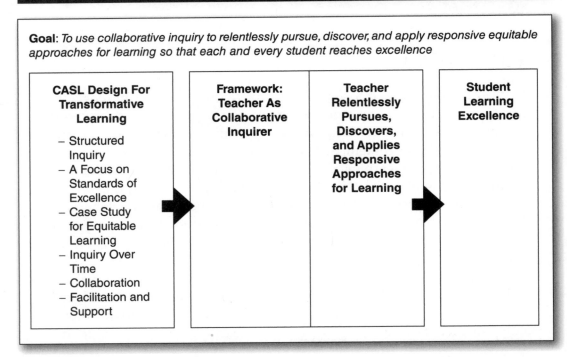

Goal: *To use collaborative inquiry to relentlessly pursue, discover, and apply responsive equitable approaches for learning so that each and every student reaches excellence*

CASL Design For Transformative Learning
- Structured Inquiry
- A Focus on Standards of Excellence
- Case Study for Equitable Learning
- Inquiry Over Time
- Collaboration
- Facilitation and Support

Framework: Teacher As Collaborative Inquirer

Teacher Relentlessly Pursues, Discovers, and Applies Responsive Approaches for Learning

Student Learning Excellence

Now take a look at the left half of the figure, which lists the six distinct and essential features of the CASL design. Although we provide ideas about how to modify CASL to fit local contexts, we believe these features must be maintained to reap the full benefits found in our and others' research. The seventh feature, the conceptual framework, is described next. Together, these features facilitate transformative learning that leads to increased cultural proficiency, teaching effectiveness, and results for all students.

- Structured inquiry
- A focus on standards of excellence
- Case study for equitable responsiveness
- Inquiry over time
- Productive and intentional collaboration
- Skilled facilitation and organizational support

A CONCEPTUAL FRAMEWORK: TEACHER AS COLLABORATIVE INQUIRER

The CASL professional learning design is grounded in the "Framework: Teacher as Collaborative Inquirer" (formerly referred to as the "Framework for Reflective Inquiry"). The framework, portrayed in the left half of Figure 1.1, and described fully in Chapter 2, outlines the teacher capacities being developed through CASL.

The framework is a synthesis of the literature on the dispositions, professional knowledge base, and thinking of a teacher who is aware of her own culture and the impact it has on her students; values the diversity of her students; and is committed to continuous learning that leads to responsive approaches for the learning needs of individual students.

We have used the framework for over two decades to guide the development of various programs for teachers during different stages of their careers (e.g., Colton & Sparks-Langer, 1993; Goff et al., 2000; Langer & Colton, 2005; Langer, Colton, & Goff, 2003; Sparks, Simmons, Pasch, Colton, & Starko, 1990). The concepts integrated into the framework are congruent with many of the professional teaching standards used for teacher appraisal systems, for example, the National Board for Professional Teaching Standards Five Core Propositions (1987), Charlotte Danielson's *Framework for Teaching* (2011), and Robert Marzano's Causal Teacher Evaluation Model (2011).

The ideas in the framework have remained fairly stable since we first published it (Colton & Sparks-Langer, 1993). The most dramatic revision reflects our current understanding of how teachers' personal filters—beliefs and feelings—influence how they construct meaning of their experiences and how they choose to respond to what they observe.

Our framework is a key decision-making tool for us (and we hope for you) because it provides a vision of the responsible and effective teacher. As such, it guides decisions about how best to implement and adapt CASL. It also serves as a diagnostic tool for facilitators and leaders to determine teachers' skills, knowledge, and dispositions and how best to support teachers' continued growth and development.

A central feature of the framework is the *collaborative inquiry cycle*, which describes how teachers build much of their professional knowledge (adapted from Kolb, 1984). This cycle is woven into the fabric of each of the CASL phases and builds teachers' skills of analysis and self-reflection, enriches their professional knowledge base, and further develops their dispositions as culturally responsive teachers.

Structured Inquiry

Teachers engaged in CASL complete five structured phases (see Figure 1.2). These phases are designed to facilitate teachers' relentless quest to discover how best to personalize their students' learning so each student reaches standards of excellence. Each phase has a specific purpose, a focus of inquiry, and a protocol that provides task directions, prompts, and the responsibilities of the study group members. Section C and Chapters 6–9 present a full description of how to facilitate each phase.

Teachers begin the inquiry process in Phase I by identifying the standards of excellence to which they will hold all of their students during the year. We refer to these standards as the *target learning area* (TLA). The TLA is an area of the curriculum that has been consistently challenging to teach as evidenced in student performance data year after year. After selecting the area for inquiry, teachers define it by describing how students will ultimately demonstrate their proficiency. We have found that the more specific teachers are about the learning outcomes they wish to promote, the more effective and targeted their instruction and assessments will be. Next, teachers identify the learning outcomes students need to master on the journey toward the success in the TLA. Finally, teachers design and administer an *initial whole-class assessment* to determine (a) the current status of their students' learning in the TLA and (b) where to begin instruction.

In Phase I, Sue's study group selected the following TLA: "To write explanatory text to examine a topic and convey ideas, concepts, and information through the selection, organization, and analysis of relevant social studies content." For the initial assessment, they asked students to read and write a summary of an article from the local newspaper.

Figure 1.2 The Five CASL Phases*

Phase I: Establishing a Focus for CASL Inquiry

What area of the curriculum is most challenging for our students?

- Define Target Learning Area
- Design Initial Whole-Class Assessment
- Begin Teacher Autobiography

Phase II: Defining Teachers' Professional Learning Goals

Which students would be most fruitful to study over time so that we may discover equitable responses?

- Analyze Initial Assessment Results
- Establish Professional Learning Goal
- Select Focus Student and Begin Biography

Phase III: Inquiring Into Teaching for Learning (3–5 months)

Which approaches are most responsive to our students' specific strengths and needs?

- Analyze Each Focus Student's Work Sample (every 2–4 weeks)
- Continue Focus Student Biography
- Continue Teacher Autobiography

Phase IV: Assessing Learning Progress

What progress have our students made? Who needs further assistance?

- Analyze Whole-Class Final Assessment Results
- Plan for Students Not Reaching Proficient Performance

Phase V: Integrating Learning Into Teachers' Professional Practice

What have we learned about ourselves and our teaching and what might we need to learn more about?

- Reflect on Teacher and Student Learning
- Set Professional Learning Goals
- Celebrate Accomplishments

---

*Throughout phases: reflect on learning and collaboration, find more information, and seek further professional learning as necessary.

In Phase II, teachers analyze their students' performances on the initial assessment of the TLA. They find patterns to determine which areas of the content are most challenging and to discover who the struggling students are as learners and people. At the conclusion of this phase, teachers have *framed a statement of their professional learning goals* and have *selected a focus student* who will help them reach these goals.

In Phase II, Sue selects Nika because he represents other students in her class who struggle to organize their thinking in writing. She also wants to study Nika because he is Native American and Sue acknowledges she knows very little about the background and culture of students in this racial group.

Phase III extends over three to five months as study groups of three to five teachers meet every few weeks to *analyze work samples from each focus student.* The story of Sue and Nika in the opening of this chapter illustrates this phase. A teacher begins by describing the focus student, the instruction that preceded the work sample, and the desired learning outcome (e.g., concept or skill). From there, the student work analysis cycle begins as the teachers make *observations* about the work using descriptive, not evaluative, words. Then the group asks questions to prompt an *analysis* of what factors may have caused the learning demonstrated in the work, for example, "What do you know about this student that might explain why she performed in this way?" "What influence might your instructional approach have had on the student's learning?" "What about the student's prior experiences might be supporting or hindering learning?"

During the *analysis*, the study group members refrain from giving advice or offering solutions. Indeed, one purpose of the work analysis is to formulate questions that might need further investigation. For example, the teacher might decide that it would be useful to hear the student "think aloud about how he did the work" before deciding what he needs. Sometimes teachers ask parents or other professionals about the student's interests and motivations. Teachers may also need to clarify how the specific understanding or skill relates to the school or district curriculum.

Finally, the group discusses a *plan*—personalized teaching strategies tailored to the specific student needs and strengths discovered during the analysis step. Each of these potential actions is examined to see if it might help the student improve (at this point, research literature and other experts are often consulted). The teacher presenting the work makes the final decision about how to respond to the student's learning needs. Once the planning step is done, the study group members *reflect* on what was learned from examining the work, how they might use what they learned, and the quality of their collaboration.

After the first student's work sample is studied, the same process is repeated for the next focus student. During the following weeks, the teachers implement the planned actions and collect the next sample of student work for another round of group observation, analysis, planning, reflection, and action. Over the months of experimentation, they come to understand their students and themselves more deeply and use their new insights to facilitate their students' learning.

Occasionally, the study group finds it necessary to suspend the student work analysis to learn more about concepts or skills in the curriculum, how students learn in the TLA, specific ways of teaching, or other areas. This may involve consulting research, theory, and experts. It is not long before they return to analyzing their students' work.

After several months of meeting in study groups, teachers complete Phase IV by assessing their entire class's performance to *determine progress toward the TLA*. The tasks during this phase are very similar to those in Phase II, with one exception. The analysis of the students' learning gains ends with significant reflection on (a) what contributed to the students' successes, (b) what responsive approaches might help those not succeeding, and (c) what additional professional learning might teachers still need to help those students who are not yet reaching the TLA.

Throughout the CASL inquiry phases, we ask teachers to keep written notes about their insights and questions. Their notes include learning about themselves, their teaching and their students' learning of the TLA, and any questions for further inquiry. This written dialogue with oneself is a powerful means to reframe problems, create new understandings of the nature of student learning, communicate information about students, and document teacher growth.

In Phase V, teachers prepare their *final reflections*. They step back from the process, review their notes, and write about their growth, their students' progress, what they might do differently in future years, and what additional professional learning they still need.

The culmination of Phase V is the CASL celebration, during which participants share with other teachers and leaders what they and their students have learned throughout the year. Section C provides details about how to engage in each of the CASL inquiry phases.

At the CASL celebration for Sue's group, the energy level in the room was noteworthy as Sue and the other teachers shared their successes. Every teacher saw impressive gains in their students' expository essays. Sue shared what she learned about using primary sources as a way to present multiple perspectives in history. She also pointed out how she was able to actively engage more students when she took the time to get to know them as people because she could then connect their backgrounds to the content being taught. Sue and her social studies colleagues let the principal know that they would like to learn more about teaching writing.

A Focus on Standards of Excellence

When teachers clearly define the TLA in Phase I, they are establishing the standards of excellence to which all their students will be held. Culturally proficient teachers believe that each and every student is capable of reaching high and rigorous standards, regardless of race, ethnicity, socioeconomic status, cultural background, learning style, disability, or life experiences. They see such standards as the intellectual, social, and moral competencies that students will use throughout their lives to claim respect and dignity and to critically examine beliefs and policies as responsible citizens.

With the *standards of excellence* well defined, teachers begin their quest to discover ways they can personalize learning for each of their students.

Case Study for Equitable Responsiveness

Equity ensures that every effort is made to eliminate potential barriers to learning to afford all students every opportunity to succeed. Providing equitable learning opportunities is no easy task, in large part because teachers regularly face unpredictable situations in their classrooms and no single approach works for every student or for all outcomes. As Ball and Cohen wrote, "No amount of knowledge can fully prescribe appropriate or wise practice" (1999, p. 10). The challenge for teachers, then, is to figure out which strategies work for whom, and in what combination and sequence.

Teachers usually connect their instructional insights to *specific cases* of student learning rather than to uniform best practices. Such expertise is called "case knowledge" (Shulman, 1987). For these reasons, teachers in a CASL study group select a focus student from their class who represents a cluster of students who exhibit similar learning challenges in the TLA and whose cultural backgrounds are different (and perhaps not well understood) by their teachers. What teachers discover about facilitating the learning of the focus student will help them personalize instruction for others in the cluster and future similar students. To further broaden the study group's learning, each teacher selects a student with different learning challenges so that every teacher learns how to address multiple student needs. The case study process also builds teachers' capacity to learn from their own practice, which prepares them to face future classroom dilemmas and challenges.

Inquiry Over Time

Collaborative inquiry is most powerful when teachers look at an individual student's work over time for four very important reasons. First, educators usually agree that deep learning of complex outcomes rarely results from a single learning experience. It is much easier—and faster—to teach a fact in history, for example, than a concept such as racism. Through longitudinal studies of students' evolving understandings, teachers test out various strategies and scaffolded learning experiences. Based on the results, they reconstruct their theories of how best to help individual students reach the learning targets (Putnam & Borko, 2000).

A second reason to extend the inquiry is that it takes time for teachers to develop relationships with students and parents to the point where both feel comfortable to share stories and facts about themselves. Through such interactions, teachers gain useful insights about their students.

Another benefit of this long-term experimentation and reflection is that teachers discover gaps in their knowledge and skills and any beliefs that may be hindering their students' learning. Over time, they either improve in these areas or seek out specific professional learning opportunities.

A final reason for extended inquiry is that it takes time for teachers to develop trusting relationships with their colleagues. Such rapport allows fellow group members to bring a struggling student's work to the group without fear of being judged or criticized. For such transformative learning to happen, colleagues need to feel comfortable both sharing and hearing new perspectives. A culture of collaboration, although slow to develop, is worth its weight in gold when it comes to discovering responsive teaching approaches for struggling learners.

Productive and Intentional Collaboration

The way teachers interact when they are not in the classroom influences the success of any professional learning program. Like CASL, the most productive environments are those in which teachers regularly engage in collaborative conversations—*dialogues*—around meaningful and relevant issues (Darling-Hammond, 1998; Sparks, 2002). During such times, assumptions are revealed and examined, and teachers allow their thinking to be open to the influence of others.

Dialogue is a central process of the CASL system because it invites multiple interpretations, helps teachers examine limiting assumptions, and unleashes teachers' creativity and expertise (Love, Stiles, Mundry, & DiRanna, 2008). A major consequence of collaborative inquiry is *collective efficacy*—a sense that teachers can overcome learning challenges when they rely on one another's expertise (Goddard, How, & Hoy, 2000).

Collaboration, however, does not happen automatically. For teachers to move beyond a culture of "polite" conversation (Little, Gearhart, Curry, & Kafka, 1999) toward deep analysis of teaching and learning, groups need to intentionally develop, practice, and reinforce *working agreements* and *communication skills*. Furthermore, such dialogue becomes possible only through intentional facilitation and leadership.

Skilled Facilitation and Organizational Support

Few innovations are sustained without skilled facilitation and organizational support. The CASL facilitator guides teachers to the kinds of thinking, problem posing, and analysis necessary for transformative learning. A skilled facilitator can ensure that working agreements are developed and followed, that everyone develops the necessary communication and analytical skills, and that teachers stay focused on student learning. The facilitator also helps teachers to reflect on their beliefs and assumptions, identify their own learning needs, and seek additional support when necessary.

Support from school administrators is also critical to the success of the CASL professional learning design. We have identified seven things that school leaders have done to support the implementation of the CASL design (each is described in Chapter 4):

- develop an interest in CASL,
- establish collaborative teams,
- provide time to meet,
- identify the target learning area(s) for inquiry,
- provide resources,
- provide incentives and celebrate victories, and
- model a commitment to collaborative inquiry.

WHAT ARE THE BENEFITS OF CASL?

We recognize the investment of time and money that any new professional learning program represents. You are probably wondering what evidence we have that CASL makes a difference in teachers' professional practice and in student success. To answer this question, we explore recent research on the characteristics of effective professional learning. Then we share the findings from studies of CASL.

Professional Learning Research

As mentioned in the Introduction, researchers (Blank & de la Alas, 2009; Croft, Coggshall, Dolan, & Powers, 2010; Darling-Hammond, Wei, Andree, Richardson, & Orphanos, 2009; Desimone, Porter, Garet, Yoon, & Birman, 2002; Garet, Porter, Desimone, Birman, & Yoon, 2001; Hawley & Valli, 1999; Hord, Roussin, & Sommers, 2009) have found higher levels of student achievement and teacher expertise in schools where professional learning

- focuses on students' learning of important content;
- is sustained over time;
- facilitates a cycle of continuous improvement where teachers assess students, share expertise, and find solutions for authentic problems of practice;
- is school- or classroom-based, and integrated into the workday; and
- develops collaborative teams with collective responsibility for student learning.

These same findings are reflected in the *Standards for Professional Learning* (Learning Forward, 2011). The standards define the essential characteristics and conditions for designing, implementing, and evaluating professional learning that increases educator effectiveness and student learning.

Studies of CASL

Since the CASL learning design aligns closely with the research on effective professional learning, it is not surprising that research on CASL has yielded impressive outcomes. Since 1999, ten studies (Colton & Langer, 2001; Goff, 1999; Gray, 2009; Langer, 1999, 2001; Langer & Colton, 2006, 2007, 2008, 2011; Loyd, 2006) of over 300 elementary and secondary teachers in CASL study groups show valuable benefits to students, teachers, parents, and organizations. Figure 1.3 presents the major studies that we have conducted with the location, sample, author, data sources, and results.

With all this experience and data, the benefits of CASL are numerous. Figure 1.4 lists them.

Figure 1.3 Studies of CASL

Forest Hills School District, Michigan (5 years of CASL, 2007–2012)

- 90 teachers in all K–6 buildings; Language Arts
- Suburban, with increasing diversity each year
- Study of teacher and student learning (Gray, 2009)
- Study of implementation and outcomes (Langer & Colton, 2011)
- Data: Test scores, teacher portfolios, study group interviews.

Results:

- District writing assessment scores increased 131%.
- Improvements in Language Arts were linked to CASL, among other improvements.

(Continued)

(Continued)

- Teachers, facilitators, and leaders sustained implementation over a 5-year period.
- Trained facilitators provided distributed leadership of study groups.

Four Ann Arbor, Michigan Elementary Schools (3 years of CASL, 2004–2007)

- 30 teachers in Grades K–5; Language Arts and Math
- Diverse socioeconomic status and ethnicity
- Study of teachers' and students' growth (Langer & Colton, 2007, 2008)
- Data: Questionnaires, portfolios, teacher reflections, principal reflections

Results:

- Teachers gained skills to personalize their teaching and could link that knowledge to students similar to the focus students studied.
- The documentation of interventions and student learning results provided an alternative to test-based decisions about Special Education placement.

Adrian Community Schools, Michigan (3 years of CASL, 2004–2007)

- All 40 teachers in two middle schools; all subjects
- Rural; low-income
- Study of teachers' use of CASL inquiry for middle school curriculum design (Langer & Colton, 2007)
- Data: Questionnaires, teacher reflections, principal interviews, and logs

Results:

- Teachers developed into collaborative teams and used norms, standards, and assessment results to create and revise project-based curriculum.
- Teachers clarified understanding of standards and felt more capable of helping students reach them.
- Over two-thirds of teachers reported using more active teaching strategies, authentic assessment, collaborative skills, and shared leadership.

Paddock Elementary, Michigan (3 years of CASL, 2002–2005)

- All 15 teachers, Grades K–2; Language Arts
- Rural; low-income; Title I
- Study of changes in teachers and in student learning (Langer & Colton, 2006)
- Study of four teachers' discourse during study groups (Loyd, 2006)
- Data: Reading assessments, teacher questionnaires, interviews, recorded study group sessions, written reflections, and observations

Results:

- Medium to large pre- to post-test effect sizes in reading achievement.
- Teachers' grew in confidence and ability to move students forward.
- Teachers increased their ability to interpret assessments and help students succeed.

- Teachers recognized gaps in their professional knowledge base and reported a need for professional development in these areas.
- Teachers approved policies to make CASL study groups a regular part of their schedules.

George County, Georgia (2 years of CASL, 1996–1998)

- 49 K–12 teachers; writing across the curriculum
- Low-income; Title I
- Study of teachers' growth and student learning (Goff, 1999)
- Data: Interviews and portfolios
- Results reported in Figure 1.4

Michigan Schools (6–12 months of CASL, 1998–2000)

- 75 K–12 teachers, various subjects
- Various schools with diverse settings
- Study of teachers' growth and student learning (Langer, 1999, 2001; Colton & Langer, 2001)
- Data: Surveys and portfolios
- Results reported in Figure 1.4

Figure 1.4 Benefits of CASL Inquiry

Benefits to Students

- Improved student learning in writing, reading, and other content areas
- Increased student clarity about intended learning

Benefits to Teachers

- Commitment and confidence in ability to promote student learning
- Cultural competence
- Analytical and reflective inquiry skills
- Growth in professional knowledge: content, student development and learning, personalized instruction (pedagogy), assessment design and interpretation, and contextual factors
- Alignment among classroom standards, assessments, and instruction
- Collaborative and group facilitation expertise
- Awareness and self-assessment of professional practice and needs
- National Board for Professional Teaching Standards certification

Benefits to Parents and Organizations

- Parent clarity about learning targets and student progress
- Curriculum alignment within and across grade levels
- Professional development targeted to teachers' needs
- Ongoing, institutionalized collaborative inquiry into student success

Benefits to Students

The most important benefit of CASL is the impressive learning of the students whom teachers have typically found challenging to reach. Of the 55 K–12 students studied by Goff (1999), 90% showed improved learning in their work samples (Goff, Colton, & Langer, 2000).

More recent CASL studies showed significant increases in the entire class's learning of elementary-level reading and writing skills (Langer & Colton, 2006, 2007; Langer & Colton, 2011; Loyd, 2006). As one first-grade teacher said, "I have done assessment in the past, but have never taken the time to pinpoint my students' results on a chart to discover areas of strengths and weaknesses." Another teacher said, "Analyzing the work of a student I'd struggled with, and trying different strategies has made all the difference."

Benefits to Teachers

Commitment to and Confidence in Ability to Promote Student Learning

One of our most consistent findings is that CASL teachers report and demonstrate a heightened commitment to student success, and they feel more confident (efficacious) in their ability to support student learning.

As one middle school teacher stated,

> Before CASL, I felt helpless. I would think, "The students aren't doing well . . . are they studying?" I didn't have the training to analyze their work. I would justify the lack of learning by thinking "Well, they just don't have the background" or "They missed something in an earlier class." Now I ask myself, "Is there something I could do or say or some type of instruction that would get the light bulb to come on?"

After participating in CASL, teachers were less likely to write off some factors as "out of my control" and would try to overcome the many barriers that interfere with learning. For example, in the early sessions, one group of teachers made many hopeless references to poor children from a particular part of town. As they inquired into their learning and experimented with different strategies, the teachers' sense of efficacy grew and they believed they could have a positive effect on those students' learning, despite the economic challenges.

Cultural Competency

It is an uncomfortable fact that teachers tend to have less success with students who are least like them in terms of background and culture (Lynn, Bacon, Totten, Bridges, & Jennings, 2010). That is why we encourage teachers to select a focus student who represents some aspect of diversity in their classroom along with a common content-learning challenge.

When teachers select a focus student who is very different from them, they gain new understandings and more flexible perspectives about why students from diverse backgrounds appear to struggle. This awareness results in part from looking at how teachers' own values and beliefs affect their interpretations of student behavior. These new ways of looking can be helpful in finding culturally responsive ways to teach their other struggling students.

As one teacher said, "It's hard to filter out your own bias." Another reflected, "I'm more mindful of my own philosophy, theories and beliefs because I've had to verbalize them." Gray (2009) concluded, "The deeper and sharper focus on student needs had pushed them away from operating out of preconceived notions about their students . . . they didn't make assumptions about students' needs based on background or economic status but saw each child with specific learning needs" (p. 38).

Analytical and Reflective Inquiry Skills

Many teachers have reported growth in the analytical and reflective inquiry skills required to explore the link between their teaching and students' learning. CASL changed their way of thinking by helping them discover, define, and analyze their students' learning needs. Then the teachers could identify teaching practices to correct the misunderstandings or fill in the gaps. As one teacher stated, "We become frustrated because we can't get students to produce what we want. This process gave me a better insight into why they couldn't do what I wanted."

It is encouraging to see this type of analytical thinking about student performance become an automatic "self-questioning script." At first, teachers followed the analysis process in a step-by-step manner. In time, however, the inquiry stance became second nature. "It is automatic; I do it without thinking. The change is embedded. Before, I had to force it. I used the question sheets. Now I do it automatically."

Professional Knowledge

We have also seen teachers gain valuable professional knowledge about their curriculum, students, methods, assessment, and contextual factors. For example, a high school science teacher discovered that her expectations for writing assignments were not clear because she was not sure how to teach writing. After seeking help from an English teacher in the study group, she was able to clarify outcomes and use new instructional strategies. She noticed (and documented) marked improvement in her students' writing.

Alignment Among Standards, Assessments, and Instruction

A large part of school reform involves the alignment of curriculum guidelines with assessments and instruction. As a result of their experience with CASL, many teachers realized that they could improve in this area. For example, one teacher noted, "If they were busy, then I hoped they learned something. But now I know." This teacher explained that she had dutifully followed the teacher's edition of the textbook, but now she uses her assessment of student understanding of the standards to help plan her instruction. Another elementary teacher stated, "This experience has changed my understanding of my subject matter to the extent that it has made me think more about this gap between teachers' expectations and students' actual successes (or lack thereof)."

Collaborative Sharing of Expertise

We frequently receive comments about the opportunity to problem solve with other teachers. As one teacher explained, "We talked about different things that we could do. It helped to be able to work with someone instead of just trying to do it on your own." In her reflections, one teacher stated, "I have learned a great deal from other teachers during this process." We have also seen wonderful mentoring of new teachers occur in the study groups, for example, sharing of rubrics and assessment ideas. One first-year teacher stated, "It taught me to re-look and talk to everybody and get help."

Professional Awareness and Self-Assessment

During CASL sessions, many teachers come to surprising realizations about their professional practice. Typically, these are private, internal "a-ha" moments. For example, they may realize that they do not have a thorough understanding of a crucial concept in math or that a particular assessment does not really get at the target learning area or standards.

Some teachers awaken to the uncomfortable fact that they have prematurely given up on a student, possibly due to their own cultural background. CASL is designed to provoke such insights in an environment of respect and commitment to student success. It is a safe place to admit a professional or personal shortcoming.

As one teacher remarked, "It made me look at my teaching styles. It made me really think about what I was doing and why I was doing it. I understood myself more." A common statement found in the final reflections is, "I now know I need more [professional] training on [e.g., teaching of reading for comprehension]."

NBPTS Certification

The first group of 49 CASL teachers included 12 who applied for National Board for Professional Teaching Standards (NBPTS) certification. All 12 went through this rigorous teacher-assessment process and received the certification. They reported that the CASL project helped them immensely, especially in writing their analyses of student learning and the reflections on their practice.

This remark summarizes many of the ways CASL benefits teachers:

I think about teaching differently. I spend more time talking with students and listening to what they are saying. I ask, "Why did you do it this way?" The process made my strategies better and I feel like I have more ability in the classroom. I am a better teacher because I have a lot more confidence and I can figure out what their problems are.

Benefits to Parents and Organizations

We are happy to report that the CASL system also benefits parents and organizations. The teachers' clarity about what they want their students to be able to do in the target learning area results in *clearer communication with parents* and other teachers. As one principal stated, "Parents love the fact that you can use work samples to talk to them about their children. 'This is where your child started, and this is where he ended up.'" A parent shared, "I've seen my child's portfolio from the beginning and . . . compared to now, he's achieved so much. . . . It's such a big difference."

As teachers begin to discuss standards and assessments within grade levels, a higher degree of curriculum consistency can be reached. When such discussions occur across grade levels, teachers begin to delineate a logical sequence of skills from grade to grade. As teachers in one school compared the writing rubrics for each grade level, they found inconsistencies in what was required and made changes to close the gaps. Such insights can have a positive effect on *curriculum alignment* and school improvement efforts.

The detailed information about students' learning is also useful in setting *school improvement goals* and for documenting student growth that results from curriculum and instructional interventions. One school found that its teachers did not thoroughly understand the specific nature of their students' reading problems. After using a reading assessment and charting the results, they were able to find programs tailored to the needs of the students.

The student-learning data gathered early in the year can assist with school *decisions about the allocation of resources*. For example, as a result of analyzing each classroom's data on language-arts skills, staff at one school decided that some classrooms needed more paraprofessionals than others. Since all teachers were involved in interpreting the assessment data together, they agreed that this was the best way to help students succeed.

Professional-learning planning is often easier after CASL because teachers are aware of where and how they need to grow. When teachers are masters of their own destiny, they are more likely to value what they learn and integrate it into their professional knowledge base. After studying students' writing in science, some teachers requested more professional learning on the teaching of writing. In other groups, teachers might request professional learning in cultural proficiency after hearing others struggling with reaching children from cultures different than their own. As one principal said, "It allows you to use your limited professional development monies in a more precise manner that meets teacher needs and student needs."

One of the greatest benefits to the school community is the *culture for collaborative inquiry* developed through CASL groups, schools, and districts. As teachers and other leaders join together with the explicit purpose of helping students grow in a particular learning area, they develop a sense of collective responsibility, moral purpose, and collegiality.

SUMMARY

When schools implement all of CASL's distinct and essential features with fidelity, the result is increased cultural proficiency, teaching effectiveness, and student success. The story of Sue and Nika illustrates just what can be accomplished when teachers engage in such transformative learning.

Sue's level of collective efficacy soared as a result of her CASL inquiry. She ended the year believing that with the help of her colleagues she could tackle any future challenge that may come her way. Her group's inquiry not only enriched her professional knowledge about how to teach history and writing, her study of Native American students revealed how limiting one's own cultural lenses can be when setting student expectations and designing lessons. As a result, Sue left the school year with a long summer reading list around issues of culturally proficient instruction.

2 Why CASL Works

The Framework: Teacher as Collaborative Inquirer

In this chapter, we present our "Framework: Teacher as Collaborative Inquirer" (see Figure 2.1), formerly "Framework for Teachers' Reflective Inquiry" (Colton & Sparks-Langer, 1993). Since the mid-1980s, we have been designing and studying innovative programs for pre-student teaching (Sparks, Simmons, Pasch, Colton, & Starko, 1990), student teaching (Colton & Sparks-Langer, 1992), teacher induction, teacher supervision, and professional learning (Goff, Langer, & Colton, 2000; Langer & Colton, 2005). We recognize that teaching for student success is full of dilemmas and does not lend itself to simple formulas. That is why we have been seeking to develop what we call *the perennial skills of teaching expertise: teacher collaboration, inquiry, and reflection*. Through our experience and research, we have gained a vision of the collaborative inquirer and a process for building the necessary capacities to meet this vision.

We changed the name of the framework to reflect current research that suggests that collaboration and inquiry play a critical role in effectively facilitating teachers' professional growth and development (Ball & Cohen, 1999; Borko, 2004; Dana & Yendol-Hoppey, 2014; Darling-Hammond et al., 2009; Gearheart & Osmundson, 2008). Furthermore, even though we removed the word "reflection" from the title, teacher reflection operates throughout the CASL phases as teachers think about their questions, insights, and the value of collaborating with colleagues.

The framework provides the theoretical underpinnings for the Collaborative Analysis of Student Learning (CASL) and portrays (1) a vision of the teacher as a collaborative inquirer and (2) how teachers develop the dispositions, skills, and knowledge necessary for responsible and effective teaching.

The framework is CASL's North Star. The framework includes four interconnected components: Professional knowledge base, collaborative inquiry cycle, filtering system, and dispositions of an accomplished teacher. This vision helps guide CASL teachers in the identification of their own professional learning needs and also their decisions about how best to engage in and/or facilitate the CASL inquiry phases to fit the needs or challenges that may arise.

Before unpacking the different components of the framework, we paint a portrait of our vision of a *collaborative inquirer*. Next, we describe the essential knowledge, skills, beliefs, and dispositions possessed by accomplished teachers who are committed to creating equitable pathways to learning so that all students reach standards of excellence. At the end of this chapter, we provide general ideas about how best to develop the capacities and dispositions captured in the framework.

A VISION OF THE COLLABORATIVE INQUIRER

Collaborative inquirers possess the will and skill to relentlessly and successfully pursue and apply equitable approaches that support their students' achievement of excellence. This commitment is driven by the teachers' unwavering sense of moral and collective responsibility to prepare all students to function and perform well in school and in society, regardless of the students' cultural background, race, socioeconomic status, and gender. Collaborative inquirers "believe that all culturally and linguistically diverse students can excel in academic endeavors when their culture, language, heritage and experiences are valued and used to facilitate their learning and development, and they are provided access to high quality teachers (teaching), programs, and resources" (Klinger et al. 2005, p. 8).

Collaborative inquirers facilitate their students' learning by coming to know them as people and learners, and then using what they learn to identify and apply appropriate and effective evidence-based culturally relevant teaching. Their "pedagogy empowers students intellectually, socially, emotionally, and politically by using cultural referents to impart knowledge, skills and attitudes. These cultural referents are not merely vehicles for bridging or explaining the dominant culture; they are aspects of curriculum in their own right" (Ladson-Billings, 1994, pp. 17–18).

With their recognition that no two children are the same, collaborative inquirers also realize that no one teaching approach works for all students. As a result, they operate from an *inquiry stance,* which Wells (1999, p. 21) has defined as

. . . a stance toward experience and ideas . . . to wonder, to ask questions, and to seek to understand by collaborating with others in the attempt to make answers to them. At the same time, the aim of inquiry is not "knowledge for its own sake" but the disposition and ability to use the understandings so gained to act informedly and responsibly in the situations that may be encountered both now and in the future.

Maintaining an inquiry stance allows teachers to make judgments based on thoughtful analysis, problem solving, experimentation, and assessment. Through the inquiry process, teachers continually transform their beliefs, improve their analytical thinking skills, and develop a rich and well-organized knowledge base that allows them to quickly think through situations and make difficult decisions in the heat of the moment (Anderson, 1984; Berliner, 1986; Colton & Sparks-Langer, 1993).

Successful collaborative inquirers regularly seek out the support and expertise of their colleagues because they know "collaboration provides perspective, diversity, and space for teachers to consider questions about student learning that can provide new insight unavailable in inquiry processes that are done individually" (Literacy and Numeracy Secretariat, 2010, p. 3).

Finally, collaborative inquirers are concerned not only with the immediate effectiveness of their actions on student learning; they also consider the long-term *moral consequences* of their actions (Van Manen, 1977; Zeichner & Liston, 1987). As responsible educators, they think about the far-reaching effects that decisions may have on students as citizens, workers, and parents. They want to guide their students toward both "academic success and effective human relations" (Lindsey, Martinez, & Lindsey, 2006, p. 32).

THE FRAMEWORK: TEACHER AS COLLABORATIVE INQUIRER

Although the Framework: Teacher as Collaborative Inquirer can be applied to any case of teachers' decision-making (e.g., during planning, teaching, or evaluating), it is central to each of the five CASL phases. Each of the components of the framework is illustrated here through Sue Baker's analysis of Nika's work samples during Phase III, "Inquiring Into Teaching for Learning."

Professional Knowledge Base for Teaching

When teachers analyze their students' learning, they draw on their own professional knowledge base (see the right side of the circle in Figure 2.1) to interpret what they see. With more experienced teachers, the categories of knowledge are woven into intricate webs of meaning, which teachers draw upon to interpret their students' performance and to plan appropriate courses of action. Less-experienced teachers' webs are leaner and less elaborate. As teachers engage in inquiry over time, they deepen their understanding of teaching and learning, resulting in a more complex knowledge base.

Of the seven categories of knowledge, five—content, students, pedagogy (teaching methods), context, and case knowledge—are adapted from the seminal work by Shulman (1986, 1987). Although some educators include

Figure 2.1 Framework: Teacher as Collaborative Inquirer

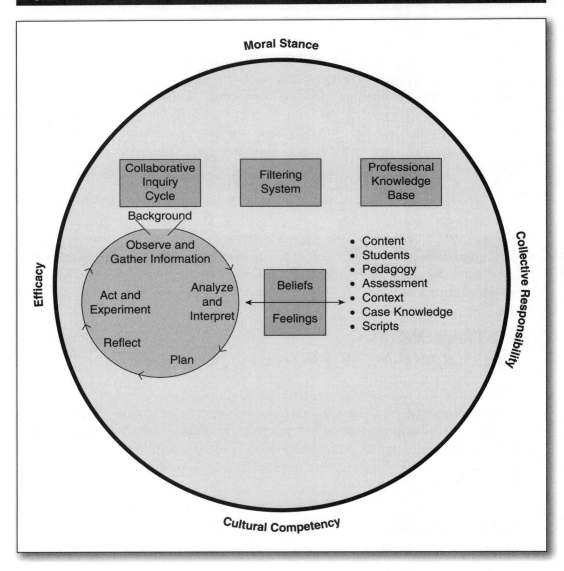

assessment with pedagogy, we prefer not to do so because of the central role of assessment in the CASL process. The last category, *scripts*, comes from the work of Resnick and Klopfer (1989) and is described later in this chapter.

When teachers analyze student work, they draw on a rich and sophisticated understanding of the subject matter and curriculum being taught *(content)*. This understanding is informed by national, state, and local standards and benchmarks.

Consideration of the *students* includes such things as their cultural backgrounds, development, and learning styles. Without this understanding, the teacher cannot select the appropriate instructional methods *(pedagogy)*.

Shulman (1987) coined a term that brings these three categories together: *pedagogical content knowledge,* which refers to the methods that teachers use to portray specific concepts or ideas for a select group of students. For example, over many years of experience, a kindergarten teacher learns which strategies work best with which students and for which types of outcomes. She discovers that young children with limited language development learn best through hands-on inquiry lessons when learning scientific principles.

Collaborative inquirers also apply what they know about the strengths and weaknesses of various *assessment* tools to monitor student progress and identify individual learning needs. For example, a teacher might detect that a student did not do well on a task because the test did not adequately assess what was taught.

Collaborative inquirers draw on their knowledge of content, students, pedagogy, and assessment to hold students to high expectations, to organize the learning in meaningful ways, and to create lessons that are culturally relevant. But one other element is crucial to success: the *context* in which the event or learning is taking place. Context includes such factors as the time of day; current events; the cultural background or socioeconomic status of the students, parents, and community; and state policies and politics. The context may very well affect what works and what doesn't in any learning situation. For example, if there was a racial clash in a student's neighborhood that gets carried over onto the morning school bus, a high school teacher's lesson plan for that day is likely to require changes in order to allow classmates to discuss the event.

Teachers also rely on *case knowledge* (Floden & Buchman, 1990)—vivid insights into content, students, pedagogy, and context—while working with a specific student. Case knowledge, or practitioner knowledge, as Heibert, Gallimore, and Stigler (2002) refer to it, is "typically detailed, concrete and specific" (p. 6) and is developed in response to particular challenges. Cases from their personal or professional experiences are easier for teachers to remember than are research findings because cases carry with them "powerful emotions, and . . . tacit knowledge, knowledge gained through experience" (Lambert et al., 1995, p. 22). Collaborative inquirers consider how "their present situations link to their own prior experiences—what they know and have experienced about the students, the content being taught, the methods being employed, and the present context—before taking the best course of action" (Colton & Sparks-Langer, 1993, p. 47).

The final element of a teacher's knowledge base is *scripts*—automatic routines for action or thinking. With experience, teachers acquire the ability to handle teaching routines with little conscious thought. They also develop automatic self-questioning (metacognitive) routines that help them analyze their actions and decisions. One goal of CASL is to practice and "install" automatic, self-questioning scripts that help teachers inquire into and reflect upon multiple sources of information or knowledge before deciding what to do about a particular situation.

To see the various aspects of the knowledge base in action, let's return to Sue and Nika. During the first month of school, and before convening the school's CASL study groups, Sue provides preliminary instruction *(pedagogy)* around writing. In October, her study group selects the target learning area *(content)*: "To write an explanatory text to examine a topic and convey ideas, concepts, and information through the selection, organization, and analysis of relevant content." To identify her struggling learners, Sue asks her students to read and write a summary of an article from the local newspaper *(assessment)*. As a result of analyzing her students' performances, she selects Nika as her focus student because he, like so many others in her class, struggles to organize his thinking in writing. She selects him also because she knows very little about Native American students *(students)*. Since her school borders on a reservation *(context)*, Sue has a relatively large group of Native American students who tend to perform lower than their white counterparts. Sue feels inadequately prepared to work with these students and trusts that her CASL inquiry will develop her *case knowledge*.

As Sue continues analyzing Nika's work, she is guided by such questions *(scripts)* as "What does the work tell me about how Nika is making sense of the social studies content? What areas of writing are still hard for Nika? How appropriate was my assignment? Have I provided adequate instruction and practice? How might I be more responsive to Nika's needs? What do I know about Nika's cultural background?" Eventually, even in the absence of her group, Sue asks herself such questions automatically.

The Collaborative Inquiry Cycle: Constructing Meaning

A central feature of the framework is the collaborative inquiry cycle (see the left side of Figure 2.1), which describes the conscious processes of teachers' analytical thinking, reflection, and decision-making (adapted from Kolb, 1984). As teachers become more skilled in this way of thinking, they develop the "automatic *scripts* of inquiry" that we mentioned earlier, which allow them to regularly study and improve their practice. Many teachers with whom we have worked refer to this cycle of continuous improvement as "CASL thinking."

Each of the five CASL phase protocols engages teachers in all six steps of the collaborative inquiry cycle. Here, we describe each step of the cycle and illustrate it with Sue's study group as they analyze Nika's work sample in Phase III.

Share Background

In an effort to build a common context for understanding what teachers are observing, the first step in the collaborative inquiry cycle involves the sharing of background information about the evidence that teachers are going to analyze. This first step helps teachers understand when and how test scores and other student performance data were generated and collected. In Phase III, the presenting teacher also shares information about the student and the work sample.

> Before Sue shares Nika's writing, she reminds her group about her decisions from the last study group (e.g., the next student learning outcome, what strategies she would try, and what student work she would bring to this session). She also provides her colleagues with some new biographical information about Nika.

Observe

In the observation step, the study group members compare the work to the provided scoring criteria. The teachers identify the strengths and weaknesses in the work without providing possible explanations for the student's performance. As they hear others' observations, teachers begin to broaden their lenses for looking at the work, resulting in increased layers of meaning (Carini, 1979).

Pat Carini (1979), a well-known researcher and observer of children, cautions against what she calls "habituated perception." She says that when teachers only see the familiar—what they always look for—they miss the true meaning of what is before them. After all, it is impossible to see everything, so we only notice what jumps out at us, given our habitual lenses. Carini (1979) suggests that when teachers give up preconceived or familiar ideas, they begin to see things, perhaps always there, for the first time. These might include important clues that can help them address individual needs, such as a student's prior experiences, cultural background, interests, or learning style. Expanding one's lenses also reduces the risk of jumping to the wrong conclusions and taking ineffective or harmful action.

> Sue is not at all surprised when her colleagues comment on how sloppy and disorganized Nika's paper is, for those are the same observations she has made. What does surprise her, however, is when her colleagues help her see how Nika uses negative adjectives when describing the "white men" and positive adjectives when referring to the Native Americans. This observation raises her curiosity about what was going on with Nika.

Analyze and Interpret

After making observations, "teachers begin to analyze the information [clues in the work] to develop mental representations—or theories—that help them interpret the situation at hand" (Colton & Sparks-Langer, 1993, p. 49). In order to develop reasonable theories about what they see in the work, teachers need to engage in flexible thinking and avoid jumping to conclusions by withholding judgment while they entertain a range of possible interpretations. Examining multiple interpretations before deciding what to do about a learning challenge is a central feature of CASL's inquiry process. Teachers also need time to consider and re-evaluate their assumptions and biases (filters) about what they are seeing. This critical analysis helps teachers accurately frame the problem so they can be more intentional and focused on the actions they decide to take.

There are two primary strategies that teachers use to arrive at a reasonable explanation for the student's performance: (1) drawing on their professional knowledge base and (2) dialogue.

Drawing on Professional Knowledge Base. At the start of the analysis step, teachers mentally inspect their professional knowledge base to see what information might be useful in the interpretation of what they are seeing. This includes drawing on their case knowledge to determine what from their experience is similar (or at least relevant) to the current situation.

When engaging in this analysis, teachers also ask each other questions that mediate their thinking and encourage them to draw on their professional knowledge base, including the following example questions:

- Content: What does the student understand? What misconceptions may be present?
- Students: What characteristics of the student might have influenced this performance? What do we know about the student (e.g., cultural background, prior experiences, learning style)?

- Pedagogy: How well did the instructional strategies work and why? What has worked in the past with this student?
- Assessment: How well did this assignment work in giving us information about the student's understanding?
- Context: What conditions may have affected this performance (e.g., time of day) and why?

As teachers hear an array of perspectives, they naturally question the validity of their own. Through dialogue, the group can critically examine each idea as it surfaces.

Dialogue. Dialogue is the centerpiece of the analysis step of the collaborative inquiry cycle. Unlike discussions, during which decisions are being made and people are advocating for their own ideas, the purpose of dialogue is to co-construct meaning (e.g., Ellinor & Gerard, 1998; Lambert et al., 1995; Senge, 1990; Senge, Kleiner, Roberts, Ross, & Smith, 1994; Yankelovich, 1999). During dialogue, teachers are asked to refrain from giving advice or solutions (solutions are presented only during the planning step). Instead, teachers engage in conversations "where people expose their own thinking effectively and make that thinking open to the influence of others" (Senge, 1990, p. 9). Teachers critically examine each idea for the underlying assumptions and possibilities prior to making any judgments about which interpretation is most plausible. As teachers hear an array of perspectives, they may naturally discover the lack of logic in their own thinking (Bohm, 1965), often leading to ideas never imagined.

Sue shares with her study group her frustration about Nika's poor writing performance and her belief that he has completely given up on doing well in her classroom. While presenting the work, she reflects on the earlier observation of his many negative adjectives to describe those who moved westward. She wonders where all of his anger is coming from. Sue and her colleagues explore several explanations. Sue, however, gravitates toward one in particular: that Nika's negativity and sloppiness might represent his strong alliance with his people and his antagonism toward the pioneers for what they did to the Native Americans. As the group explores this hunch by examining the book and resources, Sue acknowledges that the resources being used are heavily biased toward the settlers, which has probably upset Nika. This insight shifts Sue's assumptions about Nika as a learner and causes her to change her course of instruction.

Sometimes while teachers are analyzing students' specific performances, questions and curiosities arise that require additional knowledge, resources, or investigation. Quite often, the teacher's knowledge base does not include the necessary information to understand or improve the student's learning.

During the CASL process, the facilitator helps group members identify when they need additional information and how best to gather it. Some questions may require the teacher to gather information from those who know the student. Other questions may require additional professional learning and outside resources, especially when there are major gaps in the teacher's or the group's knowledge base. The specific ways the group decides to gather the information is determined during the planning step.

Plan

After analyzing the student's performance (work sample) from various perspectives, the teacher formulates hunches (hypotheses) about which interpretations are most sound. Then study group members dialogue about what actions the presenting teachers might consider taking to help the focus student progress further toward the learning outcome. The group talks about each proposed idea in terms of the short-term and long-term academic, social, moral, and intellectual consequences. After weighing the alternatives, the teacher chooses a course of action. Dewey (1933) suggested that teachers need to mull over several possibilities before acting. They need to ask, for example, "What could be done next with this student? Why would this be appropriate? What might happen as a result of such action?" The ultimate plan of action is left to the presenting teacher because the teacher has the ultimate responsibility for what happens in the classroom.

Next, the study group explores ways to address the questions that surfaced during the analysis stage and any additional curiosities. Teachers may acquire more information in many ways, including collaborative dialogue with a more skilled or knowledgeable individual (Pugach & Johnson, 1990), professional readings, conferences, workshops, or classroom observations of colleagues' teaching. In many cases, the questions posed will require gathering information from the student, the student's parents, or another educator. Teachers share this new information with their colleagues during subsequent sessions.

> Sue will contact the district social studies curriculum director for additional suggestions for primary sources. She will also talk to Nika to check out whether her assumptions about the source of his anger are accurate. Sue will use what she learns from Nika and the director to revise her lessons and final assessment.

Reflect

At the conclusion of each CASL session, teachers step back and take stock. They ponder what they have learned that might benefit their own students, and they consider how to address any professional learning needs they may have. Donald Schon's (1987) seminal work highlights the important role that self-reflection plays in helping teachers clarify their understandings and effectively adapt their behavior. Schon argued that more is actually learned by reflecting on one's experiences than is learned by engaging in the experience itself.

As important, however, is to openly share how teachers felt about their group's interactions. Did they encourage balanced participation? Did the group stay focused on the task at hand? Were all perspectives considered? This is the time to talk about and resolve any conflicts or private concerns. Little (1999) wrote that without such honest sharing, the productivity and passion of the group may fall prey to "polite conversation" that merely scratches the surface of the problem. Only in a trusting setting will teachers dig deeply enough to discover ways to benefit those students they are studying.

Teachers are also encouraged to compose their thoughts in writing, either during or after the session. We view teachers' reflective writing as "frozen thought" about their professional decisions and actions. Such reflections allow teachers to hold their ideas still long enough to critically examine them—to reframe problems, consider multiple points of view, and construct new meanings and interpretations about their experiences, about their students, and about teaching and learning in general. These reflections can be shared with colleagues at any point during their inquiry.

Sue shares her appreciation for what she called the CASL "group think." Without the dialogue, she says, she may never have realized how influential her white middle-class perspective is on her practice. As a result, she commits to always presenting multiple perspectives in history to her students. She looks forward to reviewing an array of primary sources that she can use in future units.

The group's reflection on their collaborative process yields the insight that they are still interrupting one another, and they resolve to give one another the honor of listening to and delving into one another's thinking before putting their own ideas on the table.

Act

Finally, the teacher implements her plan of action by first finding additional information that may inform her efforts. In her classroom, she uses the responsive strategies that were crafted with her study group. After several days of instruction, the teacher collects the next work sample from the same student, and the study group process begins again with the background and observation step. Through this process of observing, analyzing from multiple points of view, weighing alternative plans, and acting, teachers learn to naturally engage in the cycle of inquiry even when not in the study group—the essence of the collaborative inquirer.

Sue works with her colleagues and the district curriculum director to select some primary sources that represent Native American and other minorities' experiences during westward expansion. Through conversations with Nika, she discovers how important it is for Nika to see his cultural background reflected in her curriculum. She gets support from her colleagues to revise her final assessment so students are expected to share multiple perspectives on these events in history. She also talks through what she is going to ask of Nika's father when he visits the class.

Several weeks after Sue has implemented the selected strategies, she returns to her study group with a new student work sample. The group does another round of analysis to examine the effectiveness of the actions they planned at the previous study group session.

Sue brings to the study group not only Nika's final essay but all of her students' essays because she is so proud of what they have accomplished. In addition to the improved quality of the writing, each paper shows great empathy for the struggles of *all* people involved in the westward expansion. The other minority students, who struggled in a similar fashion to Nika, also benefited from her new approach to the unit, as evidenced from their papers. The other teachers inquire into whether Nika's dad might also come to their classes. Sue leaves the study group with a commitment to personalize her instruction in the future by using more primary sources.

Filtering System

The arrows between the collaborative inquiry cycle and the professional knowledge base (see the center of Figure 2.1) illustrate the interplay between these two aspects of teachers' thinking. Teachers draw extensively on their knowledge base as they make the interpretations and decisions required by the collaborative inquiry cycle. In turn, their engagement in the cycle develops new meanings that replace or enhance parts of their knowledge base. However, the interplay between these two elements of teachers' expertise is mediated by a powerful influence—the filtering system.

Teachers' filtering systems are made up largely of beliefs and feelings. The system often drives the degree to which teachers are willing to persist in the face of challenges to help each and every student meet standards of excellence. The system can "lock up" teachers' willingness to engage in the inquiry process, thus allowing them to remain stuck—avoiding their own moral purpose and responsibility for student learning or relying on *deficit thinking* that puts the blame for poor performance or behavior on the students because of the cultural group or families to which they belong (Valencia, 1997). The influence beliefs and feelings have on teachers' thinking and behaviors is explained next.

Beliefs

Beliefs are "consciously held, cognitive views about truth and reality" (Ott, 1989, p. 39). As mentioned in Chapter 1, our beliefs provide us with some predictability for understanding and reacting to our experiences. In some cases, however, teachers' actions do not appear to match their espoused beliefs. This may be because their deep-seated assumptions (untested beliefs)—the generalizations or theories teachers create from their experiences to explain what they encounter—do not always match their stated beliefs. Yet such assumptions are strong forces in guiding behavior, as the following example illustrates.

Imagine a teacher who, over the course of several years, has had several African American boys from a particular housing project. They are usually very disruptive and disengaged from learning. She believes that no matter what she does, these students do not respond positively. In subsequent years, when faced with other students from the same housing complex, she might just say "I can't help these students either." The underlying belief is that African American males from this neighborhood do not care to get an education. This familiar interpretation ends the responsibility of the teacher right there. Educator Marchese (1997) wisely pointed out that such assumptions—unfounded beliefs—"may be objectively wrong, or bigoted, or dysfunctional, and block fair and open encounter with the new or different" (pp. 79–95). Such beliefs can be very limiting when trying to discover and use responsive approaches for learning for such students.

Entrenched beliefs are difficult to change, especially if there is strong emotion associated with the experience (Yero, 2002, p. 102).

Feelings

Not only are many of our beliefs deep seated, they often carry with them personal feelings that may interfere with a person's willingness to persist when things aren't going his or her way. As Hoffman noted, "Whenever we have to make decisions about how to act we always perform an unconscious mental compromise between our judgments and our emotions" (Hoffman, 2011). A person who is highly frustrated or angry may be less willing or able to engage in the analytical thinking required by the cycle, may have trouble accessing relevant knowledge, or may just react without further thought. A few examples of these feelings are frustration ("No matter what I do, nothing works!"), interpersonal conflicts ("This student bugs me." or "I resent this teacher in my group because . . . "), or fatigue or poor health ("I just am not up to this.").

Why do we spend so much time talking about a teacher's filtering system? Have you ever had someone say to you, "Wait a minute. You are jumping to conclusions." We all have heard that judgment. Why? We naturally jump to conclusions because we carry around in our heads what Senge (1990) referred to as mental models—"deeply ingrained assumptions, generalizations, or even pictures or images that influence how we understand the world and how we take action" (p. 8). Our *assumptions* (unfounded beliefs) are particularly difficult to test because they are invisible and we are usually unaware of them (Senge, 1990). As such, we often react to situations without ever testing our assumptions or interpretations.

Teachers continuously observe their students in action and make split-second decisions based on their beliefs. They do this by climbing up what Argyris (1985) called the "ladder of inference." The ladder is "a useful tool for becoming more aware of our thinking and working to understand the origin of many misunderstandings and conflicts" (Ellinor & Gerard, 1998, p. 83). A full explanation of the ladder can be found in Senge et al. (1994). As teachers move up the ladder, they filter what they see and what sense they make of it based on prior experiences and established beliefs (Argyris, 1985). In very short order, these untested beliefs (assumptions) lead to actions.

Imagine if Sue's mind had climbed up the ladder in the following way. The bottom rung represents Nika's initial written work *(student work)*. Immediately, Sue uses her filtering system to select what she wants to pay attention to, or *observe* (second rung) in the paper. In Sue's case, she habitually looks for neatness and organization. She notices that Nika's paper is sloppier than usual and that his thoughts are not hanging together. Sue begins to *construct meaning* (third rung) by comparing and contrasting what she sees with what she knows, believes, and has previously experienced with her students' writing. Sue believes Nika's poor performance is due to a lack of motivation and effort on his part.

Such lack of motivation is not new to Sue. Sue finds that students who lack motivation, no matter what approach she takes, tend to do poorly in her class. Therefore, based on these experiences, Sue starts *formulating the assumption* (fourth rung) that Nika is not going to be successful. Based on this assumption, Sue *draws the conclusion* (fifth rung) that there is nothing more she can do to motivate Nika. Sue *acts* (top rung) by telling Nika she is concerned that he is in danger of failing her class unless he decides to work harder. Sue's frustration leads her to believe that the responsibility to improve is now left to Nika.

The problem with these split-second climbs up the ladder is that teachers run the risk of framing the problem incorrectly and thus solving it inappropriately. They may also end up solving problems the same way every time, regardless of the success rate. When these actions fail, teachers may blame it on someone or something else. Consequently, if a professional learning design does not include an examination of teachers' limiting, deep-seated beliefs, there is little likelihood that there will be transformative changes in practice (Bocchino, 1993; Hunzicker, 2004; Pohan, 1996). With Sue and Nika, Sue initially jumped to a conclusion and almost gave up on Nika. Fortunately, before taking her frustrations out on Nika, Sue sought out support from her study group.

Dispositions of Collaborative Inquirers

In this section, we describe the fourth component of the framework—four teacher characteristics that we now call dispositions. *Dispositions* describe specific teacher attitudes and ways of being that we believe are exhibited and used by collaborative inquirers to dissolve some of the hindrances to teacher excellence posed by limiting feelings and beliefs.

Clearly, for Sue to persist in her quest for equitable approaches through collaborative inquiry, she needed to possess a minimum of four dispositions—moral stance, collective responsibility, cultural competency, and efficacy.

Moral Stance

Collaborative inquirers feel a personal and professional sense of responsibility to maintain or enhance the well-being of each of their students (Gilligan, 1982; Noddings, 1984). They are firmly convinced that their efforts to help students learn and succeed are of vital importance. Therefore, they resist the "pull" to give up on particular students and are willing to take on the challenges that make the job difficult.

To accomplish such ends, they first and foremost take time to come to know their students as learners and people. They inquire into their students' cultural backgrounds, prior experiences, passions, strengths, and needs, and they use what they learn to connect with and motivate their students.

As responsible educators, they continually reflect upon their students' performance and the far-reaching effects that their decisions may have on their students as citizens, workers, and parents. Collaborative inquirers also stand up for the inequities that face their students. As such, they are driven to look for and change inequities in their classroom and schools.

Collective Responsibility

Collaborative inquirers feel a sense of shared responsibility for the success of students in their building and are eager to work with their colleagues to accomplish this. They know that student success is highly reliant on high-quality teaching, so they feel a professional obligation to both seek the expertise of others and help their colleagues grow. In turn, their inspiration comes from sharing both challenges and successes with other educators.

Cultural Competency

Culturally competent teachers believe that all students are capable of reaching high and rigorous standards regardless of race, ethnicity, socioeconomic status, cultural background, learning style, disability, or life experiences. They also know that their students' success is dependent upon their ability to create a culturally responsive learning environment; one that does not ask the students to give up who they are—"to assimilate to a dominant cultural identify" (Howard, 2015, p. 7). To fulfill their moral and professional purpose, they continuously reflect on their own cultural identities, biases, and experiences and the influence of these factors on their practice and their students' learning.

Culturally proficient teachers explore the cultural backgrounds and prior experiences of their students, the students' families, and the communities in which the students live. Such teachers use what they learn to create meaningful relationships and learning experiences. They know that students are more likely to engage in the learning when they have positive relationships with their teachers.

Collaborative inquirers use information about their students to identify and apply appropriate and effective evidence-based instructional practices and culturally relevant teaching that values their students' backgrounds and prepares them intellectually, emotionally, and politically for a responsible and productive life.

Culturally competent teachers also remain flexible in their thinking and their approaches to learning. They know that in order to be effective, they need to be able to "put themselves in another's shoes." For example, they might "try on" a child's way of thinking, about why it might (or might not) be important to learn to read. When certain approaches are not successful with students, collaborative inquirers willingly change course, seek support from colleagues, and pursue further professional learning.

Efficacy

Efficacy refers to the belief that one's effort can make a difference—that student learning is not just a result of luck. An efficacious teacher realizes that student success is a result of commitment and careful planning, analysis, and decision-making. Such teachers are willing to experiment and take risks because they believe that they can make a difference in the lives of their students. These teachers are constantly finding ways to improve and grow.

Collaborative inquiry can create a sense of "shared efficacy." As teachers work together to solve problems, they draw on the diverse understanding and expertise of the group members. This distribution of knowledge and skills results in a "shared belief in [the group's] conjoint capabilities to organize and execute courses of action required to produce given levels of attainments" (Bandura, 1997, p. 477). In a study conducted by Goddard, How, and Hoy (2000), collective teacher efficacy was positively associated with student-level achievement in both reading and mathematics achievement.

> Sue's success in teaching Nika how to write his views about westward expansion is partly due to her strength of *moral purpose*. She really cares about helping her students find their voices and clearly express their ideas in writing. With the help of her study group *(collective responsibility)*, she examines her personal beliefs about low-income students *(cultural competency)*. The result is a deeper understanding of the influence that her own cultural background has on her practice *(cultural competency)*. Her study group also helps her to see the value of using primary sources in her teaching, especially with students of color. This insight boosts her own and the group's sense of *efficacy and collective responsibility.* It also leads to Nika's success in her classroom.

CASL slows things down for teachers so they can examine the automatic responses that arise from their deep-seated belief systems. We call the collaborative inquiry cycle "the pause that refreshes." It enables teachers to reflect on the underlying theories or generalizations embedded in their belief systems and to develop new interpretations for their observations and, thus, new responses. These new ways of seeing usually soften and transform the limiting influence of the filtering system. One result is that teachers grow not only in their professional knowledge base but also in the dispositions of moral stance, cultural competency, collective responsibility, and efficacy.

DEVELOPING COLLABORATIVE INQUIRERS

As our vision of the teacher as a collaborative inquirer evolved, so did our ideas about how to help teachers grow professionally. We recognized that the traditional top-down, one-shot professional development that presents new ideas and skills unconnected to teachers' daily work is not sufficient for transforming teachers' practice. Instead, we believe that the most powerful professional learning design combines inquiry with collaboration.

Research in cognitive psychology tells us that teacher learning is an organic process of active construction rather than an accumulation of facts and discrete pieces of information (Putnam & Borko, 2000). For teachers to assimilate new ideas into their professional practice, they need opportunities to pose their own questions, to view situations from multiple perspectives, to examine their personal beliefs and assumptions, and to experiment with new approaches. CASL provides the structure and the time for teachers to engage in such inquiry.

According to research (Borko, 2004; Nelson & Slavit, 2008; Nelson, Slavit, Perkins, & Hathorn, 2008; Putnam & Borko, 2000; Zeichner, 2003), teachers who engage regularly in collaborative cycles of inquiry develop many of the capacities described in the Framework such as

- transforming their beliefs and practices about teaching, learning, and their students;
- reporting increased student learning;
- developing a stronger sense efficacy;
- regularly engaging in the analysis of data to assess their impact on learning;
- taking more responsibility for their own professional learning;
- developing internalized scripts (or habits of mind) to analyze student learning or other challenges from multiple perspectives before taking action;
- developing skills and dispositions of collaboration; and
- engaging in increased collaboration with colleagues.

These results, however, don't just happen because a group of teachers are put in a study group. To successfully reach these outcomes, collaborative inquiry needs to occur in a trusting environment. Section B of this book provides a fuller explanation of the importance of building a culture of collaboration and various ways to accomplish such a culture through specific practices, supports, leadership, and facilitation.

SUMMARY

Our quest for deeper understanding of the knowledge, skills, and dispositions of a collaborative inquirer is ongoing. The Framework: Teacher as Collaborative Inquirer represents our current understanding. In our search, we have identified and designed a variety of strategies and processes that foster in teachers the professional knowledge, thinking, and characteristics described. As will become evident in subsequent chapters, the CASL professional learning design represents our concerted effort to integrate what we have learned into a structured system of collaborative inquiry.

SECTION B

Building a Culture
for Collaborative Inquiry

Few innovations can survive without the right organizational culture and support. Rosenholz (1989) and others (e.g., Ladson-Billings & Gomez, 2001; Little, 1993; McLaughlin & Talbert, 1993) have observed that the way teachers interact with their colleagues is critical to the future of school restructuring and its effects on students (Darling-Hammond, 1998; Darling-Hammond & Richardson, 2009; Darling-Hammond, Wei, Andree, Richardson, & Ophanos, 2009; Sparks, 2002). The most productive environments seem to be those in which teachers regularly interact and engage in positive and productive collegial conversation around meaningful and relevant issues (DuFour & Mattos, 2013; Darling et al., 2009). During such times, beliefs are revealed and examined and teachers allow their thinking to be open to the influence of others.

These kinds of interactions are possible when appropriate processes and supports are put into place to establish *rapport* and *trust* among study group teachers. Under the right conditions, harmony (rapport) can be established quickly, whereas trust is established over time as individuals become confident that they can rely on their colleagues to behave in specific ways. Based on the work of Tschannen-Moran (2004) and Bryk and Schneider (2004), trust exists among teachers when they can predict that their colleagues will (a) always have their best interest at heart, (b) present things in a truthful manner, (c) fulfill their obligations and promises, and (d) "make themselves vulnerable to others by sharing information, influence and control (Zand, 1997)" (Tschannen-Moran, 2004, p. 25). Finally, trust exists when teachers believe that every member holds some piece of the answer to the puzzle and when they are encouraged to remain open and respectful for all views and perspectives. If these collaborative cultures built on trust are to exist, they have to be planned into the system as a way of doing daily business (DuFour & Mattos, 2013).

For CASL to result in transformative learning—"thoroughgoing changes in deeply held beliefs and habits of practice" (Thompson & Zeuli, 1999, p. 20)—it must be embedded in a supportive school culture in which there is constant attention to building rapport and trust, and in which adequate time, space, and support are provided for teachers to openly and collaboratively reflect on, inquire into, and experiment with new beliefs and practices. With the appropriate working agreements and communication skills, facilitation, leadership, resources, and structures, teachers can move beyond the typical polite conversation that so often interferes with deep analysis of teaching/learning issues. Instead, they can engage in conversations that transform the deep structures that guide their own practices.

The chapters in this section detail the structures, supports, and resources that are needed to reap the greatest benefits from CASL. Chapter 3 describes the working agreements and communication skills that are essential for developing trust among the teachers as they engage in CASL study groups. Chapter 4 explains the support that principals need to provide in establishing and maintaining a school culture for collaborative inquiry. Chapter 5 describes in detail the role of the facilitator in teaching, modeling, and coaching teachers as they relentlessly pursue, discover, and apply responsive approaches to learning so that every student reaches standards of excellence.

3 Working Agreements and Communication Skills for Collaborative Inquiry

As described in the opening of this section, a collaborative culture of trust and openness is crucial to teachers' learning and the productive analysis of student learning. Teachers can feel very vulnerable when they share work from their less successful students. Trust in fellow group members allows teachers to bring such students' work to the group without fear of being judged or criticized. Openness is required because many solutions require a transformation in perceptions, knowledge, or beliefs. In fact, it is often the old way of thinking about a situation and dealing with it that results in the lack of students' and teachers' success.

Specific *working agreements* and *communication skills* provide the psychological safety you need to share your perspectives, inquire into those of others, and reconsider what you have been doing and how you have been thinking about it.

This chapter presents two important ways to develop this sense of safety and willingness within your study group:

1. Working agreements that help the group function in collaborative ways

2. Specific communication skills that promote and maintain a trusting environment while also supporting teachers to stay open to new ways of thinking and being

Much of what we present here will be familiar if you have had extensive training in Cognitive Coaching™ (Costa & Garmston, 2002), Coaching For Results Global (Kee, Anderson, Dearing, Harris, & Shuster, 2010), Adaptive Schools (Garmston & Wellman, 2009), social work, counseling, facilitation, or other interpersonal communication systems designed to develop rapport and problem solving. If this is the case, you may wish to skim this chapter and focus your attention on how these skills are used during the CASL phases as described in Section C. The role of the facilitator in helping develop these crucial aspects is described in Chapter 5.

WORKING AGREEMENTS

Working agreements can be thought of as *ground rules* that define the behavioral expectations of group members. To maintain trust, group members need to know that they can rely on their colleagues to behave in a particular way. This predictability helps set the stage for all future learning. Before beginning to analyze student work, participants need to agree upon and record their group's working agreements. Once established, the group is responsible for revisiting and monitoring the agreements to make sure that they are understood and practiced by all.

Although all schools have working agreements, they are rarely written and are often unclear. Individuals new to the organization may struggle to decipher them by watching the behavior of others. For example, many teachers see getting to meetings on time as a common courtesy, especially when time is limited. When teachers are habitually allowed to arrive late, however, the unspoken message is that such behavior is acceptable. This kind of behavior tends to frustrate those who are punctual, and may cause them to act in ways that interfere with the group—for example, by unconsciously responding negatively to everything a latecomer says, regardless of its value.

By establishing a written agreement for the starting time, the group is likely to avoid such conflicts. If someone does arrive late, it may take only a subtle reminder that an agreement has been broken. If tardiness continues to be a problem, the group needs to rethink the starting time, the consequences for arriving late, or both. We have found that such conflicts

Figure 3.1 Working Agreements Chart

Areas to Consider When Establishing Working Agreements	Sample Agreements for Each Area
Time • What is our beginning and ending time? • Will we start and end on time? • How will we use our time?	**Time** • Start on time; end on time. • Set and honor realistic time lines.
Participation • How will we encourage everyone's participation? • Is it okay not to participate? • When sharing individual student work, what is the role of study group participants? • How will we encourage listening? • How will we encourage sharing of ideas? • How do we support experimentation of new strategies? • What from the session remains confidential?	**Participation** • Seek to understand before being understood. • Criticize the ideas, not members. • Support each other's experimentation. • Practice forming new habits of mind. • Pay attention to self and others. • Challenge the limits of our potential. • Hold experiences and revelations of others with care. • Protect confidentiality.
Focus • What should be the focus of the conversation? • How might the group keep the conversation focused?	**Focus** • Focus on issues of teaching and learning related to the presented student work.

rarely happen when the agreements are collaboratively determined, made explicit among all group members, and periodically reviewed.

Groups can develop working agreements in a variety of ways. They may discuss what is important to them in a learning situation and from there identify the agreements that support those conditions. Alternatively, the group can save time by beginning the conversation with some general categories, such as those in Figure 3.1. Given adequate time to explore each category, group members are generally able to write a set of statements that describe the desired expectations. The Introduction to Section C contains a detailed plan for developing the study group's working agreements.

For example, when developing their working agreements, a group may decide that it is important for a teacher to be able to share his interpretation of a student's work without encountering criticism or personal judgments. The group members may discuss this idea and decide that they will actively seek to understand what a person is saying before responding or stating their own opinions. To make this expectation explicit, the group might establish the norm "Seek to understand, before being understood" (Covey, 1989).

We have found the following agreements to be particularly beneficial in creating productive and engaging CASL study groups:

- Practice forming new habits of mind
- Pay attention to self and others
- Challenge the limits of our potential
- Protect confidentiality
- Hold experiences and revelations of others with care

Regardless of what the agreements are, group members need to talk about why each agreement is important to them and what it looks like in practice. For example, if the group identifies "Paying attention to self and others" as a working agreement, the group members need to talk about why this is so important and discuss multiple ways of meeting this expectation. One way in which members might demonstrate that they are "paying attention to self" is to monitor their "air time" when sharing ideas. This allows others to have ample time to weigh in on the subject. Similarly, "paying attention to others" might mean observing people's reactions to any given comment to make sure that no one is offended.

Dialogue about the specifics of your working agreements helps build consensus and clarifies the expectations for the entire group. A few years ago, Amy was facilitating the development of agreements with an elementary staff. One teacher put the idea of confidentiality on the table. Amy asked the group members to share their thinking about what should stay in the group and what was fair game to talk about with others. One teacher shared how she had told something to a colleague in confidence (or so she thought) after a heated debate. Days later, she learned that half the staff had heard about it. After much dialogue, the group agreed that the specifics shared about students or teachers would remain confidential. Without such a dialogue, trust might have been easily broken as each staff member interpreted confidentiality differently.

For the working agreements to be fully functional, the group members should monitor their behaviors. At the beginning of the first few sessions, members should review the list they added to the CASL Poster. It is also a good idea to ask everyone to select one agreement they find particularly challenging to follow and to pay extra attention to it during the session.

Before closing a session, the study group should reflect on how well they followed the working agreements. If the group is not doing as well as expected in a particular area, then it is important to talk about how the group can improve its efforts. The group may also decide at some point to revise the agreement list. Such a review helps the agreements become an integral part of the group's interactions. When the working agreements become "an established part of group life and group work [then] . . . cohesion, energy,

and commitment to shared work and to the group increase dramatically"
(Garmston & Wellman, 1999, p. 37).

COMMUNICATION SKILLS

If the working agreements are the ground rules, then the communication
skills are the *tools* that the group members use to help each other find ways
to become as effective as possible with their students. We've stressed the
importance of transformative learning during CASL study groups—the
consideration and reframing (if necessary) of beliefs and feelings (filtering
system) that may be limiting teachers' effectiveness with particular students,
especially those whose cultural backgrounds are different from those of
the teachers.

To explore this terrain—let alone the possibility that teachers may need
to shift their own practice—requires respect, honesty, and a safe place to
learn. It also requires specific communication skills that encourage teachers
to dig below the surface to consider ideas and perspectives that may not
have occurred to them previously. This is a tall order for a study group.
Yet, we have seen this kind of transformation when teachers trust one
another and use specific ways of interacting to discover new responsive
approaches to facilitate student learning.

Although there are many different communication skills that one can
use to support collaborative inquiry, we focus on six: committed listening,
pausing to interpret, matching verbal and nonverbal cues, paraphrasing,
probing, and putting ideas on the table. We have found these to be particularly integral to engaging in productive dialogue, which is the central process
used for professional learning in the CASL inquiry (see Figure 3.2).

Figure 3.2 CASL Communication Skills

CASL Communication Skills for Productive Dialogue
Committed Listening Pausing Matching Verbal/Nonverbal Cues Paraphrasing Probing
• Probing for Clarity • Empowering Probes (Presuppositions) • Probing for Beliefs
Putting Ideas on The Table

This chapter begins with a definition and rationale for why *dialogue* is at
the heart of CASL. Next, we describe each of the communication skills and

describe how they are used to facilitate teachers' increasing understanding of the relationship between their teaching and student learning. An illustration of how each skill might be used during a CASL session is also provided. Specific ways for teaching and developing the communication skills are described in Chapter 5: Facilitation of Collaborative Inquiry and in the introduction to Section C.

Dialogue

How group members communicate with one another is fundamental to building a culture for collaborative inquiry and transforming one's beliefs and practices. Although there are two primary ways to converse with colleagues—dialogue and discussion—CASL relies heavily on dialogue. Whereas *discussion* is most often used by groups to arrive at a single idea or solution by supporting and defending opinions and suggestions, *dialogue* encourages study group members to expand their thinking by suspending judgment and taking the time to inquire into their own perspectives and those of their colleagues. The intention of dialogue is *not* to force the group to come around to your perspective as the right one, but rather to *build shared meaning* about what the work demonstrates about how the student learns and which approaches will be most responsive to addressing the student's learning needs. Engagement in dialogue often results in a change in beliefs, knowledge, and behaviors. As stated so eloquently by David Bohm, an American theoretical physicist who contributed to our understanding of dialogue, "A change in meaning is a change in being" (Ellinor & Gerard, 1998, p. 241).

A major benefit of dialogue is that it slows down the decision-making process for teachers, who have the ultimate responsibility for determining what to do next with their students. It provides the time, space, and collegial support for teachers to reflect on the accuracy of their own interpretations of the work and the effectiveness of potential responses to their students' learning needs. Dialogue influences the thinking, beliefs, and practices of all members, which is why each CASL phase concludes with reflection on the process.

To reap the full benefits of dialogue, teachers need to value and respect the ideas of others and remain open to being influenced by what they learn. They have to believe that the answer lies within the group and that together they will come to a responsible and effective solution. This is accomplished through the integration of the following six communication skills, beginning with committed listening.

Committed Listening

When we think about dialogue, we usually think about talking, or conveying our message using words. We are taught that if we want to be understood, we need to present our ideas clearly and succinctly. But if all we do is clearly articulate our ideas, how do we know whether anyone understands what we meant to say? How will we be encouraged to examine, clarify, or change our thinking?

It is through committed listening that people share and construct meaning around ideas (Wood, 1999). Such listening is one of the most essential skills in dialogue because

> Listening is the doorway in which we allow the world to enter. How we listen, to what and to whom we listen, and the assumptions we listen through all frames our perception of reality. Listening may be the single most powerful creative act we perform; we listen and create reality based on what we hear in each moment. (Ellinor & Gerard, 1998, pp. 98–99)

Committed listening is voluntary, active, and complex. The first step in this process is to *attend fully*. Friere defined attending as "taking in and making meaning of the totality" (quoted in Wassermann, 1994, p. 94). It doesn't mean that you have to agree with what is said. To attend to the entire message, focus on both the speaker's words and the nonverbal behaviors that accompany the words. In fact, it is difficult to understand the entire message unless you listen for what is *not* said aloud. Think about this example. A teacher might say, "Go ahead; please explain your position." This message can take on many different meanings depending on the teacher's body language and voice tone. If the teacher has arms folded and shows a frown, the message is different than if the teacher is leaning forward with a smile. Therefore, if you truly wish to understand what a person is feeling or saying, you need to pay close attention to all verbal and nonverbal cues.

Whereas we involuntarily hear many things, listening requires a concerted effort on our part to commit to *fully understand* what is said. "To interpret someone on her or his own terms is one of the greatest gifts we can give another. What we give is personal regard so deep that we open our minds to how another sees the world" (Wood, 1999).

Committed listening requires a commitment, on our part, to hear the message. As the Chinese characters shown in Figure 3.3 suggest, listening requires the focused attention of our ears, eyes, and heart.

Listening in the manner described is not always easy, and it requires "practice and execution" (Sparks, 2005, p. 54). Too often, we are so eager to interject our own thoughts that we miss much of what the other person has said. A helpful strategy, when you are first learning to attend fully, is to ask yourself periodically how well you are attending. Ask such questions as, "How well did I understand the person's thoughts and feelings?" "How often did the person have to repeat the message?"

Figure 3.3 Chinese Characters for Listening

These Chinese characters for listening combine the "ear of the attentive listener" (both characters on the left) with the "eye that is unswerving" (top right) and the "rectitude of the heart" (bottom right). Together the characters suggest that listening requires "focused attention, power, or faculty" of ears, eyes, and heart.

"Am I thinking about how to respond before I have listened to the entire message?"

As you become more conscious of distractions, you will find it easier to set aside your thoughts and shift your focus back to the person speaking.

Nonproductive Listening

To help you become a *committed listener,* we present four of the most common patterns of non-productive listening used during conversation—judgmental, autobiographical, inquisitive, and solution listening (Ellinor & Gerard, 1998; Garmston & Wellman, 2009; Kee et al., 2010).

Judgmental Listening

Judgmental listening is a quick way to shut down the dialogue and destroy any trust previously developed. Attending requires us to suspend our reactions or judgments and to tune in fully to "the how and the what" of the speaker's message.

Whether you agree or disagree with an idea, either one can limit your ability to listen. When you hear something you agree with, you may limit the opportunity to hear and consider other perspectives. You may begin listening only for comments that support your own position. Should you share your approval of one idea, it can immediately discredit any additional thoughts presented.

When you disagree with what is being said, you may immediately attempt to find flaws in the person's idea, causing you to become overly critical. You may simply tune out what is being shared. Or you may begin to associate the bad idea with the person and view that person in a negative light. In either case, you are sending the message that others are not as capable or competent as you; in other words, "It is difficult, if not impossible, to be genuinely curious about someone's opinion and try to reach some deeper understanding of what the person is thinking when you have already judged it as stupid or uninformed or even dangerous" Ellinor & Gerard, 1998, p. 70).

The following are examples of judgmental statements or thoughts:

- "I like Sue's idea of how to motivate Nika."
- "I have already tried that, and it doesn't work."
- "How can he even present that idea when we're talking about students of color?"

To attend fully, you need to learn how to suspend judgment by detaching yourself, personally, from the ideas that are being presented. You need to be able to release yourself from certainty about your own opinions and ideas so that you can explore the possibilities presented without rushing to a particular position.

Autobiographical Listening

Autobiographical listening happens when the topic being talked about causes the listener's brain to make a connection to a personal experience or feeling, and that connection becomes the focus of your listening or the conversation. It is one thing if you are aware of the connection and can set it aside to be fully present. It is another if you shift the conversation to telling your own story or comparing your story to the speaker's. Although you may think that this is a way to communicate your understanding, it actually draws the attention away from the speaker and on to you. As soon as you notice your own autobiographical listening, it is important to refocus your attention and words to what the speaker is sharing.

Imagine that if after Sue shared her frustrations with Nika, a colleague started describing how upset he was with his own student for the same reasons. Sue may never have learned that Nika's lack of engagement in class was due to her one-sided presentation of the westward expansion.

Inquisitive Listening

Inquisitive listening happens when the listener's curiosity about something gets in the way of continuing to listen. Your curiosity may lead you to ponder or ask about a detail that has little to do with the issues being discussed.

This kind of nonproductive listening takes your (and the group's) attention away from what the teacher is sharing For example, when a teacher shared that his student's mother changed to a part-time job so she could be home to meet her child after school, one of his colleagues asked what kind of work the mother did. The teacher stopped sharing and appeared to lose his train of thought. Noting this, the facilitator redirected the group so as not to lose focus on the work. When you catch yourself wanting to ask such questions, remind yourself that the purpose of your listening is to support the teacher's thinking and learning and not to satisfy your own curiosity.

Solution Listening

The intent of this last pattern of nonproductive listening is to provide answers, solve the teacher's problem, or offer advice. Teachers are known for their problem-solving skills, so you might be inclined to offer a solution rather than attend to what the person has to say. With this kind of listening, you are likely to start filtering what you hear because you are looking for ideas that support your own solution. You may even stop listening so that you can prepare how you are going to advocate for your idea to make sure it is accepted. Remember that the whole purpose behind dialogue is to explore *alternative perspectives* before arriving at a single solution.

During the planning step of the inquiry cycle, the teachers started presenting a string of ideas for how Sue should respond to Nika's anger. No one stopped long enough for Sue (or anyone else) to explore the potential that each idea might have in resolving the issue. The noise level even got louder as individuals attempted to argue for their own suggestions. The facilitator quickly recognized that this serial sharing was of little use to Sue and reminded the group to slow down so that each idea could be carefully examined for its potential use.

As these patterns of nonproductive listening demonstrate, attending fully is not easy to do. As Dennis Sparks, the former executive director of Learning Forward, suggests, "Without constant vigilance, it is easy to backslide into inattention, to redirect the speaker to better serve our interests, or fall into argument or debate rather than provide genuine acceptance" (Sparks, 2005, p. 54). Committed listeners need to maintain mindfulness and monitor their attention constantly. Remember that you are present to support your learning and that of your colleagues. One key way you can avoid nonproductive patterns of listening is to pause.

Pausing

Before responding to what is said, it is essential to pause so that you can mentally process what you have heard and formulate an appropriate response (Ellinor & Gerard, 1998). Pausing before responding

- allows the listener time to process the comment and frame his response;
- allows the speaker time to gather his thoughts, clarify what was said, or provide additional information;
- helps the listener to suspend judgment;
- communicates to the speaker that something worthwhile has been shared; and
- promotes time for all to reflect on what was said and to see how it squares with their current understandings.

While pausing, you need to consider both the *content* of the message and the *feelings* behind the words. The feelings are revealed by the speaker's body language and the tone that accompanies the response. During a pause, you can take a "dual perspective" (Wood, 1999, p. 185) by interpreting the message from the speaker's body language and tone along with the speaker's point of view.

When the listener pauses, the speaker has time to reflect on what she just said and perhaps elaborate on or clarify her own thinking before others jump into the conversation. According to Garmston and Wellman (1999), with additional processing time, "more thoughts are organized into coherent speech" (p. 39). For example, Sue may say, "You know, I'm not sure if Nika can really do this type of work!" Immediately jumping in with a comment about Sue's low expectations of Nika may be less fruitful than just waiting for her to realize what she has said and reconsider her assumption.

The pause also allows the group members to put a check on their own reaction and resist nonproductive listening patterns (i.e., solution listening). This can result in the teacher clarifying her own insight. For example, during a pause, Sue might add to her comment by saying, "Well, I'm assuming he can't, but I guess I need to check that out," thereby showing the group that she is aware of her own thinking. But if it becomes clear that Sue is *not* aware of her own assumptions, then the listeners will have had time to think of a response that will help her come to this realization on her own while maintaining her dignity. Examples of effective responses are provided in the next sections.

A pause can also communicate that a teacher has shared a valuable idea that merits consideration. Imagine that Sue shows work illustrating that her students have begun to make progress and says that she thinks it is because she finally understands how different this child's learning style is from other students in her class. The group members can pause, which will give Sue time to add her own explanation of the child's learning style and the strategies that have been so helpful. If she does not provide this level of detail, the group members can follow up by paraphrasing or probing for more information about what she has done and why she thinks it has worked.

Finally, a key feature of dialogue is time to reflect on what is being said, to identify connections, and to formulate the questions that will take the thinking to a different level. Everyone in the group needs to pause in order to do this.

As you can see, a pause before responding can be extremely powerful. Yet this is a very hard skill for most of us to learn, because we are just too eager to interject our views. We sometimes jokingly tell teachers to sit on their hands during a pause so that they won't speak (this is especially helpful for those of us who talk with our hands!). Once you have attended to the message and paused to interpret it, you can decide how to respond.

Responding allows us to communicate our interest, understanding, and reflections about what has been said. If the response is open-ended and nonjudgmental, the speaker will be inclined to share more information, clarify what he is thinking, and perhaps change his thinking as a result.

Teachers in CASL study groups use the following three types of responses to help one another analyze and reflect on teaching and learning: Matching verbal and nonverbal cues, paraphrasing, and probing. Each serves a unique and critical role in promoting and maintaining a trusting environment while also supporting teachers to stay open to new ways of thinking and being.

Matching Verbal and Nonverbal Cues

Matching verbal and nonverbal cues shows the speaker that the listener is "with him" by matching

- body orientation (e.g., facing fully, leaning forward or backward),
- eye contact (although not all cultures accept direct eye contact),
- facial expressions,
- gestures, and
- voice tone and rate.

By matching the speaker's body posture, gestures, voice tone, rate of speech, or some combination of these, you communicate that you heard the message from the speaker's point of view (Costa & Garmston, 1994; 2002). The matching is a quick and subtle action. For example, if a teacher expresses himself with hand motions, you can begin your response with a similar gesture as a way of acknowledging you heard what was shared. When someone frowns while describing something, then you might do the same. To avoid a sense of mockery, do not continue to gesture throughout your response.

Matching *nonverbal cues* is particularly useful when the listener observes signs of discomfort from the speaker. For example, should a teacher put his head down while sharing a situation that is particularly difficult for him, the other teachers might respond by not making direct eye contact when responding, thus giving the person a bit of space.

Matching the *voice tone and rate* is another way of communicating that the teacher is being heard in an accepting way. When, for example, Peter leans forward and rapidly explains in a high-pitched voice a breakthrough with a particular student, the person responding would match the speed and tone, perhaps by saying quickly, "You sound really happy about that, Peter!" To lean back and say the same thing slowly in a deep voice may leave the teacher feeling alone in his enthusiasm. If you start your response at the same tone and speed, he will know that you caught his enthusiasm. Once he knows you heard him, you can slow down your speech.

Matching behaviors in this way is subtle and often unrecognizable by the teacher who is sharing, but it quickly puts him at ease. It lets him know that you understand and respect how he is feeling or acting. Even more important, it opens up the lines of communication so that more dialogue can occur.

Paraphrasing

Paraphrasing is one of the most valuable communication skills for establishing trust quickly. Paraphrasing is the art of letting the speaker know that you have heard and care about what she has said by restating the essence of the message in a different way. A person's first utterance is rarely the entire message. By pausing, and then restating what you think you heard, you invite the speaker to expound on the original message. This allows you to gain further insights into her thinking about a particular situation and to frame appropriate responses. As you paraphrase, remember to match the teacher's body language, voice rate, and intonation. If you detect a heightened emotional state, you can reflect that aspect in the paraphrase.

Paraphrasing keeps the focus on the speaker, which is a profound compliment to her. Rather than jumping in with your own ideas or experiences (referred to earlier as autobiographical or solution listening)—as so many of us are inclined to do—study group teachers listen to one another carefully. Responding in this manner builds trust and comfort.

Paraphrasing helps all group members check their interpretation of what was said. When listeners restate what was heard, the speaker gets to hear the message in another person's words. In this way, the speaker can check the accuracy of what others heard and correct it if necessary. We all can think of times when we misunderstood the initial message and acted accordingly, only to regret it later.

It is important to note that we are not advocating that the listener restate everything that was said by the teacher. Indeed, selecting *which part* of the message to paraphrase is an important decision; paraphrasing is a subtle way to focus the next part of the discussion on a specific aspect of what has been said. For example, Georgea might tell a long story about what happened when she asked her focus student, Kareem, about his understanding of a key math concept. The group members are listening for which piece of the story might yield the greatest insights or which piece might need to be clarified. In one part of the story Georgea mentions that Kareem "could not read the directions" and then goes on. In this example, it would be important to understand exactly what happened when the child could not read the directions. If you paraphrase that point, you can probe for more information by saying, "You mentioned that Kareem had trouble with the words. Tell us more about that. What was he struggling with?" In this way, we focus the teacher on one "nugget of gold" that can be "mined" for greater meaning and insights into Kareem's struggles.

PARAPHRASING

Listener restates a part of the message that warrants more discussion (may include the content of the message and the emotional aspects). Paraphrasing may precede a probe or question.

Purpose (Intent)

- Speaker senses that others care about what she said.
- Speaker can hear what she said and check accuracy.
- Speaker has opportunity to amplify, correct, or clarify.

Examples

Presenting Teacher:	"The students will be doing more creative writing in the future, so I want them to learn how to spice up what they do by using a variety of words."
Group Member:	"You want them to create more vibrant pieces of writing through the use of descriptive words." *(Paraphrase of content)*
Presenting Teacher:	"I just can't get them to be creative!"
Group Member:	"You are really frustrated by your students' current writing because you have worked long and hard with them to get them to use more descriptive language." *(Paraphrase of emotion)*

To practice, try paraphrasing and matching with a loved one or a close friend in your next conversation; you will be astonished at how much more you learn about what that person is thinking and feeling. And you will be surprised by the good will you have created. As mentioned earlier, Stephen Covey (1989) calls this habit of highly effective people "seeking to understand first." You cannot interact with another person in a meaningful way until you truly understand what she is trying to say. Furthermore, people usually need to feel understood before they are open to examining their ideas or viewing the world from a different perspective; both are critical to dialogue and the inquiry process.

Probing

After pausing and paraphrasing (with matching), it is time to respond and invite a deeper level of conversation about how teachers are thinking about a student's learning. Probes are either statements or questions. We introduce three kinds of probes to encourage teachers to delve more deeply into their thinking—probing for clarity, empowering probes (presuppositions), and probing for beliefs and feelings.

Probes are used in a manner that maintains the teacher's comfort and avoids a sense of defensiveness. It is important that the *intent* of the probes always be honorable by communicating respect for the teacher's ability to understand and solve complex learning problems. This means that any teacher offering an idea must never feel corrected or judged. Thus, no suggestions are given—even if they are clothed in the language of a probe—unless the teacher specifically asks for ideas.

Imagine that a member of the study group says, "You just mentioned that Maria is struggling with place value. But haven't you tried manipulatives with her?" The implication is that this teacher has not done enough. Well, we all know there is more to be done, but we do not assume that we have the answers and the teacher does not.

The essence of shared inquiry in a study group is not to fix one another; it is to deepen teachers' knowledge bases and to build in one another the capacity for reflective analysis. So, rather than implying that the "solution" is the use of manipulatives, a group member might paraphrase, and then probe for more information, "Hmmm, you mentioned place value. Tell us more about what you have done to try to help her understand place value." The teacher may mention how she used manipulatives in a small group. The next probe might ask, "How does Maria work in a group? How much does she touch the Unifix cubes when counting?" Through such a conversation, the teacher may discover that

Maria's partner is not sharing the cubes, and Maria may not have actually touched them. This leads to a discussion of how the teacher might use student roles in cooperative learning groups to increase Maria's active involvement with the cubes.

In addition to being nonjudgmental, probes need to be *open-ended*. That is, they should require more than a "yes" or "no" response. We have found that questions that start with "What . . . ?" or "How . . . ?" are usually open-ended and solicit more information. For example, we would ask, "What have you done to help the mother work with her child?" rather than, "Have you tried sending home a specific assignment?" Or "How might you respond to him the next time he doesn't turn in his work?" rather than "Did you consider how you might respond next time?" In both examples, the open-ended questions invite more information, whereas the latter questions can result in a "yes" or "no" answer.

Also, note that the question beginning with "Have you tried?" contains a not-so-hidden suggestion, which sends a message that the teacher has not thought of that tactic and has not tried it. It is better to find out what the teacher has been thinking and trying *before* others share ideas that might help the situation. (The last communication skill presented in this section addresses when and how to "put ideas on the table.") When choosing one of the three types of probes, always consider your intent.

Probing for Clarity

When sharing ideas, even in a study group, you may find that teachers often leave out important information. Either the teacher forgets to mention the information or she thinks that you can fill in the missing pieces. You may seek more information about the feelings, ideas, or thought processes of the speaker by asking her to rephrase, elaborate on, or get more specific about what was said. By probing for clarity, you show that you are truly interested in what is being said and you gain a better understanding of the thinking of your colleagues.

Sometimes a teacher may present an idea in a general or vague manner, and you need to ask for more specificity. When learning this skill, it is most natural to combine the probe with a paraphrase. For example, "You mentioned that Joe was having trouble with his spelling *(paraphrase)*. What kind of trouble have you seen *(probe)*?" One common probe is "Tell me more about that." For example, a teacher might say, "I think the problem might be Mary's attention span." You could respond, "Tell me more about that. What led you to that conclusion?" Such probes invite speakers to become clearer about the details that support what they have said.

Thinking aloud in this fashion is a strong metacognitive tool and has the advantage of helping the speaker become more conscious of and clearer about her thought processes and decisions. Note that being conscious of one's own and others' beliefs and values is a key element of the disposition of *cultural competency* in the framework presented in Chapter 2.

PROBING FOR CLARITY

Listener asks the speaker to elaborate upon or add specific detail about what was said.

Purpose (Intent)

- Moves beyond vague language or generalizations.
- Prompts the speaker to dig more deeply into his own thinking.
- Helps the speaker to become more conscious of his thought processes.

Examples

Presenting Teacher:	"My students really struggle with writing."
Group Member 1:	"What have you seen that tells you that they are struggling?"
Group Member 2:	"What specifically would you like to see in their writing that would represent improvement?"
Presenting Teacher:	"I think that peer editing might be a helpful strategy for Joe."
Group Member 1:	"What might that look like, specifically?"
Group Member 2:	What do we need to think about to make it most effective?"

Empowering Probes (Presuppositions)

Empowering presuppositions raise the speaker's *efficacy* (a disposition in the framework) by assuming that he knows (or can figure out) the solution to a dilemma. It empowers him by raising his level of cognitive functioning and building trust (Costa & Garmston, 2002). "Assuming that others' intentions are positive encourages honest conversations about important matters" (Garmston & Wellman, 2009, p. 38), which is necessary if dialogue is to grow.

We mentioned earlier that to understand a message fully, the listener has to move below the surface of the spoken words. This is because messages often carry hidden meanings. You probably remember times in your life when your mother asked, "Why didn't you do what your teacher told you to do?" The "disempowering" message behind that question is that you were not very smart and didn't even consider doing what you were asked. Such an accusation probably made you highly defensive and cut off further interaction or analytical thinking. In fact, you may have been considering doing exactly what you were asked, but, after this comment, concluded that you either were unable to do it or did not feel it was the appropriate thing to do. The problem with such "limiting presuppositions" (Costa & Garmston, 2002) is that psychologically we tend to believe what we are told and act accordingly. When the message is that we are incompetent, we are apt to shut down our thinking and disengage from the conversation.

If the goal of a study group is to maintain trust and encourage teachers to raise their level of analytical thinking, then you need to use probes that suggest (or *presuppose*) that a teacher has already considered the issue being raised. The teacher will tend to live up to these expectations because she unconsciously senses the high regard she is given by the listener.

Imagine the following situation. A teacher shares a student's writing from a recent unit on creative writing. The work is of poor quality. One of the study group members concludes (in his own head) that the reason for the poor performance is that the teacher did not provide enough models of high-quality writing (*solution listening*). Rather than suggesting this possibility and creating a defensive atmosphere, the participant pauses to suspend his judgment, and decides to see what the presenting teacher thinks. He asks, "What do you believe are some of the reasons for the quality of writing?" The implied message is that the teacher has already considered some possible reasons for what she sees in the work. In the event that she has not thought about the reasons, she will now consider some ideas or ask for some suggestions, because she will recognize the value of the question. Chances are, she will also ask this question of herself the next time she reviews students' work.

An empowering probe can also prompt a teacher to ponder an important issue of which she is not already aware. For example, a group member might wonder whether a creative writing assignment was culturally appropriate for the students. Rather than saying outright that he thinks the writing prompts that the teacher used were above the students' heads, he asks, "How did the students respond to the writing prompts you used? What sense did you get that they could relate to them?" This implies (*presupposes*) that the teacher can think (*or already has thought*) about this aspect of the assignment. If she has, she can share her thinking. If she has not, she will usually pause and consider this idea. Visual evidence of such deep thinking is evident when a person's eyes look up or sideways. This is how a group member knows that he has asked a really good question. Then, the teacher might say something like, "Well, now that you mention it, Joe's short, dry response could have been due to that—the inability to relate to the situation I posed." After such an insight, she will be sure to ask herself this question in the future. Her self-efficacy is boosted because the group *presupposed* that she could figure out an answer to her dilemma by respectfully using probing questions to help her look at a different explanation for the poor quality in the paper.

Many of the questions presented in CASL Phase III protocol are posed as empowering probes that prompt the consideration of several factors that may bear on why a student is or is not making the desired progress. These factors are drawn from the knowledge base included in the Framework: Teacher as Collaborative Inquirer. For example, Joe's teacher can be asked about any contextual factors that might have influenced Joe's writing. The teacher may then remember that Joe was worried about a crisis in the community, and that this may have distracted him from doing his best work.

EMPOWERING PROBES (PRESUPPOSITIONS)

Communicates an expectation that the teacher has already considered the question or issue being raised. The group member *presupposes* that the teacher knows something about the topic being talked about but just hasn't explicitly stated it.

Purpose (Intent)

- Saves the teacher's dignity.
- If the teacher has not thought about the topic, he will think about it.
- The teacher will ask this question of himself in the future *(self-questioning scripts)*.

Examples

Presenting Teacher:	"I want them to show me what they know."
Group Member:	"As you designed this assignment, what student outcomes did you have in mind?"
Presenting Teacher:	"My students won't like poetry unless they can make personal connections to what they read."
Group Member:	"How are you planning to draw on the students' cultural background when you teach poetry?"

Probing for Beliefs and Feelings

Probes can also be used to help individuals examine the beliefs that get in the way of finding the new understandings required to discover equitable approaches that meet students' learning needs. These probes help teachers step back and evaluate the accuracy of their thinking. Remember that, through dialogue, teachers discover solutions by revealing and examining all assumptions *(untested beliefs)* and positions. Probes for beliefs can help people see, in a dignified manner, how their thinking may be faulty.

Occasionally we find teachers who are complacent or reluctant to give up their views. Sometimes they are so sure their views are correct that they do not want to examine them closely. In such cases, we may use probes that cause cognitive dissonance or "rattle one's brain." As Einstein said, "We cannot solve problems with the same thinking that created them." Since these more challenging questions often push a person to go beyond her comfort zone, you need to be tactful and sensitive when using such probes. In fact, we recommend that these kinds of probes be left initially to the group facilitator (see Chapter 5) or to those who are most gentle and discerning with their use of the communication skills—at least until the group becomes more artful in using the communication skills.

The study group process often shakes up teachers' assumptions in a private way as they listen to their colleagues present a point of view that is different from their own. At the end of one year of CASL inquiry, one teacher told us, "After I listened to Carlos discuss how he was not going to give up on Larry, I really had to ask myself this hard question: 'Do I give up too early on a child who is not succeeding?'" She went on to explain that her low expectations were "automatic" until this crucial point when she had to rethink her assumptions about a certain child. Needless to say, she did not give up on her struggling student and she saw him make more progress than she had expected.

Sometimes it is helpful to simply paraphrase the teacher's implied assumptions, especially if you are not sure what those assumptions might be. You might just say, "It sounds like you think Joe is lazy." Although the teacher did not say this directly, it was implied, and now he has a chance to clarify or expand. Or, you might choose a more direct route and say, "I'd like to stop for a minute and check to see what you were thinking or assuming about Joe." This message implies that you believe the teacher is aware of his assumptions, in itself an empowering presupposition that may encourage him to take a second look at his thinking. Or you might ask, "What makes you feel the situation is hopeless?" This might provide some insight into why the teacher feels so discouraged. Once the assumption is out in the open, the group can use the communication skills to help the teacher explore its validity.

Another way to ask someone to examine her assumptions or beliefs in a nonthreatening manner is to ask her to consider alternative perspectives— different ways of interpreting the same experience. Consider the case of a middle school teacher, Gina, who says, "The mother doesn't care about her daughter's education because she never comes to parent conferences." Gina seems to be making the assumption that parents who don't attend conferences don't value their children's education. In this case, you might ask, "What other explanations might there be for the mother not attending conferences?" This is a gentle way of calling into question Gina's beliefs. If Gina shows little willingness to see the situation differently, you might say, "Gina has said the mother doesn't care about her child's schooling. How do the rest of us see that?" The group can then explore other explanations for the mother not attending conferences, for example, that the mother works at the scheduled time, that she may have had bad experiences with school personnel as a child and is not comfortable coming to school, or that she is from another country and doesn't understand what is being asked of her. After the group discussion, Gina may find that another interpretation of the mother's behavior is more fitting.

Viewing the world from someone else's perspective helps teachers challenge their own beliefs. For example, you might ask, "How do you think the mother thinks or feels about this issue?" This kind of probe asks Gina to look at the situation from the perspective of the mother and may yield useful insights, for example, that the mother is intimidated and needs more guidance. Viewing the world from multiple perspectives increases a teacher's *cultural proficiency*—another element in the framework presented in Chapter 2. It also helps the teacher to learn that there may be many different causes for the same behaviors.

PROBING FOR BELIEFS AND FEELINGS

Listener helps individuals examine their beliefs and feelings.

Purpose (Intent)

Asks the speaker to reconsider a belief that may be limiting her ability to pursue, discover, and apply responsive equitable approaches for learning so that each and every student reaches excellence

Examples

Group Member: "You mentioned that Nika just doesn't care and does sloppy work. How do you think Nika feels about his writing?"

Group Member: "So, the mother is uninvolved in this student's learning. What might be some reasons for this?"

Putting Ideas on the Table

Knowing when and how to "place an idea on the table" and when to "take it off" are essential skills for productive collaborative inquiry. For shared meaning to evolve, you need to release your attachment to your own perspective by "putting it on the table" for others to engage with. You can do this by signaling your intention to shift away from listening to and inquiring into another's idea and toward making your own thinking visible and open for examination by others. What you don't want to do is present your idea in a manner that is meant to *persuade and convince others that your idea is the right one*. When you do this, others may balk at giving your idea the serious consideration it deserves because of how it was presented.

As Ellinor and Gerard (1998) wrote,

> The ability to share something that you feel strongly about with your group is important. The problem arises when the way you share your view puts others on the defensive and/or shuts down the conversation. The impact you will have depends on the intention with which you put it forth. (p. 150)

There are three primary ways to put an idea on the table for shared understanding. First, *pause* to signal your intention to share. Second, *label your intentions* by using a transition stem to frame your idea. For example, you might say, "Here is another way . . . " or "Here is a different point of view . . . " or "Another possibility might be . . . " Third, use *tentative language*. Tentative language takes the certainty out of an idea and leaves it open for other possibilities. So, instead of saying "What we see *must* mean . . . ", you would say, "What we see *might* mean . . . " The use of the word "might" avoids the suggestion that there is just one right interpretation.

What the group wants to avoid is what we call *serial sharing*. This is when people just throw out one idea after another without taking the time to make sense of the ideas. This happens most often during the inquiry and planning steps of the CASL phases. Teachers are so eager to share their interpretations and ideas for action that they don't allow time for reflection about what is being said. People need time to process what they are hearing if learning is to take place. Therefore, make sure that you inquire into the thinking of the other person's ideas before putting your own idea on the table.

It is equally important to know when to take an idea *off the table*. There are times during dialogue when an idea is being over-analyzed and it is time to move on. When this happens, one might say "I believe this idea is getting in our way, so I'd like to take it off the table so we can explore other perspectives." Or "I think we have examined this idea sufficiently and it is time to move on to another idea."

PUTTING IDEAS ON THE TABLE

Release ideas in a tentative manner that invites others to engage with them.

Purpose (Intent)

- Recognizes that there is no one right answer, interpretation, or solution.
- Allows group members to understand the thinking of their colleagues.
- Allows the group rather than the individual to own the idea.
- Builds shared meaning.

Examples

Group Member:	*(Pauses)* "Here is another idea that we might want to consider..."
Group Member:	"Let me play the devil's advocate and present this idea."
Group Member:	"What is the possibility that..."
Group Member:	"One area we might need more professional learning on is how to teach reading comprehension."

PUTTING IT ALL TOGETHER

The working agreements and communication skills presented in this chapter are combined in an artful manner, depending on the goal of the conversation and the group members' readiness to critically analyze their thinking about students' learning. For example, if a person is nervous about bringing her students' work to the table, this is a critical time to pay particularly close attention to what you are saying, how it is being said, and how others are responding (working agreement: Paying attention to self and others). You want the presenting teacher to trust that you have her best interest at heart. While the teacher is sharing, group members need to use many paraphrases, empowering presuppositions, and probes for clarity. As mentioned earlier, it makes sense to avoid probing for beliefs and stick primarily to the protocol prompts until the teacher feels more comfortable.

Each step in the inquiry cycle (see Figure 2.1 page 34) benefits from careful attention to the communication skills. Here we illustrate how integral the skills are to both the analysis and planning steps of the inquiry cycle. When a CASL group studies a student work sample, the presenting teacher usually begins Step 3, *analyzing*, by sharing her interpretations of the work. After she is done, group members pause to reflect on what she said. Then, any one of them might paraphrase what was heard and use various probes to inquire further into the teacher's ideas. Be sure to take time to explore one idea at a time. Only put a new idea on the table if it appears that the group has fully understood and considered what came before.

The same sequence is used during Step 4, *planning*, when the group explores which teaching strategies might be most responsive to the discoveries they made about the focus student. At this point, you want to use a combination of probes to help the teacher evaluate the potential effectiveness of each approach offered. This helps the teacher (1) understand the idea thoroughly (i.e., not only *how* it works, but *why* it may or may not work) and (2) take ownership for the idea. Sometimes a teacher takes another teacher's idea and tries to implement it without a careful examination of why it might (or might not) work. To avoid this situation, the group needs to spend time talking about the reasons why a particular strategy is both a responsible and effective way to respond. Without this understanding, the teacher may have no idea what to do if the idea needs adapting for his particular situation. Further, the teacher needs to explore the idea and "make it his" so that if it *does* work he feels more efficacious. If it *doesn't* work, he will still feel comfortable reporting back to the group that he needs to explore other ideas.

SUMMARY

In this chapter, we have presented ideas that are crucial to positive and productive collaborative inquiry into student learning. If these skills are to be used consistently, group members need to clarify, affirm, and review their dedication to help every member grow in her ability to inquire reflectively into and to promote their students' learning. Groups must also commit to honing their use of these skills and to engaging in meaningful dialogue through practice, self-assessment, and reflection.

The most important things to remember as you learn to follow and use the working agreements and the communication skills are their purposes: (1) to establish and maintain a safe and trusting environment and (2) to encourage group members to reexamine, clarify, and transform their thinking and practice so they can help their students reach standards of excellence.

4 Leadership and Support

W herever CASL is successful, school leaders, principals, and district administrators are credited for having a clear vision, providing strong ongoing support, and encouraging teachers to take responsibility for high levels of student learning. These leaders nurture collaborative environments that promote the growth and development of the professionals within their schools. The first part of this chapter describes three leadership principles that help support the success of CASL:

1. Develop and uphold a shared vision

2. Apply pressure and support to reach the vision

3. Promote collective responsibility

After explaining each of these principles, we will share specific ways that school and district leaders can support teachers' engagement in CASL.

DEVELOP AND UPHOLD A SHARED VISION

Without establishing a shared vision of the kind of school you want to build as the leader, it is unlikely that you will get there. The vision is not simply a statement or a mission; it has a compelling aspect that serves to inspire, motivate, and engage people (Southwest Educational Development Laboratory, 2000). A school driven by such a vision usually has a climate of passion and excitement about learning and improvement. It is a place where students enjoy coming every day, an institution for which parents are grateful, and, in general, a source of pride for the community.

All of the administrators with whom we have worked had clear "mental images of a better and more hopeful future" (Deal & Peterson, 1994, p. 101) for all of the children in their schools. They developed their vision through careful study of the literature on educational leadership and school reform. They also visited schools with established learning communities, attended professional learning sessions, and engaged in dialogue with colleagues and consultants.

LORETTA'S VISION

Early in my administrative career, I realized that leadership was about using my role to focus everyone on improvement. Armed with a vision of administrators and teachers working together in a world in which their shared energies would produce motivated and successful learners, I struggled to determine what was needed to bring this vision into reality.

I found that teachers (like students) had individual strengths and weaknesses and were at different developmental stages. I sought to accelerate individual teacher growth while leading the collective to higher levels.

I tried asking teachers to identify professional learning targets and plans for improvement, but the responses focused on rather superficial goals (e.g., "I want to be better organized" or "I would like to learn how to use cooperative learning strategies in my classroom"). Although worthwhile, these goals did not lead to meaningful change. As I pressed teachers to be more specific about the connection between their actions in the classroom and student performance, I found that they did not understand how to inquire into teaching and learning.

It was during this struggle that I first discovered The Framework for Reflective Teachers (Colton & Sparks-Langer, 1993; currently called, the "Framework: Teacher as Collaborative Inquirer") and CASL—a workable system for instructional leaders who want to increase the capacity of teachers, both individually and collectively, to boost learning potential. I realized that the CASL professional learning design was just what I needed to accomplish my vision.

In schools that have a positive influence on student learning (those that reach *excellence* through *equitable practices*), the vision includes expectations of high performance for each and every student, regardless of race, socioeconomic status, cultural background, or gender. Such schools engage teachers as collaborative inquirers in discovering the best ways to support student learning (DuFour & Mattos, 2013). Major decisions are made through dialogue, and their results are studied using systematic, collaborative inquiry.

The leadership's vision "will be influential only to the extent that it is widely shared by the staff and community. Rallying support for a realistic, credible, and attractive vision of what the school might become is part of the daily work of principals" (DuFour & Berkey, 1995, p. 3). Gaining support for a powerful vision requires, time, deliberate leadership actions, and even occasional interventions (DuFour, DuFour, Eaker, & Many, 2010).

To build ownership of the vision, a committee might be composed of representatives from collaborative teams. This committee helps make decisions about various issues that support instruction and acts as a "go between" to assist administrators in making the vision a reality in the school.

By nature, some teachers are resistant to change and may be reluctant to take responsibility for the learning of all students in the school; others will need additional support in learning how to work collaboratively. The best advice is to keep your vision in front of you and to support the efforts of teachers as you apply pressure by holding them accountable.

APPLY BOTH PRESSURE AND SUPPORT TO REACH THE VISION

The principal's position is different from the facilitator in that you, as the principal, are the one who holds teachers accountable for continuous improvement of teaching and student learning. Bear in mind, however, that in addition to putting *pressure* on teachers, you also need to provide the appropriate *support* for their professional learning so that they stay committed to their own improvement. Therefore, we recommend that you continually monitor and take action to balance both pressure and support to lead your school to high performance (DuFour, 2014).

When Loretta implemented CASL in her district, one of the principals was extremely skilled at moving between pressure and support through her words and actions. The principal told the small group of teachers that they were expected to participate in CASL and then monitored the sessions through her periodic attendance. This pressure served to keep the teachers going to the meetings. But the principal also provided ongoing support by acknowledging that CASL was a learning opportunity and that she did not expect perfection. The principal rewarded teachers' work by offering them release time to meet together. As she saw new strategies being tried in the classroom, she provided positive feedback and recognition to the teachers involved.

When we asked a successful elementary principal how she supported teachers in the CASL process, she said that she monitored their progress and provided them with feedback. She did not attend every study group session, but she did make the following suggestion: "When you see them (teachers) later, talk to them . . . . Come into their classrooms to observe . . . . Talk to them about how you can see that they have taken what they've gained from their team meeting and put it into practice." Whenever you see or hear evidence of a teacher's professional growth, it is important to let her know so that she feels both recognized and appreciated. You can share a teacher's successes in a staff meeting, in a one-on-one conversation, or through a personal note.

You might also provide informal feedback to CASL study group members. For example, you may talk with a teacher in the hall as she is going to the workroom to make copies. You might mention that you observed her effectively using a strategy and that you are proud of the progress she has made. By making these comments, you will likely motivate the teacher to work harder to accomplish the shared vision of high performance for all.

If a teacher is still not invested in collaborative inquiry—for example, if his participation is limited or distracting—you may need to pull him aside and reiterate your expectations. You might also ask him what is interfering with his engagement. If appropriate and within your control, you may be able to address this teacher's concerns. If he cannot offer an explanation, you might emphasize the importance of his involvement to the success of the group. As a last resort, you may need to tell him that you are monitoring his involvement and explain possible consequences of not participating. Finally, you might consider asking the teacher to relocate.

PROMOTE COLLECTIVE RESPONSIBILITY

Little professional learning occurs unless teachers have a fire in their belly to accomplish something important. And what could be more important than sharing a passion for the learning of their students and colleagues? Stimulating teachers' collective responsibility is one way to fan the fire.

According to research in cognitive psychology, teacher learning is an organic process rather than an accumulation of facts and discrete pieces of information (Putnam & Borko, 2000). Based on our own experience and the literature, we believe that an effective catalyst for teachers' learning is their own *curiosity*. According to Wolf & Brandt (1988) "the brain is essentially curious, and it must be to survive. It constantly seeks connections between the new and the known. Learning is a process of active construction by the learner . . . ." For teachers to accommodate new ideas into their knowledge base, they need opportunities to pose their own questions, to view situations from multiple perspectives, to examine their personal beliefs and assumptions, and to experiment with new approaches.

CASL provides the structure and the time for teachers to explore their own curiosities. As teachers see the value of collaborating with their colleagues, they gain a sense of shared responsibility and passion for the learning of all.

Establishing a sense of collective responsibility for all students' learning among the staff is a critical means for reaching excellence with equity (Brinson & Steiner, 2007; Dufour & Mattos, 2013). Principals can tap into teachers' natural curiosity and establish shared responsibility by generating *cognitive dissonance*—a key ingredient in facilitating transformative learning.

Cognitive dissonance occurs when teachers are asked to test their beliefs and practices against conflicting evidence or ideas. As a result, teachers are usually eager to resolve the dissonance through collaborative inquiry. We describe three ways in which you can create such dissonance: analysis of student data, examination of the unknown, and review of research. Each has the potential to promote teachers' curiosity and help teachers consider their collective responsibility for learning.

Analysis of Student Data

You can create cognitive dissonance by sharing data that conflict with the staff's assumptions about their students' performance. It is hard to ignore a problem when the data show a major achievement gap between your Caucasian students and your African American students or when you see that your male students are doing better in science than your female students. Such data analysis can create a shared sense of urgency that doing "business as usual" is not enough; things need to change! (Darling-Hammond, 2010).

> When Loretta was a curriculum director, she asked principals and a small group of teachers to analyze schoolwide student data. The analysis showed teachers where students were struggling and also provided some clues as to why students were doing so poorly in reading comprehension of expository text. In this case, the staff used what they learned to identify their target learning area for CASL. Chapter 6 provides more information about selecting the target learning area.

Examination of the Unknown

Another way to create dissonance is to lead teachers to discover discrepancies—perhaps discrepancies between the intended curriculum and the delivered curriculum (Kotter, 2008). For example, when the curriculum director of a Michigan district began working with an elementary school, she asked teachers to identify their students' outcomes in reading. The teachers soon realized that they were not at all clear about what they hoped to accomplish. She then asked them to share what they actually taught at the first- and second-grade levels. The teachers soon discovered that there were redundancies and gaps in the curriculum and acknowledged that this was interfering with their students' progress. They immediately launched an investigation of their curriculum outcomes using student work samples to clarify the desired learnings.

Review of Relevant Research

Another way to motivate teachers to question the status quo is to have them read and discuss research studies that demonstrate how other educators in similar situations have raised student achievement.

> When Loretta met with teachers from her district in Mississippi, she shared how she came to believe that the CASL system would help address some of their students' problems. She talked about what she learned from articles on learning communities and shared her belief in teachers' collaborative problem solving. Then she led a professional learning session designed to review their students' test data. After the session, Loretta distributed articles related to the issues that had been identified through the teachers' data analysis. In subsequent meetings, teachers were given time to dialogue about how the information from the research articles might apply to their issues.

A second example of the use of research to stimulate cognitive dissonance comes from Michigan. When a group of elementary school teachers decided that they wanted to become better at teaching reading, the principal and district curriculum coordinator invited Amy to come in and talk about CASL. She shared information about the system and answered questions. She also asked the teachers to read "Power of the Portfolio" (Goff, Colton, & Langer, 2000), which describes the CASL inquiry process and supporting research. She then guided them through the assessment and analysis of their own students' reading assessment results. As they looked at the evidence and reviewed relevant literature on reading acquisition, they discovered multiple areas that needed to be addressed. As a result, they were eager to continue their inquiry.

Next, we turn to specific ways that you, as a school or district leader, can support the implementation of CASL.

SUPPORTING TEACHERS' ENGAGEMENT IN CASL

The CASL design is conducted in study groups and follows the image suggested by DuFour and Mattos (2013):

When members of a team make the results from their common assessments transparent, analyze those results collectively, and discuss which instructional strategies seem most effective based on actual evidence of student learning, they're using the most powerful catalysts for improving instruction. (p. 4)

Principals support the CASL study groups "by providing teams with time to collaborate, helping to clarify the work that teams need to do, and ensuring that teams have access to the resources and support they need to accomplish their objectives" (Dufour & Mattos, 2013, p. 4).

We suggest seven specific ways for principals and other leaders to support teachers' engagement in CASL:

1. Develop interest in CASL

2. Establish collaborative teams

3. Provide time to meet

4. Identify the target learning area(s) for inquiry

5. Provide resources

6. Provide incentives and celebrate victories

7. Model a commitment to collaborative inquiry

Develop Interest in CASL

Although *you* may know the benefits of CASL, don't assume that everyone else does, too. When your colleagues first hear about CASL, they may have questions and concerns. Unfortunately, many teachers have never experienced the power of positive, productive collaboration. Moreover, because teachers so often work in isolation, there may be little trust among colleagues and they may be reluctant to share what they do in their classrooms. Some teachers fear that the experience will take too much time out of their day and will have little payoff. In short, teachers will not be interested unless the process is seen as comfortable, manageable, and helpful for dealing with everyday student learning challenges.

Participants may need time to mull over the process, ask additional questions, and explore different scenarios before they are willing to commit to engaging in CASL. If this is true in your school, we suggest that you conduct an *introductory session* (Section C, pp. 126–138) includes an outline) and then hold other meetings to address questions that arise.

As you consider who to invite to these early sessions, we strongly encourage you to include administrators and other leaders who may be involved in supporting CASL. Also invite any teachers who show an interest in working collaboratively or those with whom you would like to pilot-test the process. If you take the time up front to build understanding and commitment, you are likely to avoid potential conflicts during implementation (Hattie, 2012).

Establish Collaborative Teams

Research suggests that when teachers form teams to intentionally study their practice, teaching and learning improve (Bryk, Sebring, Allensworth, Luppescu, & Easton, 2010). Although teachers' participation in professional learning communities is on the rise, the results of their meetings are not always productive (DuFour et al., 2010). Some people have assumed that collaborative tasks are natural and convenient for teachers. We think not. In fact, without intentional preparation and leadership, you may find that although teachers have completed a "collaborative task," it may come at the expense of precious time and bad feelings. That is why we recommend that the teams be led by a skilled facilitator, as explained in Chapter 5.

When establishing teams, consider how the teams will be configured, what meaningful work teachers will engage in, and what you want the teams to accomplish (DuFour, 2014). As you plan how to form and support the CASL study groups, you might let the following questions guide your decisions. As you consider each of these factors, it is important to invite teacher input.

- What curricular issues are we attempting to address in our school or district?
- What are the goals and purposes of implementing CASL in our school or district?
- Who needs to work together regularly to help move us toward our goals? How can we fully use the knowledge and expertise of the faculty (e.g., discipline-specific, cross-discipline, or special-needs expertise)?
- What structures exist within the school day to support collaborative work? What would be a natural and feasible way for teachers to work together (e.g., planning times, professional learning days)?

The opportunity for shared learning in CASL is tremendous because the same group of three to five teachers will meet regularly. Think about what you hope the teachers will learn and who should work together to meet these goals. For example, if you see a need for content expertise to be shared across subjects (e.g., writing across all curricular areas), you might include English teachers in each study group. Or, if there is a lack of coherence in the middle school English curriculum across schools, form study groups composed of eighth-grade English teachers across the district. Finally, in a school with several new teachers, you might ask them to work with veteran teachers so that the novices have access to the knowledge of the more experienced teachers.

Provide Time to Meet

Powerful professional learning requires sustained time, which is a scarce resource for teachers. As you plan to implement CASL, teachers will ask, "Where will we find time to do this?" "How much time will it take?" "Will we have enough time to do it right?" Since CASL requires that teachers meet regularly to examine student work samples, test results, and other data, common time is needed (Leithwood, Louis, Anderson, & Wahlstrom, 2004).

In the short term, review your school's current use of time. Think about time slots when teachers are free from classroom duties and how they can be brought together. Forming study groups may be as simple as combining teachers who have common planning times.

Finding time may require restructuring the school day or altering how time is used. In one middle school, the teachers met during a planning period once a week. In an elementary school, the principal rearranged special subjects (art, music, physical education) so that clusters of teachers could meet when their students were with the special subjects' teachers. Some schools use staff meetings for CASL study group meetings.

If state law requires your district to offer a specified number of days a year for professional learning, allot some of this time to CASL. At a Mississippi high school, CASL was the centerpiece of the school's professional learning plan and those days were allocated to the process. Finally, if teachers choose to meet before or after school, you can count it as professional learning time (e.g., continuing education units or college credits).

Identify the Target Learning Area

CASL Phase I (see Chapter 6) requires the identification of a content focus of study, referred to as the target learning area (TLA). If your school already has identified areas for academic improvement, one of those areas is a good place to start. If not, you should do some preliminary work with leaders and teachers to identify areas of needed improvement.

You could ask teams to examine achievement data and report strengths and weaknesses at a staff meeting. As teachers report their findings, discussion might evolve around patterns found across disciplines, grade levels, or different racial, cultural, socioeconomic, gender, and other subgroups. Many good resources exist to guide you in designing these data inquiry meetings, for example, Wellman and Lipton's (2004) *Data-Driven Dialogue*.

Ultimately, the teachers in your school need to know that their time in CASL is going to be well spent. Whatever they investigate as the TLA should make their work easier, improve their practice, and increase student achievement.

Provide Resources

As an administrator, you will need to find and allocate resources to support the CASL system (Marzano, Waters, & McNulty, 2005). You can anticipate meeting expenses, compensation for facilitator and participants, resources, and professional learning opportunities.

Meeting Expenses

Expenses for meetings may include food, copying costs, notebooks, and resource books. Each teacher will need to have a copy of this book and a CASL Notebook for materials and written reflections. Depending on when the teachers meet, you may want to provide refreshments (e.g., coffee and bagels in the morning or a light snack in the afternoon).

Compensation for Facilitator and Participants

The facilitator is critical to the success of the process. If she comes from outside the district, she should be compensated for her services. You may find it prudent to estimate how many times teachers will meet and then create a budget to compensate the facilitator for her time. If adequate funding is not available for the facilitator, relief from other duties may balance the workload for this person.

Funding for substitute teachers or teacher stipends may be needed to allow teachers to attend the initial CASL session and study group meetings. One administrator used money from a federal grant to hire floating substitute teachers, who rotated from classroom to classroom throughout the day. The floating substitutes allowed the teachers to leave their classes to attend their study group meetings. In another school, teachers received stipends for meeting an hour before school. If time during the day or funding is not available, the acquisition of continuing educational units (CEUs) or college credits may help teachers balance the use of after school time with personal needs.

Professional Learning Opportunities and Materials

During the process of analyzing students' learning in CASL study groups, teachers often find that, as a group, they lack sufficient knowledge or skills to meet the needs of the students they've selected to study (Leithwood et al., 2004). As they identify their own professional learning needs, you can respond by providing resources such as books, videotapes, or other materials. Teachers often request a session with experts in the areas they've chosen for further learning. Finally, you might provide funds for attendance at relevant institutes, professional learning programs, or conferences.

For example, several elementary teachers decided to watch videos and attend workshops on teaching reading comprehension. Teachers at another school invited a professor from a local university to share her ideas. Access to such resources enhances the teachers' abilities to achieve higher levels of performance with students and often serves as a powerful motivator.

Provide Incentives and Celebrate Victories

Teachers feel appreciated and are more willing to engage in new learning experiences if they feel that there is something in it for them, both professionally and personally. Guskey (2001) found that teachers often have to try something and see the positive effect on students before they are willing to integrate it into their practice. We think the same is true with CASL. Most teachers have to see the benefits before they are fully committed. Once they do, they are intrinsically motivated. Prior to that, however, they often need some external incentives.

Some of the incentives that schools have used are release time, registration to go to a conference, access to a professional library, instructional materials related to the TLA, skilled facilitation, and a pleasant quiet area to meet.

One study group had asked their administrators if they could implement a new approach to teaching reading that they had seen at another school. The district administrators provided the teachers with Amy's facilitation and said that they would be willing to support the program if the teachers' inquiry into their students' reading performance supported their request. As the teachers examined student work and learned more about reading acquisition and instruction, they decided that the new program would not meet their needs; what they needed were leveled reading books (trade books organized in incremental levels). The district was more than willing to provide the resources because they felt that the teachers had thoroughly investigated their students' needs.

Another way to motivate teachers is through ceremonies that acknowledge teachers' accomplishments and let them know that they are part of something important. "Genuine celebration is a necessity for creating a school culture in which raising and sustaining student achievement is possible" (Routman, 2014, p. 186). Note that in the final phase of CASL, study group members share with their colleagues their own and their students' learning gains (see Chapter 9). This celebration may involve the participants only, or it may involve a wider audience.

At one school, the central office administration was so excited about CASL that they asked the participating teachers to make a presentation to the school board. Afterward, the board gave the teachers plaques to formally recognize their work.

We find that for many teachers, the main motivation to engage in this process is an internal one—seeing their own students grow and make progress. Teachers also feel affirmed when one of the ideas they propose in their study group is tried by a colleague who reports that the strategy helped students make great strides.

Loretta invited Amy and Georgea to join her staff in Mississippi every few months, not just to provide additional training but to acknowledge the progress that teachers were making. Typically, during the morning session of these district gatherings, teachers shared what they had done and learned since the last large-group session. In the afternoon, they were treated to more support and training. Teachers who were frustrated because they were struggling with certain aspects of the process left with vigor and excitement. One teacher said, "I was getting frustrated, but now I am eager to go back and analyze another piece of my focus student's work."

Model a Commitment to Collaborative Inquiry

CASL is an inquiry-based way of approaching classroom and school challenges; it is a way of thinking rather than a program. Therefore, the inquiry cycle, working agreements, and communication skills need to be incorporated into as many school meetings and professional learning activities as possible. Ideally, all staff members would strive to use the communication skills during their meetings. Further, they would choose to use the collaborative inquiry cycle as part of their decision-making process. Consistent use of these tools builds a culture of trust and deliberate thoughtful decision-making.

It is important that teachers see you, an administrator, engaging in collaborative inquiry and decision-making in your own work. Teachers need to see you working with them, valuing collaboration, procuring needed resources, and creating supportive structures as they struggle to find new solutions to persistent problems.

Your leadership actions will demonstrate your commitment to collaborative inquiry. For example, if you have teacher groups review assessment results, and then use this information in making decisions, this communicates your belief in the power of collaboratively analyzing data. On the other hand, if an administrator wants teachers to work collaboratively but never involves them in decision-making, a double standard is communicated. An administrator might say he values the use of data for decision-making but then makes decisions based on political influences. Such actions call his credibility into question.

How you respond to teachers' questions can also signal to teachers that you value inquiry and dialogue. For example, a teacher might ask, "What should I do in this situation?" By listening, paraphrasing, and probing (rather than trying to fix the problem for the teacher), you can empower her to consider the possible causes. For example, you may also ask, "What have you learned so far about what is contributing to this situation?" Then you might ask, "What recommendations have you considered with your CASL team?" Another important question might be, "What data are you using to support your concerns?"

Such open-ended questions mirror the kinds of communication skills used in the CASL study groups (see Chapter 3) and offer you an opportunity to model key aspects of collaborative inquiry. At the same time, you can also subtly assess the teacher's professional thinking.

Another way of modeling your commitment to collaboration is to participate in the teacher study groups, even if you only drop in occasionally. Although one principal was not able to attend many of the group sessions, the teachers welcomed her participation and the fact that she attended early in the morning—before school began. As she became more engaged, she began to raise important questions, provide outside resources when needed, and share her insights.

When you participate in the study groups, the teachers need to know that you will follow the working agreements and use positive communication skills. Furthermore, teachers need to be able to trust that what you hear them say during the group sessions will not be used during their evaluations (Wallace Foundation, 2013). Otherwise, the trust level will be diminished and little will be accomplished. We worked in one school where the principal would come to the study groups and then make critical comments outside of the group about what the presenting teacher shared. As a result, teachers withheld ideas and were hesitant to share their students' work when she was present.

Although it is not feasible for the administrator(s) to sit in on every study group meeting, it is crucial that you monitor, encourage, support, and show interest in the progress of the team. One tool for this purpose is the CASL Study Group Log. At the end of each study group meeting, the recorder completes a short summary of what transpired during the meeting, including any resources or other requests for support. In this way, the groups know that you are aware of their progress and can be responsive to their needs.

If you cannot attend any of the sessions, it is important that you at least recognize the effort of the study group teachers. Ask them how the process is going, mention items reported to you in the Study Group Log, and encourage them to share what they are learning. If you observe teachers using a new strategy that they learned from their colleagues, provide positive feedback so that they will continue to experiment with new ideas.

SUMMARY

The CASL system is not intended as a complete fix or solution to all the issues confronting administrators, or as the only way to successfully accomplish your vision. We offer it as one professional learning design to assist you in your efforts to improve instruction for all students in your schools and districts. We encourage you to use the principles shared in this chapter in ways that work for you. Analyze the important aspects of your situation, mix your creative abilities with good judgment, and adapt CASL to meet your needs.

5 Facilitation of Collaborative Inquiry

Chapter 3 emphasized how central dialogue is to teachers' relentless pursuit to discover responsive approaches that enable each and every student to reach standards of excellence. We also pointed out that the opportunity to engage in sustained "authentic talk about real work" (Lambert et al., 1995, p. 93)—*dialogue*—has not traditionally been a part of teachers' daily experiences. Moving teachers away from mere polite interactions to the kinds of thinking, problem posing, and problem solving that result in transformative learning requires careful planning and guidance (Fullan, 2001; Lambert et al., 1995). As with the establishment of any new group, such guided participation needs to come from someone outside the study group who is more skilled than any of the members. With this support, participants soon embrace collaboration and may make comments similar to this one from an elementary teacher: "I can't imagine ever doing my work without my colleagues again. This was the best professional development experience I ever had. I want to keep meeting with my CASL study group next year."

CASL is designed to build teachers' capacity to engage in collaborative inquiry in a manner that supports them in developing the skills, knowledge, and dispositions defined in the framework in Chapter 2. Achievement of these outcomes requires *skilled* and *flexible facilitation*. Facilitation refers to the "art, craft and science of providing process leadership in a manner that enables optimal human interaction, learning and organizational performance" (Great Lakes Area Regional Resource Center, 1998). The CASL facilitator's responsibilities include preparation for each CASL session; providing guidance during each session so that the group stays focused, learns skills of collaboration, and completes the required tasks; and assessment of the group's and individuals' development of collaborative inquiry skills, professional knowledge base, and dispositions. Facilitation of CASL's collaborative inquiry process is always designed to build and sustain trust and rapport for transformative learning that leads to excellence with equity.

Although one person is designated as the facilitator, the ultimate goal is for all study group members to develop the skills of collaborative inquiry and facilitation so that they take collective responsibility for one another's learning. You want all members to actively inquire into the ideas of their colleagues rather than relying solely on the designated facilitator to do all the probing for more perspectives.

In this chapter, we suggest how a school or district might select a facilitator to guide the CASL process. Next we talk about the art of facilitation and share a vision of CASL facilitation. Then we provide a detailed description of how to prepare for the CASL sessions including such items as logistics and designing a session. Next we talk about the purpose of group and individual documentation. We also provide some general tips on how to facilitate teachers' consistent use of the working agreements and communication skills. Suggestions for teaching and supporting the agreements and communication skills are provided in the introduction to Section C: The Five CASL Phases and in Chapters 6–9. The final section in this chapter provides guidance on how the facilitator might prepare herself and grow in her facilitation.

SELECTION OF A STUDY GROUP FACILITATOR

A building-based teacher leader, department head, district-level specialist, or administrator in areas such as curriculum and instruction may be able, willing, and qualified to take on the role. Sometimes the leadership prefers hiring a consultant from outside the district to start the process. Before making a selection, keep in mind the role and responsibilities of the facilitator.

Although implementation of the CASL system does not require special training, it is helpful if the person has read this book, agrees philosophically with this approach to professional learning, and is familiar with both the Framework: Teacher as Collaborative Inquirer and the CASL phases. The selected individual should also know how to build study group members' commitment to the working agreements and to teach and model positive and productive communication skills (educators trained in Cognitive Coaching™, Coaching for Results Global™, or The Adaptive School are familiar with such skills). Furthermore, it is imperative that the facilitator be a trusted colleague or someone who can build rapport quickly with the group members. Otherwise, it is difficult to create a safe and supportive environment for learning. We find that the most effective facilitators are committed listeners, are open-minded, know their limitations, and are comfortable relying on the expertise of others.

We don't feel that it is necessary for the facilitator to be an expert in the subject matter (target learning area) being discussed by the study group. In fact, such expertise may hinder group interaction. A facilitator is there to keep the group focused and to guide the dialogue, not to provide the answers or to teach the content. If the facilitator is expected to come with all the answers, she may be more inclined to share her own ideas rather than guide the learning of others. When she is unfamiliar with the content, the facilitator is more likely to ask probing questions for her own clarification, which encourages participants to deepen their understanding.

When inviting someone other than the facilitator in to share her expertise, it is helpful to provide specific information about what the teachers want to learn. Equally important is to share the goals of CASL and to ask the "expert" to design her professional learning in a manner that allows teachers time for dialogue, analysis, and reflection.

Should the facilitator have expertise in the subject matter under investigation and is in a position to address the gaps in the teachers' knowledge base, it is certainly okay for that person to provide additional information. When doing so, however, it is important for her to let the group know that she is stepping out of the role of facilitator to present some content. When done, it is important to signal her return to facilitation. She can do this by asking the group to reflect on what they just learned and to apply it to the situation currently under investigation.

A variety of approaches have been used to select the facilitator. In one elementary school, where a grant allowed all teachers to participate in CASL, we led the initial sessions on working agreements, communication skills, and the first few CASL phases. We also facilitated the study groups for a few months to model the communication skills and provide feedback on the teachers' interactions. Toward the middle of the school year, we relinquished the role of facilitator to a trusted reading consultant in the school and we coached her through the first few sessions.

In another elementary school in which the teachers had formed their own study group, Amy and the district curriculum director joined the group and provided facilitation services. In a middle school where teachers were required to meet regularly, we sat with each group as consultants, but we encouraged teachers to accept more of the responsibility for their own facilitation over time.

Optimally, the facilitator needs to gradually move the group to greater levels of competence and independence. The process we use to do this is called *guided participation* (Rogoff, 1990).

THE ART OF FACILITATION

In guided participation, the skilled facilitator assesses the degree to which the group and its members are able to engage in collaborative inquiry and gradually moves the group to higher levels of skills. As the facilitator, you should remember that "This process requires active collaboration, communication skills, assessment of another's developmental level, and interactive dialogue" (Colton & Sparks-Langer, 1992, p. 158).

Through your facilitation, you help the teachers learn the tools of collaborative inquiry; in the process, the participants enrich their professional knowledge base. You teach these tools by building bridges (or scaffolding) from what participants already understand and can do toward new insights and skills; scaffolding occurs through teaching, modeling, and coaching (Joyce & Showers, 2002). This bridging occurs in the "zone of proximal development" (Vygotsky, 1978)—"the mental distance between a person's current problem solving ability and the ability the person can achieve if coached and supported by a more skilled individual" (Colton & Sparks-Langer, 1992, p. 158). Thus, guided participation is moving participants through the zone.

The teachers with whom you work will progress most effectively within an atmosphere of trust and rapport. You can develop and maintain such an environment by attending to what the group members say, interpreting the conveyed message, and then responding appropriately. Your response is determined by assessing each member's level of knowledge and skill compared with where the group needs to be. As the facilitator, you need to interpret what you hear and artfully and intentionally push the members to take risks and consider new ideas without asking them to take on too much too soon.

The approaches that you use to move the group through the zone of proximal development include directive, collaborative, and nondirective approaches, as illustrated in Figure 5.1. This model of facilitation approaches is adapted from Glickman's (1981) work on developmental supervision.

The Directive Approach

The directive approach is used whenever the group lacks the necessary knowledge or skills for the inquiry, for collaboration, or for engaging

Figure 5.1 Approaches Used by the Facilitator

Directive (FACILITATOR/teacher)	Collaborative (facilitator/teacher)	Nondirective (facilitator/TEACHER)
• Initiate and teach • Model • Provide feedback	• Solve problems • Identify solutions	• Listen attentively • Prompt

NOTE: Capital letters symbolize the dominant party in the conversation.

students in learning. In either case, the facilitator assumes the bulk of the responsibility for directing the group's learning and interactions (see "FACILITATOR/teacher" in Figure 5.1) by *initiating, teaching,* and *modelling* certain practices for collaborative inquiry and, when appropriate, helping group members plan how they will address their own professional learning needs.

When modeling is called for, you need to demonstrate the behavior in tandem with an explanation of why it is being used. As the skills are taught, ask the group to practice them with your *guidance* and *feedback*. As the group becomes more knowledgeable and skilled, step back into a collaborative approach and give most, if not all, of the responsibility to the group.

If study group members are in need of additional professional learning, actively engage them in planning how they will address their learning needs. At this point, you take a collaborative approach.

In the early phases of CASL, you will probably use a more directive approach by doing most of the summarizing and labelling as you help teachers clarify their own professional knowledge and language. As their level of expertise increases, group members will be able to do their own summarizing, with perhaps only an occasional reminder from you as an equal. When this happens, you move toward a nondirective approach.

The Collaborative Approach

A collaborative approach is used when the situation calls for participation of equals. This typically happens when the group needs to problem-solve or plan a course of action together. As facilitator, you'll need to listen carefully to what the group members are saying and help them make an appropriate decision by engaging them in dialogue, paraphrasing what you hear, probing for more clarity and ideas, and reflecting on what is being said.

Should you have your own ideas, feel free to put them on the table to be examined by others. Just make sure that you are transparent with the group about your intent.

The Nondirective Approach

Once the group becomes mostly autonomous, you need to interject an idea or question only when the group needs a quick reminder about what to do next or when you see them glossing over an important learning opportunity. For example, when a teacher shares an assumption and no one in the group probes into what the teacher means, you need to interject, "I believe an assumption has been raised; what question might you want to ask?"

At times, you may want to provide the group with specific feedback about how they are progressing in their use of collaborative skills so that they can ultimately critique themselves in this area. You may need to remind the group to write reflections before the session is over. Or, you may ask the group members to reflect on what more they may need to learn. For example, if they have tried the same approach to address the students' learning needs for three sessions in a row and they are getting the same results, you need to help the group to either pick another strategy or consider getting additional professional learning.

When you feel that at least some of the group members have acquired the necessary analytical and communication skills to take on some responsibilities for facilitation, which is the ultimate goal, take a back seat and observe their interactions. You may interject your ideas periodically to answer questions or monitor progress. When this happens, you are there to monitor the group's progress and to make sure that the members stay focused on the task at hand.

Flexing for Various Purposes

Teachers enter the CASL study group with different knowledge, various levels of functioning, and individual views on the issues discussed. Your goal is to encourage the group to share diverse perspectives while continuously assessing members' levels of understanding and appropriately moving them through the zone of proximal development.

Although Figure 5.1 may suggest that facilitators move teachers through the "zone of proximal development" in a linear fashion, this is not the case. The approach that you use is totally dependent upon the teachers' consistent use of the communication skills and the teachers' level of development of the outcomes defined in the framework. For example, there might be times when you will need to stop the group and redirect its focus; help group members learn more because they are coming up dry when trying to find a solution; or teach, re-teach, model, or coach a skill, especially the communication skills. We recommend that you keep your eye on the teacher learning outcomes that you are trying to accomplish and remain flexible in your approach by using your best judgment and intuition to decide how to effectively respond. The following sections describe a few common moves that you might find reason to use when facilitating CASL. Other facilitation tips are embedded in Chapters 6–9.

Identify a Teacher's Assumption

Until trust and rapport are established, the facilitator will usually be the one to ask the more difficult probes—empowering presuppositions and probes for surfacing teachers' beliefs and feelings. Imagine that a teacher makes the comment, "Until Sara learns English, there is nothing I can do to help her write a constructive response in mathematics." To help the teacher examine her assumption about students whose native language is not English, you might ask, "So you believe that it is not your responsibility to help her with her English?" The teacher pauses and then responds by saying, "I guess what I really am saying is that until she knows English this is going to be hard for her and I unfortunately, don't know how to help her."

After the teacher responds, stop the action (we call it a "stop and frame"—we often use our hands to signal time out), and explain to the group that a probe was used to label a teacher's assumption. Remember that an assumption is an untested belief. Explain the intent of your question, which is to see if you have interpreted the teacher's assumption correctly. In addition, you are ensuring that the teacher is aware of her assumption and you are encouraging the group to examine whether the assumption was accurate. Notice Sara paused to think about what she said before responding to the probe. She acknowledged that what she was really feeling was unprepared to help the student. This interchange opened the door for the facilitator to guide the group to explore ways to help English language learners during the *planning* step.

As the facilitator, you explain the purpose of the probes only *after* the teachers respond, so that the group can see the results of the question—the additional thinking and information that were prompted. This example illustrates how you can use a directive approach to introduce a new or more complex communication skill in the heat of the group's inquiry.

As the teachers recognize that your function is to keep them safe from criticism, they will relax and begin to ask these questions of themselves.

Identify Gaps in Teachers' Professional Knowledge Base

As you work with teachers, it is also important to listen for where there are gaps in their professional knowledge base. For example, if, as you listen to teachers engage in the inquiry cycle, you feel that the group needs expertise that is not readily available, help the teachers identify what they need to know and how they might find the needed information.

In most cases, you'll be able to help teachers acquire the additional information between study group meetings.

Occasionally, however, a group may discover that they need to learn new skills or understandings before going on to the next phase or task. In such situations, we advise that the group take a hiatus from analyzing student work and instead take the time for further professional learning. As the facilitator, you help the group judge how much time to take. When the group is comfortable with their knowledge and skills, they should resume analyzing student work.

> As Georgea and Amy worked with a group of middle school teachers on reading, it became quite apparent that the teachers' knowledge of reading strategies was lean. After consulting with the teachers, Georgea and Amy arranged for the district reading specialist to meet with the teachers to provide additional professional learning on how to integrate reading strategies into the curriculum.

Facilitating the Flow of Curiosity

Sometimes, teachers' curiosity gets the best of them and they deviate from the protocol. This is not always a bad thing. In fact, letting teachers explore their own questions or ideas in the heat of the moment often results in very important insights about teaching and learning. You'll need to decide what is in the best interest of the teachers' learning. Should you refocus their attention on the step of the protocol? Or should you let them take a journey down their own path of inquiry?

At times, we let teachers travel into uncharted waters because we anticipate that doing so will deepen their understanding about themselves, their students, or their curriculum. If after a time, the new direction doesn't seem fruitful, you can certainly bring the teachers back to the task at hand.

The Kettering Elementary School teachers were studying how to increase reading fluency. Their hypothesis was that increased fluency would lead to improved reading comprehension.

During a CASL session, the first-grade teacher shared that her students were having difficulty understanding the last story they read, which she assured her study group was at the right reading level for her students. She was surprised that the students were struggling because their reading fluency was right on target.

The teacher explained the story in the following manner. "A family was camping near a large lake. When they woke up in the morning, the sun was in their eyes, so they decided to move their campsite to the direct opposite side of the lake. The family arrived at the lake later that afternoon. When they arrived at the new location, they found that the sun was back in their eyes." After summarizing the story, she explained that her students didn't seem to understand the story. They didn't know what time of day it was at the end of the story, why the sun was back in the family's eyes, or how many days it took to get to the other side.

The other group members became quite curious about the students' struggle and immediately started sharing all kinds of explanations for the students' performance. The presenting teacher shared the multiple strategies that she had used to explain why the sun was in the family's eyes at the end. Others started thinking about alternative ways in which the teacher could have taught the concepts that were in the story so that the students could understand how the rotation of the earth makes it appear that the sun rises in the east and sets in the west . Amy let the dialogue go on for quite a while because there was so much energy behind the conversation. Her instinct told her that there was something to be learned about teaching reading if she let it go on long enough.

Then it dawned on her. Amy recognized that to understand the story, the students would need to understand two complex concepts. Therefore, Amy asked the teachers two questions. The first was, "At what grade do children learn about the rotation of the earth and its relationship to the sun?" The other question was, "When are children developmentally able to understand temporal relationships?" Amy wanted teachers to consider how a child's developmental level and prior experiences are both important to understanding the story. She also saw this as a gap in the teachers' knowledge because they were not considering these issues when analyzing the work. It was a great time to push the teachers' thinking!

The teachers knew that their first-graders have a hard time with concepts of time, but they didn't know when students typically develop an understanding of this concept. Amy suggested that the answer might be found in the work of Piaget. When no one volunteered to find the reference needed, the principal offered to find it and bring it to the next meeting.

According to Piaget (Flavell, 1963), first-graders are not likely to understand the passage of time unless it is explicitly stated. For example, they can tell you time of day if the story says either "It was night time" or "It happened in the morning." But they cannot infer time from contextual clues. If the story said, "The boy had already eaten lunch and was waiting for dinner," they would be unable to identify what time of day it was.

After discussing what they learned, the group concluded that they needed to examine a book for both readability *and developmentally appropriate concepts* before assigning it. Otherwise, students would not be able to comprehend what they read. They also recognized that they needed to spend more time just studying how to teach comprehension. The group decided, with Amy's help, to spend at least a month reading articles and viewing videotapes about how to teach young children how to understand what they read.

PREPARATION FOR FACILITATION OF CASL

In our experience, effective facilitators plan for both the expected and the unexpected. In this section, we identify the key tasks for which a CASL facilitator is responsible:

1. Planning with the school leadership

2. Addressing logistics

3. Getting acquainted with the teachers and the context

4. Becoming familiar with the standard CASL session design and tools

5. Arranging the space for CASL sessions

6. Gathering necessary materials

For each of the six categories, we highlight issues that you might encounter and explain how you might address them. We cannot emphasize strongly enough the importance of thinking about these issues as you prepare for each study group meeting so as to avoid pitfalls that might hinder the accomplishment of the CASL goals. We also suggest that you review all of the other chapters in the book for a thorough understanding of the theories and processes of CASL.

Although the facilitator plays a critical role in preparing for CASL, we strongly encourage you to do the bulk of your planning in collaboration with the school leadership (e.g., principal, assistant principal, school leadership team, teacher leaders).

Planning With the School Leadership

Many of the logistics and operations are impossible to plan without involvement and oversight from the school leadership. While Chapter 4 is devoted to this topic, a few essential ideas are offered here.

As soon as you know that you will be facilitating CASL, schedule a planning meeting with the school administrator(s). Use your time together to learn all you can about the expertise and prior experience of the teachers with whom you will be interacting and the context in which CASL is being implemented. This is also the time to address logistical details related to the composition of the study group as well as the timing and location of group sessions.

Teachers' Expertise and Prior Experience

You want to honor teachers' prior experiences and expertise when designing CASL sessions. Although you can learn much from the teachers themselves, it is also helpful to ask the school leadership such questions as

- What areas of expertise will the teachers bring to the group?
- Have the teachers had formal professional learning in the skills of facilitation (e.g., communication skills, Cognitive Coaching, Adaptive Schools)?
- Are any of them mentoring other teachers?
- What school improvement goals are the teachers working on?
- Have any of the teachers done other forms of collaborative inquiry (e.g., action research)?
- Have any of the teachers ever been members of a study group?
- What other professional learning have they had related to the target learning area?

Contextual Background

You will want to ask the leadership about the context in which you will be working. You need to find out whether the group has identified its target learning area (TLA), whether there are pressures from the outside that are influencing the focus of the inquiry, and whether there are competing demands on teachers' time.

When you ask about the TLA, find out if one has been identified and, if so, what it is. If the TLA hasn't been selected, then work with the principal to plan how to select it (see Chapter 6). If the teachers have already identified a TLA, ask what process was used to select it. Did the principal choose it, or did teachers help? This gives you insight into how decisions are made in the school.

If the teachers and principal worked collaboratively, you can build on that experience. You will want to find out why they picked the particular target. Perhaps they picked it because the district mandated that they choose it from a list. Is it an accreditation or school improvement goal? Does the target represent a new area in the curriculum? Is the community pushing the school or district to address the target area selected?

This last question helps you explore the external pressures that may push teachers to take on a certain focus. Another example of community pressure might include school improvement teams focusing on "the basics" because parents are concerned that their children won't be prepared for college.

As a facilitator, you may need to help the school leadership consider the feasibility of implementing the CASL phases at this time. Find out whether there are other school or district initiatives that might be competing with or supporting the CASL design. If the teachers are engaged in too many other initiatives, it may be hard for them to commit high-quality attention to this one.

Logistics

Once you get a general sense of the expertise of the staff and the context in which you will facilitate, you and the leadership need to roll up your sleeves and address the specific logistics—e.g., the composition of study groups, scheduling and timing of CASL sessions, and arrangement of space.

Composition of Study Groups

Consideration of the composition of each study group is extremely important. To reap the greatest benefits, you will want to form groups of teachers who will learn the most together, given their daily responsibilities and your intentions for professional learning and school improvement. We recommend that each group remain together through all five CASL phases.

We recommend a group size of three to five members. A larger group may have the advantage of multiple perspectives and a wider knowledge base to inform the inquiry. However, larger groups may have trouble finding time to analyze all of their focus students' work samples in a reasonable amount of time. The smaller size allows the group to complete each focus student's work analysis once every two or three weeks during the months spent in Phase III. If there is too much time between samples, teachers have difficulty knowing what they did that influenced student learning. Smaller groups also encourage balanced participation and more consistent use of the communication skills. As you compose your CASL study groups, consider the following possibilities, along with their benefits and challenges.

Group Members Share Same Subject Area and Same (or Close) Grade Level. This configuration is ideal for learning the CASL process. Teachers who are responsible for developing student learning in the same grade and content can dig deeply into how students at this developmental level construct meaning in the target learning area. They already share the same content knowledge and understanding of the needs of students in their grade level. Further, such groups are invaluable to the professional growth and development of teachers new to the grade or content.

Another benefit of grade-level teams is that they are in charge of so much curriculum development. They can bring their working agreements and communication skills to those tasks. Further, when they need to make a decision about any issue related to their team, they are likely to gather evidence and analyze the issue from many angles before planning their actions

Group Members Share Same Subject Area but Different Grade Levels. In cross-grade groups, teachers can learn how students construct meaning and proficiency with given content standards at different ages. Such "vertical teaming" helps members learn how teachers in the grades below and above them develop and assess students' learning. These understandings lead to a more coherent curriculum across the grade levels. For example, many elementary schools inquire into a TLA related to language arts because all teachers are responsible for student learning in this area.

Group Members Share Different Subject Areas but Same Grade Level. This configuration makes sense in middle or high schools where interdisciplinary teams share the same students and are responsible for developing student learning across the curriculum. Some interdisciplinary teams study learning areas (e.g., writing, reading, interpreting graphs) that cut across disciplinary areas. In such groups, teachers may learn how to make cross-disciplinary connections among their subjects and help students transfer skills and concepts across classes. Further, they can see how their own students think and operate in different subject areas, which is often a valuable clue to crafting responsive approaches.

We are often asked how to include the following individuals in CASL groups: counselors; consultants; and teachers of special education, art, music, and physical education. Our answer is that every person in the group needs to have something to contribute and needs to select a focus student of her own by completing Phases I and II. The perspectives of teachers who work with the focus students in nonacademic situations can be very enlightening.

Scheduling and Pacing of CASL Sessions

In preparation for the implementation of CASL, you need to (a) create a master schedule for CASL sessions and (b) determine how much time you will need to spend developing the communication skills and engaging teachers in the CASL phases. Ultimately, you and the study group are responsible for the pace and progress of their shared inquiry. Suggestions for creating a master schedule and pacing teachers' engagement in the CASL phases is provided next.

Master Schedule for CASL Sessions. In Chapter 4, we recommend that the principal find a regular meeting time for the CASL study group so that teachers can plan accordingly. You may have to help the principal think this through.

In an effort to establish job-embedded professional learning, many study groups meet once a week during the school day and once during the time slot reserved for staff meetings. When staff meetings are used for CASL, principals often reduce the time spent on announcements about policies and news by putting such information into an email message or newsletter.

Pacing Teachers' Engagement in the CASL Phases. You and the teams are in charge of the pace and progress of your shared inquiry. While we have listed the phases in a deliberate order, the amount of time that you take with each phase will depend greatly on the study group teachers' prior knowledge and the allotted time for CASL. Figure 5.2 shows how the phases can be scheduled and how you might organize the pacing of the sessions. Note that no one phase must be completed in only one CASL session.

Who is in the room when you facilitate CASL inquiry will also influence the timing and scheduling of the sessions. For Phases I, II, IV, and V, you may choose to facilitate two or more groups in the same room. However, in Phase III, it is best to facilitate each study group separately as the groups analyze the work samples of their focus students. This hands-on facilitation will allow you to read the study group's progress and engage them in decisions about next steps.

During Phase III, it may take up to 45 minutes to analyze one student work sample. (Some of this depends on the length of the work.) Therefore, a four-person group will need at least three hours per month of meeting time. You will want to work with the school schedule and the district contract to find ways to provide this time.

Figure 5.2 Scheduling CASL Phases and Developing Productive Collaboration

CASL Session: Title, Timing, and Topics	Development of Working Agreements and Communication Skills

Introductory Session
 	
Timing
 	
Prior spring, late August or early September (one day or two half-days)
 	
Topics
 	
• CASL Goals and Benefits
• The Five Phases
• Framework: Teacher as Collaborative Inquirer
• Working Agreements
• Communication Skills
	• Develop Working Agreements
	• Teach New Communication Skills
	
	  o Dialogue
	  o Listening
	  o Pausing

Phase I: Establish a Focus for Collaborative Inquiry
 	
Timing
 	
Begin before school starts and finish in September, OR begin in September or early January (one half-day or full day if combined with Introductory Session)
 	
Topics
 	
• Target Learning Area
• Initial Whole-Class Assessment
• Teacher Cultural Autobiography
	• Review Working Agreements
	• Review Communication Skills
	• Teach New Communication Skills
	
	  o Matching Verbal and Nonverbal Cues
	  o Paraphrasing

CASL Session: Title, Timing, and Topics	Development of Working Agreements and Communication Skills
Phase II: Define Teachers' Professional Learning Goals **Timing** Two-four weeks after Phase I is completed (one half-day) **Topics** • Initial Assessment Results • Professional Learning Goal • Focus Student Biography	• Review Working Agreements • Review Communication Skills • Teach New Communication Skill ○ Probing for Clarity

Phase III: Inquiring Into Teaching for Learning
 	
Timing
 	
After Phase II is completed (For 3–5 months, meet every 2–4 weeks to analyze focus student's recent work; add time for further professional learning as needed.)
 	
Topics
 	
• Focus Student Work Analysis
• Focus Student Biography
• Teacher Cultural Autobiography
	• Review Working Agreements
	• Review Communication Skills
	• Teach New Communication Skills
	
	  ○ Empowering Probes
	  ○ Putting Ideas on the Table
	
	(In second Session of Phase III: Teach Probing for Beliefs and Feelings)

Phase IV: Assessing Learning Progress **Timing** Late spring or end of semester (one-half day or 90 minutes if teachers bring completed performance grid with them) **Topics** • Whole-Class Final Assessment • Plans for Non-Proficient Students	• Review Working Agreements • Review All Communication Skills
Phase V: Integrating Learning Into Teachers' Professional Practice **Timing** One or two weeks after completion of Phase IV (Reflection: 2 hours; Celebration: 1–2 hours) **Topics** • Reflection: Teacher and Student Learning • Professional Learning Goals • Celebration	• Review Working Agreements • Review All Communication Skills

Where additional curriculum work or assessment design is required, you may extend the time to complete Phases I and II. Sometimes teachers are stumped by a challenge in the middle of Phase III and will choose to use one or more sessions to pursue new understandings instead of analyzing their focus students' work. Chapters 6–9 provide detailed guidelines for what we call *further professional learning*.

We want to caution you, however, about taking time away from the CASL phases to engage in further learning. We have seen some groups want to stick with designing curriculum as a way of avoiding the risk of trying out the instruction and revealing the actual results of their efforts (e.g., through work samples). It's important to always move back into looking at the actual evidence of student learning as quickly as possible.

Our experience has taught us that it is best to spread the study group sessions out across the academic year (or semester, if in high school). That said, the CASL Introductory Session (see Section C: The Five CASL Phases) might be held in the spring of the prior school year. Teachers may also begin to analyze large-scale performance data in the spring to prepare for beginning Phase I the following fall. Completion of the rest of the phases needs to wait until teachers meet their new students at the beginning of the school year since the inquiry tasks focus on those students.

Arranging Space for CASL Sessions

The space in which the groups meet has a big influence on their productivity. You will want to select a room that is free of interruptions and noise. The room should have a dedicated place for CASL meetings, with the Framework Poster (Figure 2.1) and the CASL Poster (Figure C.3) set up so that everyone can see them when the facilitator refers to them at critical points during each session. The Framework Poster provides a visual display of the capacities teachers are utilizing and developing during their CASL inquiry. The CASL Poster (Figure C.3) portrays the group's purpose, its working agreements, and the CASL communication skills.

The space also needs to allow for each member to see the information written on the Recorder Sheet. During each session, a recorder is keeping track of the group's ideas on a sheet provided for that purpose. This sheet might be posted on an easel, wall, in the middle of the table, or on an electronic projector. The important point is to make sure that all study group members can easily see and read the information on the Recorder Sheet.

The seating arrangement of the study group is another important consideration. Regardless of whether you have multiple study groups meeting in the same room (during Phases I, II, IV, and V) or you have only one study group, you will want to arrange the space so that the group members are able to easily see one another and the materials that they are analyzing. This usually means that the three to five group members either sit around a small round table or gather around the end of a rectangular table.

Gathering Necessary Materials

Essential tools to facilitate the group's work include a flip chart with markers in several colors, a pad from which individuals may take paper, and sticky notes. Make sure the CASL Poster (Figure C.3) and the Framework Poster (Figure 2.1) are available for all to see. Also include materials required for the specific CASL tasks of the day: the protocol for the current phase, the Recorder Sheet, and a Study Group Log for the administrator. Chapters 6–9 list the specific materials necessary for each phase.

We suggest that each teacher be provided with a three-ring binder (notebook) with a separate tab for each of the five phases. Each tab will contain a protocol with the teacher's notes on it, along with student work and other relevant documentation (listed at the end of Chapters 6–9).

One school discovered a clever way to organize the documentation for the focus students that each group studied. Within the Phase III section of the notebook, they included extra dividers, one for each of the study group's three to five focus students. When the study group finished analyzing a work sample, they placed it and the related materials into that student's section.

These CASL notebooks are often shared during Phase V, when teachers celebrate their own insights and the learning progress of their students.

Getting Acquainted and Building Rapport With the Teachers

Before the first CASL session, it is helpful for the facilitator to get to know the participating teachers and the context in which the group will work. The information gathered from the teachers in tandem with that from the school or district leaders can help you adequately prepare for the first few meetings. If you have already worked with the teachers, you can integrate what you have learned from those experiences into your planning.

Here are just a few suggestions about how you might begin to build rapport among the teachers with whom you will work. Schedule informal meetings with each study group during their planning time, lunch, or immediately before or after school. You might even offer to meet them for coffee off campus after school hours. It is best to give them choices for meeting times.

If you are not from the local area, you might suggest using videoconferencing and scheduling the conversation for a time that is mutually convenient.

The CASL Session Design and Supportive Tools

With logistics addressed, you are ready to prepare for your first and subsequent CASL sessions. In this section, we introduce you to the CASL session design template that is used when planning any session. The unique considerations for facilitating each phase's tasks are highlighted in Chapters 6–9.

We recommend organizing study group sessions into three segments: (1) opening the session, (2) engaging in professional learning, and (2) organizing for the next session (Figure 5.3). Each segment of the agenda relies on specific tools to guide teachers through an array of activities and tasks. The purpose of each segment and a description of the supporting tools are described next.

In describing each tool, we use a facilitation strategy called "What, Why, How." This strategy provides the teachers with explicit information about *what* is coming up, *why* it is worthwhile to engage in (its purpose), and *how* group members will be engaged (what they will be doing). This strategy is used to help teachers focus their attention on the upcoming activity.

Figure 5.3 CASL Study Group Session Design

Opening the Session

- Greeting
- Grounding
- Framing the Session

  o CASL Goal
  o Session Outcomes
  o Agenda
  o Working Agreements
  o Parking Lot

- Distributing Materials
- Identifying Roles

Engaging in Professional Learning

- Developing and Applying Communication Skills
- Completing Collaborative Inquiry Tasks
- Reflecting

  o After Each Activity
  o On the Day's Learning

Organizing for the Next Session

- Taking Actions Planned During Session
- Pursuing Further Professional Learning as Needed

Opening the Session

The opening of any session sets the tone for all that follows. You want to ensure you have created a psychologically safe space that supports collaborative inquiry and calls participants' attention to the goals and outcomes for the day. The tools used in this segment include: (a) greeting, (b) grounding, (c) framing the session, (d) distributing materials, and (e) identifying roles. These tools are used to establish rapport and to establish the group's focus.

Greeting

- **What:** A greeting is a way of calling attention to your presence and indicating your intention to establish a relationship with others.
- **Why:** Informally greeting teachers and asking them how they are doing as they arrive to a CASL session helps quickly build rapport.
- **How:** For the first session, informally greet teachers as they arrive for the session. Then at the start of the session, greet them and share some background information about yourself, if appropriate. Explain why you are excited about facilitating CASL. Include a statement of what your facilitator role will include. At the start of subsequent meetings, you can informally greet teachers as they arrive and ask them how things are going.

Grounding

- **What:** Grounding is a process that helps individuals transition their attention and energy from their everyday classroom responsibilities to the interactions and tasks of their study group.
- **Why:** A teacher's day is filled with pressing concerns and issues that don't go away just because they are in a CASL session. A grounding allows teachers time to transition from the world outside their group to the tasks at hand. In addition, a grounding helps the group

  o gather information,
  o develop relationships (rapport and trust),
  o practice committed listening,
  o bring all voices into the room,
  o express their hopes and concerns, and
  o connect with past, present, and future content.

- **How:** Start by describing the purpose (Why) of the activity. Then ask participants to jot down some thoughts about a list of questions posted on chart paper, in preparation of sharing them with the group. Writing some of the ideas down allows each person to prepare and discover his or her responses ahead of time. Encourage all teachers to share, because it is important for all voices to be heard. Jotting ideas ahead of time allows teachers to decide what they are comfortable sharing.

The questions posed will vary from session to session (except for the last one in the list below). Teachers are always asked the last question: how they are feeling about being with the group that day. The other questions can range from teachers sharing their expectations for the day to connecting to something that was shared a previous day or raising questions that are floating in their heads.

The grounding for the first meeting usually asks teachers to share their name and position (unless they already know one another), their expectations for their participation in CASL, and their feelings about being here (this one is always asked).

Here are some sample questions you might use:

- "What are your aspirations for your staff as a professional community of learners?"
- "What are your concerns about this work?"
- Always ask "How do you feel about being here?"

After allowing two or three minutes of writing, ask members to speak to each question, one at a time, in round-robin fashion with one member sharing at a time. When one teacher is speaking, the others engage in committed listening, with no cross-talk or responding.

The facilitator names the first speaker (e.g., the person who traveled the farthest distance to get to the building) and then each person shares, in sequence. Grounding provides practice time for committed listening without responding.

Framing the Session

- **What:** Framing the session provides teachers with an overview of the structure of the day.
- **Why:** Facilitators do this to "set a tone for participation and productivity—to describe the purposes of the work, how it relates to a larger context, and how it benefits participant interests" (Garmston & Wellman, 2009, p. 101). Members will perform at their best when they know what to expect.
- **How:** Review the CASL goal, session outcomes, agenda, working agreements, and parking lot:

○ CASL goal and session outcomes. Start by reminding the group of CASL's long-term goal as written on the CASL poster "We use collaborative inquiry to relentlessly pursue, discover, and apply responsive approaches for the success of students we have struggled to reach and teach." This goal should be written at the top of the CASL Poster that lists the group's working agreements and communication skills. After sharing this long-term goal, it is helpful to post the session outcomes so that all can follow along as you review them. Review the agenda next.

○ Agenda. Sharing the agenda provides guidance about "where the group is going" and "what the group will be doing" during the session. The agenda items are directly linked to the session outcomes. If you choose to post the agenda, you only need to provide a list of the main topics. We suggest you not include times for each topic to allow for flexibility as you observe and analyze the behaviors of the group. A formal written agenda is most appropriate for the Introductory Session and Phases I and II, IV and V, when you may be working with more than one group or if you are facilitating a session longer than an hour. When you start guiding the group through Phase III, however, you may refer teachers to the steps in the protocol that make up the agenda for the session.

○ Working agreements. Once the group has established the working agreements, list them on the CASL poster. Then at the beginning of each meeting, refer teachers to them on the poster. Ask each group member to review the list and pick one they are going to pay particularly close attention to during the session. If during previous sessions the group identified a working agreement that the members were having difficulty following, you might ask them to revisit that one. Then clarify how the group might help members remember to follow it (e.g., identify a hand signal to remind folks).

○ Parking lot. A *parking lot* is a large piece of chart paper where teachers can list any items that arise that aren't on the agenda or aren't relevant to what is currently being talked about. The ideas are believed to be important and need to be addressed at some point, either later in the session or at a more appropriate time in the future (e.g., a future meeting, outside of the group). The listed items may include feedback about the session, questions that are bubbling up, or thoughts someone is having. We use a labeled piece of chart paper for the parking lot on which teachers can post their comments and feedback during breaks. We provide Post It notes for this purpose.

- Use of the parking lot helps keep the teachers focused and moving forward with the specified agenda. The notes are often used to capture important thoughts or questions when participants don't want to distract the group from the given task. It honors teachers' curiosity, questions, and construction of insights. It also provides space for those who have thoughts they hesitate to share for whatever reason. Feedback provided on the parking lot can be used to plan future sessions.

- At the first CASL session, you'll want to introduce the What, Why and How of the parking lot. Let teachers know that their feedback and questions are important to assuring a quality learning experience. When teachers raise questions or comments that at that moment are not relevant, invite them to put the idea on a Post-it Note and then during the next break put it on the parking lot.

- You need to make a habit of checking the parking lot during breaks so you can determine when would be an appropriate time to respond. When the comments are used in planning the next session, we often read some of the comments aloud at the beginning of that session to show how we have adjusted our plans in response to the feedback.

- Sometimes at the end of a session we explicitly invite participants to provide feedback on their way out the door. For this exercise, subdivide the paper into three sections, and label each as follows: "+", "Δ", and "?". Each of these sections serves a specific purpose: the "+" section includes feedback related to the question "What is going well?"; the "Δ" section includes feedback related to the question "What improvements are needed?"; and the "?" section includes feedback related to the question "What questions still remain for you?"

- When working with several study groups at a time we usually place the parking lot off to the side so it doesn't distract the group from the work in front of them. If we are facilitating a single study group we ask teachers to put their parking lot ideas on a Post-it Note and to leave them on the table on a small sheet labelled "parking lot." The facilitator can walk around and look at them during a break or after the session.

Distributing Materials. Distribute all relevant materials at this point. In Phase III, remember that the student work samples do not get passed out until *after* the presenting teacher provides background about the work and the student.

Identifying Roles. Before starting into the protocol, be sure to assign someone the role of taking notes on the Recorder Sheet and to fill in the Study Group Log. Also, appoint a time-keeper, if appropriate (especially if the group has limited time).

Engaging in Professional Learning

Once the opening activities have been completed, the study group is ready to learn the skills of collaborative inquiry.

It is during this segment that the teaching of the communication skills and the completion of the phase tasks occur. Figure 5.2 provides guidance for how to schedule the content listed. The explicit ways the facilitator and teachers accomplish these outcomes is outlined in detail in Section C (Chapters 6–9).

Developing and Applying the Communication Skills

- **What:** The communication skills that support teachers' collaborative inquiry include: Committed listening, pausing to interpret, matching verbal and nonverbal cues, paraphrasing, probing, and putting ideas on the table.
- **Why:** The communication skills promote and maintain a trusting environment while also supporting teachers to stay open to new ways of thinking and being.
- **How:** The content and processes for developing the communication skills vary based on the group's interactions, individual development, and which CASL phase the group is embarking on (see Figure 5.2). As the skills are being introduced, refer to the CASL Poster (Figure C.3), which lists the skills. Answer questions teachers might have about any of the skills. As you see fit, have individuals silently assess their level of consistent use and which ones they might need to work on for that session. If the group has struggled to use a skill during the previous session, remind them of that and ask how you might support them in improving.

Completing the Collaborative Inquiry Tasks

- **What:** A key supportive tool used in this segment is a *protocol*. Each CASL phase has a protocol designed around the collaborative inquiry cycle. Protocols are a structured process or a set of prompts and guidelines for a specific activity that focus the group's attention on an intended outcome.

- **Why:** Protocols provide an order to the activity, define a structure for conversation, identify responsibilities for participants, and build and sustain trust. Protocols are important tools for ensuring focus; providing space for all voices; balancing participation: and bringing transparency to work, thinking, beliefs, and values. For CASL, the protocols also support suspension of judgment, multiple and diverse perspectives, and shared construction of new understandings.
- **How:** The CASL phase protocols include

  o a clear statement of purpose,
  o specific directions,
  o defined responsibilities,
  o prompts for facilitation, and
  o supports for working agreements and communication skills.

Reflecting

- **What:** Reflection happens when we pause to ponder, explore, and question our experiences so we are able to construct meaning from them.
- **Why:** John Dewey (1933) recognized that it is the reflection on our experiences—not merely the experience itself—that leads to learning.
- **How:** There are at least two times when you will want to ask the group to pause and reflect so they can construct understanding and learn from their thinking.

  o After each activity. It is important to have teachers reflect after each individual activity. For example, when you introduce the idea of dialogue, you will have teachers engage in a strategy called First Turn, Last Turn (see Section C, p. 132). In this activity, teachers silently read a passage from this book and highlight sentences that resonate with them. Once done, a teacher starts by reading one highlighted passage to the group. In round-robin fashion, each teacher shares her thoughts about the sentence read while the teacher who read just listens. The teacher who started gets the last word and shares why she selected the passage and how it resonates with her. The cycle is then repeated, starting with another teacher. Invariably, when teachers are asked to reflect on this activity, they share how they found that committed listening had helped them to crystallize their own thinking, which is the whole reason to engage in this experience. You will remember committed listening is a core feature of dialogue.
  o On the day's learning. Step 5 of each CASL phase protocol involves reflection as well. The purpose of this reflection is to

transfer learning from the study group to teachers' practice, build collective responsibility, and improve their collaborative skills. When time allows at the end of a CASL phase, we ask teachers to reflect, first in writing, on what they learned from the inquiry that they might use with other students and on how well the group followed the working agreements and used the communication skills. Then they are encouraged to share their reflections with the group.

Organizing for the Next Session

Before the group leaves, it is important to make sure that everyone knows how to prepare for the next CASL session. This involves both (a) taking the actions that were planned during the session and (b) pursuing further professional learning as needed.

- **What:** Before closing the session, you'll want to do a little planning.
- **Why:** As the teachers plan for the subsequent session, it holds everyone accountable for their future professional learning.
- **How:** The facilitator provides an overview of the next session, highlighting what teachers need to do and bring. These items are listed at the end of every protocol under Step 6, Acting. For example, in preparation for Phase III, you will want to identify which teacher(s) will bring student work to the next session. Or, if, earlier in the session, the group planned to gather additional information, you'll want to remind them to act on their plans. This is the time to also talk about how they might want to engage in additional professional learning.

GROUP AND INDIVIDUAL DOCUMENTATION

During each CASL session, there are times when teachers are either asked to publicly make note of the group's thinking, or to make individual written notes or reflections (see Figure 5. 4). These two categories of documentation are described next.

Public Notes of Group Thinking

- **What:** Public notes capture the thinking of the group, therefore providing a visual record of ideas and agreements that may otherwise be difficult to follow and retain.

Figure 5.4 Group and Individual Documentation

Public Notes of Group Thinking	Individual Notes and Written Reflections
• CASL Poster (Goal, Working Agreements, and Communication Skills) • Study Group Log • Recorder Sheet • Charts as Needed	• Protocols • Cue Card for Communication Skills • Student Performance Grids • Teacher Cultural Autobiography • Focus Student Biography • Written Reflections • Self Assessments

- **Why:** Individuals see their ideas accurately depicted to promote ownership and trust. The immediate recording of ideas on chart paper supports accuracy and encourages others to contribute. It also provides a record to be used during subsequent sessions (e.g., the CASL Poster (Figure C.3) with the working agreements generated by the group).
- **How:** During each CASL phase, an individual is assigned the role of recorder and is asked to document on the Recorder Sheet the ideas generated during the inquiry. Another teacher (or the recorder) is asked to complete the Study Group Log, to make copies for each group member and the principal, and to distribute the completed log to everyone.

While the group develops its agreements, the facilitator and recorder take responsibility for writing them on the CASL Poster. Other ideas are charted publicly when the entire group needs to analyze and reflect on them, for example, in Phase IV, when the teachers share the areas in which their students are still struggling after several months of CASL inquiry.

Individual Notes and Written Reflections

- **What:** Teachers are asked to maintain a CASL notebook in which they keep their own notes and written reflections for each phase.
- **Why:** We view teachers' analytical writing as "frozen thought" about their professional decisions and actions. It allows teachers to hold ideas still long enough to critically examine them—to reframe problems and consider multiple points of view. Individual notes and written reflections can also be shared with others. The CASL notebook allows another person to see a record of the students' learning and the teacher's growth (e.g., in a teacher evaluation conference or a parent conference).
- **How:** The facilitator prompts the teachers to write at different times throughout their engagement in CASL. Some of the writing is done

prior to a session, whereas other writing is done while in the study group. For example, teachers are encouraged to review the protocol prompts in Phase III and to jot down some notes about the student's work before sharing the work at the table. Teachers are given the forms for Teacher Cultural Autobiography and Student Biography to complete prior to a CASL session so that they have ample time to ponder and reflect on the questions.

During Phases I–IV, individual note-taking helps teachers capture and summarize ideas and questions generated at the CASL meetings so that they can refer to them later. Written reflections during Step 5 of each phase allow them to reflect upon and form conclusions about their own learning and the learning of their students. Reflections on the group's productivity and use of collaborative skills allows them to consider how they might improve in these areas during future sessions.

In Phase V, the writing of the final reflections can prompt many important insights—both comfortable and uncomfortable. It allows teachers to look at concrete evidence, gathered over time, of how their students are learning. Usually, teachers find it gratifying to see in black and white how much their students have learned. But if they see that a student is not performing adequately, they have to confront the responsibility of figuring out what to do about it. Determining a course of action can provide valuable direction for future professional learning efforts. The final reflections engage teachers in analyzing what to do next, both with their students and with their own professional growth.

During a CASL session, teachers are encouraged to add information to their cue card for communication skills, their Cultural Autobiography, and the Student Biographies of their own and their colleagues' focus students. They are also encouraged to jot notes on their personal copies of the protocols as they hear others talk about the evidence being presented.

Finally, there are points throughout the year when the facilitator has the teachers complete a self-assessment to measure their consistent use of the collaborative skills. These are also kept in the CASL notebook so teachers can track their progress.

DEVELOPING CONSISTENT USE OF THE WORKING AGREEMENTS AND COMMUNICATION SKILLS

As stated in Chapter 3, the working agreements and communication skills are useful because they can build "the kind of environment that supports deeper reflection and conversation" (Miller & Kantrov, 1998, p. 56).

Directions for establishing a set of shared working agreements is described within the agenda for the Introductory Session (Introduction to Section C, p. 131). In addition to creating working agreements, teachers need to learn how to monitor the group's adherence to them, both during and after a study group session.

When an agreement is not followed, group members should feel comfortable enough to gently remind others what is expected. A reminder can be as simple as pointing to the agreement on the CASL Poster and saying, "Remember what we agreed to." Before adjourning a CASL session, the teachers are always asked to reflect on how well they have followed the agreements. You should model this process and provide feedback to the group until you are confident that they can do it on their own.

As for the communication skills, once you have taught them you need to coach the teachers and monitor their use of the skills that they have learned. You may even need to reteach a skill. During the CASL phases, much of your attention is on the teachers' use of the communication skills as the basis for building trust and engaging in the inquiry process. Help teachers understand why these skills are so important and encourage their use. As illustrated in Figure 5.2 , the simpler skills are taught and practiced during the first few CASL sessions. The more challenging probes (empowering and probing for beliefs) are introduced and practiced as the teachers become more comfortable with the first set of communication skills and there is a high level of trust.

As the teachers practice their newly acquired skills, keep a watchful eye on group dynamics and on how consistently the teachers use the collaborative skills. Look for opportunities to help participants refine their skills. At the early stages of learning, members are often awkward in their use of paraphrases and simple probes. They tend to respond to comments made by others before making sure they accurately understand what was said and often forget to ask open-ended questions. For example, a teacher might say, "Don't you think the student misunderstood place value?" This question elicits a simple yes-or-no answer and may put the speaker on the defensive. At these moments, stop the action and ask individuals to think about the intent of the question. What are they trying to learn from the teacher, or what do they want the teacher to think about? Give them time to restate the question. One way to restate this question would be "What misconceptions does this student exhibit on this piece of work?" This question is more empowering and opens the way for multiple possibilities. It also helps teachers focus on content issues. After the presenting teacher has a chance to share, stop the action again and talk about what information was elicited by the new question. Most often, the group will see that the more open-ended question encourages a teacher to share more information and gain more insights.

In a study group at an elementary school, a teacher was asked to talk about Bobby, a student demonstrating reading problems. Kathy responded "Bobby is large for his age and older than his classmates. His parents are very supportive and help him at home. But Bobby would rather play than work at reading. Although he does get some things done, it's always a major effort on Bobby's part. His comprehension and fluency levels are way below first-grade expectations."

After she shared this information, someone in the group asked Kathy what she thought was hindering Bobby's progress in fluency (a paraphrase and probing question for more information). Kathy responded, "His auditory blending and phonemic awareness is intact. But where he falls apart is when he tries to use the cross-checking strategies" (cross checking involves checking to see whether the word the learner put in the sentence makes sense in the story). Kathy shared, "What Bobby does is just push through the story without monitoring what he read." Then another teacher jumped in and said "Is that the case whether you do the picture walk or not?"

At this point, Amy, who was facilitating the group, stopped and summarized the conversation. She pointed out that Kathy had just shared what gets in the way of Bobby's fluency. Then she turned to the teacher who asked the last question and said, "You asked Kathy about picture walks. Sounds like you had a useful thought there. What is it that you are trying to learn from Kathy or have her think about?" The teacher said, "I want to know under what conditions Bobby has these problems." Amy then asked the teacher to reframe the question without making it a yes or no question. Then the teacher asked Kathy, "Under what conditions does Bobby have these problems?" Kathy then answered with greater detail. Amy then asked the questioner what was learned from this answer. Finally, Amy pointed out to the group that by asking an open-ended question, the group received more information than a simple yes-or-no answer. Kathy continued, "Based on what I have seen, my goal for Bobby is to integrate a sense of story as a decoding strategy."

After she said this, someone piped in and asked, "How are you going to do that?" Although this is an open-ended question, Amy stopped the group again and asked whether everyone was clear about the learning outcome for Bobby. Amy asked this question because she wasn't clear about the desired outcome, and she sensed that there were others in the same boat. Several teachers acknowledged that they were fuzzy on what Kathy hoped to help Bobby accomplish. Amy pointed out that it pays to slow down and probe for clarity before jumping to strategies so that the teacher doesn't try a strategy for the wrong outcomes. Amy asked someone to reframe the question, and this time a teacher asked, "What will you see if the learning outcome is accomplished?" Kathy then described the performance she hoped to see from Bobby.

With trust levels high, and the use of basic communication skills honed, you can begin to push or challenge the group to inquire more deeply into the ideas of another person. Teachers need to feel a real sense of trust before they are willing to create cognitive dissonance with their colleagues. You can help build the trust early on by modeling how to use *empowering presuppositions* and *probes for beliefs*. When you model these probes, point out why you used them and highlight the results. Initially, teachers are quick to move away from the dissonance created by these probes. You need to help them live with the discomfort for a while. Otherwise, transformative learning will not occur. When they observe how you support them through the discomfort, they will be more willing to engage in and create cognitive dissonance in the future.

At the end of a year of studying the progress of first- and second-grade students in reading comprehension, the teachers at another elementary school found that their students' reading fluency had increased but that their comprehension had not. This discrepancy created much cognitive dissonance in the minds of the teachers. The teachers looked at the data and said that they would just have to work harder next year. They did not question one another about why there was a discrepancy.

This was a perfect opportunity to encourage teachers to "live in the dissonance" by suspending judgment and exploring possible explanations. To start the conversation, Amy asked what their initial assumptions were about the relationship between comprehension and fluency. The teachers shared that they thought that high levels of fluency would lead to higher comprehension. Then Amy asked the group to explore possible explanations for why their preconceived belief did not play out this way. Some teachers surmised that the lack of comprehension was because the students weren't applying the decoding strategies when they read. Others thought that it might be because the students didn't understand the questions they were being asked—questions about story elements. Those who agreed with this hypothesis noted that they had not explicitly taught the story elements, so students probably wouldn't know what was being asked on the assessment. Still others wondered whether they just didn't know how to teach comprehension.

Ultimately, the group had a lengthy discussion about what skills are needed in order for students to comprehend a story at the child's reading level. The group assessed their own knowledge and realized that they knew far too little about teaching comprehension and its relationship to other reading skills. They decided to keep comprehension as the target learning area for another year. In this case, the teachers' cognitive dissonance provided motivation for further study. They were willing to continue pursuing this understanding because they felt the support of the facilitator and the group.

When working with a study group, always remember to model positive and productive communication skills. You will maintain rapport with the teachers, and they will learn much from your expertise.

GROWING IN YOUR FACILITATION

This section provides some general ideas about ways to support your own learning as you begin to facilitate CASL inquiry.

Start Small

When first learning to facilitate CASL inquiry, it may be wise to limit the number of teachers and study groups with whom you work. Skilled facilitation is a mix of tools, lenses, skills, and art. While we provide protocols and processes to achieve significant learning, there are no fixed scripts. Be conscious of your own learning curve; rather than juggling large numbers of teachers and groups, protect time and energy to reflect on your own learning as well as that of the group and its members. You might want to read the book first and then engage two or three colleagues, as a trial run, with Phases I, II, and III.

Co-Facilitate

It can be helpful to join with another person to plan and lead the study group sessions. Another perspective can be quite valuable in reflecting on what you have observed in the group and individuals and in interpreting those observations from multiple perspectives. Over the past decade and a half, we have found that co-facilitating and then inquiring into the results of CASL sessions has helped us improve the design and facilitation of the CASL design.

Pursue Additional Learning

Your own development will be enhanced through in-depth learning about many of the facilitative tools that we have presented. Learning from experts coupled with practice in coaching individuals and facilitating groups will contribute to your artistry with CASL. We each have benefited greatly by attending sessions with the following masters of facilitation: Bob Garmston and Bruce Wellman (Adaptive Schools), Art Costa and Bob Garmston (Cognitive Coaching™), Bruce Wellman and Laura Lipton (Data Driven Dialogue), and Kathy Kee and Karen Anderson (Coaching For Results Global).

Inquire Into the Group's Learning and Your Role in Facilitating It

You might use the inquiry cycle to observe and analyze the group's needs and progress just as you would use it to study student work samples. We offer some questions below to guide your own inquiry into your group's learning using a modified version of the inquiry cycle. You might analyze your work with the teachers using such prompts as the following.

1. After facilitating a CASL study group, take about 30 minutes alone to reflect on the experience, preferably in writing.

   - Examine the "work" produced by the group: Study Group Log, Recorder Sheet, your own notes, the group's self-assessment of their collaboration, and other products generated by the group.

- Recall and jot down any moments during the session when a significant learning (e.g., an insight) occurred. Do the same for moments when the learning may have been jeopardized (e.g., someone was critical of another's ideas).

2. Use the questions below to write out your reflections.

- Observing: What are you noticing about the group members'

    (a) *learning* (e.g., knowledge base, filters, inquiry cycle, dispositions)? and

    (b) *collaboration* (working agreements and communication skills)?

- Analyzing: What might have caused what you observed?
- Planning: Given these insights, what might you do next?
- Reflecting: What might you want to pay attention to next time in terms of the group members' development? What evidence might be most useful to you as you reflect on the session afterward? How might you summarize your reflections on this session?

3. Meet with a trusted colleague to dialogue about your reflections.

- Share your evidence of the study group's learning.
- Use the questions you wrote about to guide the dialogue.

4. Set a goal or an inquiry question for your own learning.

EXAMPLE OF FACILITATOR INQUIRY

- Decide on your own *inquiry question* (e.g., How does the use of paraphrasing influence the development of my study group teachers' dialogue and discoveries?).
- Devise method to *observe* and *record* specific evidence that might help answer the question (e.g., Have a co-facilitator script only the paraphrases and what comes afterwards from a teacher).
- Observe the evidence (e.g., Paraphrases are rarely used by the group members. When one is provided, however, teachers' subsequent language becomes clearer and more precise about what the student learning outcome for that sample looks like when it is seen in the work).
- Analyze the meaning of what was recorded (e.g., Paraphrases are not provided because of interruptions and the fast pace of each step in the protocol. Maybe pauses and self-monitoring of non-productive listening are not there; perhaps the group members are not aware that they are not providing paraphrases, or when opportunities to paraphrase arise, they forget specific ways to do so).

- After selecting the plausible interpretations for what was observed (e.g., that they were not aware or forgot), make a *plan* to address this need (e.g., Show the value and purpose of paraphrasing by showing the group a script of their own paraphrasing so they can see what happens when it is done. Ask the teachers what makes paraphrasing hard for them. Based on what you hear, you might review non-productive listening and give them time to create a reminder card to use during the session. Finally, be sure to provide specific praise.

SUMMARY

Without a doubt, facilitating a CASL study group is one of the most rewarding professional experiences we have ever had. Amy often says there isn't another 7:30 a.m. meeting she would attend with such enthusiasm. To watch a group of teachers become a learning community in which ideas are shared, problems are studied and solved, support to take risks is provided, and learning is celebrated, is worth every minute spent planning and working through the tensions of the group dynamic. This chapter provides a blueprint for how to facilitate your own groups and come out with a winning team.

SECTION C

The Five CASL Phases

The central goal of CASL is to create the conditions for transformative teacher learning. As teachers engage in collaborative inquiry, they discover new ways of problem solving, reframe their personal attitudes and cultural beliefs, and build new knowledge and practices. As a result, they are able to create responsive and equitable learning environments so each and every student reaches excellence. The CASL phases, conducted in collaborative study groups, create and support the conditions for teachers' transformative professional learning.

Let's take a moment to consider the essential features of CASL that are listed on the left half of Figure 1.1 (p. 14). You already have read about the Framework: Teacher as Collaborative Inquirer (Chapter 2), Working Agreements and Communication Skills (Chapter 3), Leadership and Support (Chapter 4), and Facilitation (Chapter 5). The CASL phases combine these vital aspects with the last three essential features: Standards of Excellence, Case Study for Equity, and Structured Inquiry Over Time.

After we give you an overview of the five phases, we provide an outline for a workshop to prepare teachers and leaders for beginning their CASL inquiry.

CASL PHASES OVERVIEW

For the readers who like to have the big picture before delving into the details of each phase, we now provide a brief overview of them. In Chapter 1 (pp. 16–19) you read a narrative describing how Sue's study group progressed through the five phases. In this section, you will find an overview (Figure C.1, pp. 124–125) that lists each of the phases along with the Introductory Session. Finally, you have a graphic illustration of the phases (Figure C.2, p. 126).

Phase I begins by considering grade-level performance data to establish the content focus for inquiry, referred to as the *target learning area* (TLA).

The TLA is a set of complex outcomes (standards) that are developed in multiple units across the year. Before Phase II, the group members design and administer an initial assessment to determine their own students' current performance relative to the TLA proficiency criteria. Each member also begins a cultural autobiography.

In Phase II, teachers analyze their own classroom assessment results. Each teacher uses the patterns found to select a focus student who will help the group members discover responsive learning approaches for students they often struggle to reach. To understand their focus students' cultural backgrounds, teachers gather biographical evidence.

Phase III extends over a period of months as the group studies successive TLA-related work samples from each of their focus students. The analysis of a work sample yields understandings about the students as people and as learners. These insights guide the design of the instructional approaches that are used in the following weeks. After implementing the approaches, teachers collect another work sample and bring it to the group as evidence of the focus student's current performance. Then another round of work analysis and experimentation with new approaches begins. As personal and cultural insights are discovered, teachers continue to update their students' biographies and their own autobiographies.

After several months in Phase III, teachers begin Phase IV by giving to their entire class a summative assessment of the TLA-related outcomes. They analyze this evidence, determine progress, and set new inquiry goals. Finally in Phase V, teachers reflect upon their students' learning, their own growth, and future professional learning needs. Then they celebrate their progress in a sharing session.

Keep in mind that teachers use the essential tools of collaboration—the *working agreements* and *communication skills*—as they engage in dialogue during each of the phases.

Figure C.1 Overview of CASL Phases

Goal: *To use collaborative inquiry to relentlessly pursue, discover, and apply responsive equitable approaches for learning so that each and every student reaches excellence.*

Introductory Session

What is CASL and how will it benefit us and our students?

- CASL Goals
- The Framework: Teacher as Collaborative Inquirer

- CASL Design and Features
- Working Agreements and Communication Skills

Phase I: Establishing a Focus for Collaborative Inquiry

What area of the curriculum is most challenging for our students?

- Define Target Learning Area
- Design Initial Whole-Class Assessment
- Begin Teacher Autobiography

Phase II: Defining Teachers' Professional Learning Goals

Which students would be most fruitful to study over time so that we may discover equitable responses?

- Analyze Initial Assessment Results
- Establish Professional Learning Goal
- Select Focus Student and Begin Biography

Phase III: Inquiring Into Teaching for Learning (3–5 months)

Which approaches are most responsive to our students' specific strengths and needs?

- Analyze Each Focus Student's Work Sample (every 2–4 weeks)
- Continue Focus Student Biography
- Continue Teacher Autobiography

Phase IV: Assessing Learning Progress

What progress have our students made? Who needs further assistance?

- Analyze Whole-Class Final Assessment Results
- Plan for Students Not Reaching Proficient Performance

Phase V: Integrating Learning Into Teachers' Professional Practice

What have we learned about ourselves and our teaching and what might we need to learn more about?

- Reflect on Teacher and Student Learning
- Set Professional Learning Goals
- Celebrate Accomplishments

---

*Throughout phases: Reflect on learning and collaboration, find more information, and seek further professional learning as necessary.

Figure C.2 Each teacher in a study group goes through all five phases.

CASL Phases for Sue Baker

All Students	Focus Student	All Students
Tracy		Tracy
Sandy	**Nika**	Sandy
Terry		Terry
Marty		Marty
John		John
Mary		Mary
Nika*		**Nika***
Tamika		Tamika
Etc.		Etc.

Phases I and II

Establish Focus;
Analyze Class
Assessment;
Select Focus
Student (* Nika)

Phases III (3–5 months)

Inquire Into Teaching
for Learning:
Analyze Work Samples

Phases IV and V

Assess Progress;
Reflect on Professional Learning;
Celebrate

ADAPTING THE CASL PHASES FOR LOCAL NEEDS

The CASL system is designed to flex with the specific contexts, teachers, and students involved. For example, some groups take longer to develop the psychological safety required to share their struggling students' work samples. Other groups need more time to develop deep understanding of the target learning area or assessment basics before moving on to the other CASL phases. For this reason, at the end of each phase, we have described common adaptations that may be needed by your groups.

We recommend that the facilitator(s), teacher leaders, and administrators meet regularly to monitor and adjust the pacing and structures for the CASL phases. When making such decisions, the crucial question is, "What will best support the desired learning outcomes for teachers and students?"

Given this background, let's move into the introduction of CASL to teachers.

THE CASL INTRODUCTORY SESSION

The Introductory Session helps participants understand how and why CASL inquiry works. Many participants have information concerns at this point, for example, "What will we be doing, and why is it important?," "Where will we find the time?" or "How does this fit with what we are already doing?" This workshop offers answers to such questions.

Once teachers understand that CASL conversations focus on the students that they have been challenged to reach, they may have some personal concerns about the safety and confidentiality of the group. They want to know that their efforts will be respected, that their motives presumed positive, and that the study group's conversation will be non-judgmental and kept private. In this session, teachers begin to learn how to collaborate in safe and productive ways. Next, they will closely examine the CASL goals, design, and benefits. Finally, they will prepare to begin Phase I in the next session.

Preparation and Materials

Group Size

One or more teams of three to five teachers, grouped according to purposes for collaborative inquiry. See Chapter 5, pp. 100–101, for more information on grouping decisions.

Timing

Conduct the session either in the spring, or early in the school year. Allocate one full day or two half-days.

Materials

- This book. Give one book to each teacher before the session, and ask them to read the Introduction and Chapter 1 (if they have time, also read Chapter 2).
- CASL Notebook (with five dividers and two blank sheets of paper in each section). Prepare one for each teacher.
- Committed Listening Self-Assessment (Figure C.4, p. 135). One copy for each teacher
- 5 × 7 index cards (four per teacher, placed on table)
- Chart paper (one blank piece for each study group, placed on table)
- Post-it Notes (placed on table)
- Posted for all to see:

  o Agenda (Copy from this chapter onto chart paper)
  o Teacher Learning Outcomes (Copy from this chapter onto chart paper)
  o Framework Poster (Figure 2.1, p. 34)

Teacher Learning Outcomes

The first day's session is designed to develop in participants the capacity to

- value the goals of CASL study groups,
- understand the CASL professional learning design and its benefits,
- develop and commit to the study group's working agreements, and
- communicate in ways that promote trust and depth of thinking.

Agenda

Opening

- Greeting
- Grounding
- Framing the Session
- Distributing Materials
- Identifying Roles

Engaging in Professional Learning

- CASL and Professional Learning
- Study Group Working Agreements
- Communication Skills for Productive Dialogue: Listening, Pausing
- Framework: Teacher as Collaborative Inquirer

  o Dispositions and Professional Knowledge Base
  o Collaborative Inquiry Cycle and Filtering System

- CASL Features, Phases, and Benefits
- Reflecting on Learning and Collaboration

Organizing for the Next Session

- Preparation for Phase I. Establishing a Focus for CASL Inquiry
- Reading for next time: Chapters 2, 3, and 6

Opening the Introductory Session

Greeting

If you know the teachers, take time to clarify your role and your interest in CASL. If not, introduce yourself and then clarify your role and interest.

Grounding

a. Writing. Ask each study group member to jot his or her reactions to the two statements below and their response to the last question:

   (1) *All students should be held to the same standard.*

   (2) *Students can reach those standards if teachers use the same best practices for all students.*

   (3) *What do you hope to gain from participating in CASL, and how do you feel about being here today?*

b. Sharing. Within each study group, one person takes notes as, one at a time, each member shares what he or she wrote about the first two statements. When each teacher is speaking, the others listen with full attention on the speaker. (If you have multiple teams in the room, ask each team to identify one response to the quotes that they would like to share with the rest.)

c. Sharing. Ask individuals to share with their group their feelings about being here today. If you can respond right away, do so. If the question or concern cannot be addressed immediately, you may ask them to write it on a Post-it Note to place on a sheet called "the Parking Lot" in the back of the room. Assure them that you will consider their ideas in depth and respond individually, later in the day if possible.

Framing the Session

a. Outcomes and Agenda. Show the Agenda and Teacher Learning Outcomes, ask what questions they have, and respond.

b. Parking Lot. Draw attention to the sheet posted in back of room. Explain that this is where they can put their questions or concerns (written on Post-it Notes) at any time. (For more information, refer to Chapter 5, pp. 109–110.)

Distributing Materials

a. Make sure everyone has his or her copy of this book.

b. Pass out CASL Notebooks.

c. Refer to the chart paper and index cards on the table.

Identifying Roles

Ask the group(s) to identify one person who will serve as the group recorder.

Engaging in Professional Learning

Professional Learning and CASL

a. Purpose (Why). Say something like, *You each have had valuable professional learning experiences, and we want to tap into those to help you see how and why CASL works.*

b. Professional Learning Experience. Ask individuals to think about a powerful professional learning experience that transformed their practice and/or beliefs. With a partner, share the experiences, and then jot down the conditions that made the learning so powerful.

c. Professional Learning Research. Have pairs compare their list with the one in Chapter 1 (p. 23)—the characteristics of powerful professional learning derived from research.

d. CASL in Action

- Sue and Nika Case. Explain that they now will read about CASL in action and consider this question: *Which of the characteristics of professional learning that you already listed (or that were on page 23) did you also see in the case?*
- Reading. Individuals silently read Sue and Nika case at beginning of Chapter 1 (pp. 10–12).
- Pairs. In pairs, teachers compare what Sue is experiencing in her study group with the lists of characteristics that the pairs just created.
- Sharing. Have pairs share their answers. Point out how the characteristics are integrated into the CASL design and that is why it is so powerful.

e. Transformative Professional Learning

- Purpose (Why): Say something like, *The reason the research shows a positive impact on students is because this kind of professional learning results in transformative, not just additive, teacher learning. Let's take a minute to unpack what we mean by this.*
- Mini-Lecture. Explain the difference between additive learning (adding on new strategies or content) and transformative learning (change in beliefs and/or behavior). Explain how both happen in CASL but that real change happens most often when we transform our beliefs and assumptions (Chapter 1, p. 5).

f. Culture. Ask teachers to read the definition of "culture" from Chapter 1, p. 12. Clarify how such beliefs are formed through years of experiences and that they can be difficult to change.

g. Theory of Change. Direct teachers' attention to Figure 1.1, p. 14. Explain that this figure shows how the CASL design ultimately impacts "Student Learning Excellence" (in the far right box).

h. CASL Goal. Now teachers look at the box that says "Teacher Relentlessly Pursues . . . ". Ask teachers to talk in pairs and then share with the group how they think Sue's study group was fulfilling this goal in the case the teachers just read.

Study Group Working Agreements

a. Purpose. Explain why the working agreements are important to achieving the CASL goals (refer to Chapter 3, pp. 52–54).

b. Mini-Lecture. Explain what working agreements are and show examples from Figure 3.1, p. 53.

c. Individual Writing. Each person in the study group silently writes his own most important agreements, *one agreement per Post-it Note.*

d. Sharing and Categorizing. One at a time, each person reads one of her notes, explains why it's important, and places it next to a similar one in the middle of the table. Then the next person does the same. Keep going around the table until all Post-its are clustered in like-piles in the center.

e. Agreements. Label each cluster with a working agreement statement, for example, "Be on time."

f. Recording. Ask the recorder to write on the chart paper using the format shown in Figure C.3 on p. 132:

- Write at top: "Our CASL Poster."
- Then write: "Our Goal: We use collaborative inquiry to relentlessly pursue, discover, and apply responsive equitable approaches for learning so that each and every student reaches excellence."
- On left side: List each of the group's working agreements, as they are developed.

g. Creating Meaning. For each agreement listed, ask group members to give concrete examples of what maintaining or ignoring the agreement would look like.

h. Consensus. Group members come to consensus on their agreements, with the understanding that they can be modified later.

Figure C.3 The CASL Poster

Our Goal: We use Collaborative Inquiry to relentlessly pursue, discover, and apply responsive equitable approaches for learning so that each and every student reaches excellence.	
Our Working Agreements	**Communication Skills for Productive Dialogue**
<ul><li>Presume positive intent</li><li>Pay attention to self and others</li><li>Maintain confidentiality</li><li>(Add others as determined by group)</li></ul>	<ul><li>Committed Listening</li><li>Pausing</li><li>Matching Verbal & Nonverbal Cues</li><li>Paraphrasing</li><li>Probing for Clarity</li><li>Empowering Probes</li><li>Probing for Beliefs</li><li>Putting Ideas on the Table</li></ul>

Productive Dialogue

a. Purpose. The group's exploration of multiple interpretations through open and trusting dialogue is the key to fulfilling CASL's goals.

b. Dialogue. All silently read the section in Chapter 3 about dialogue on page 56. Highlight three or four passages that seem significant (points of agreement or disagreement, interesting facts, or curiosities).

c. Practice. Give directions for the "First Turn, Last Turn" activity and check the group's understanding of the directions.

   (1) Select the "First Turn" speaker in the study group. This person reads to the group one of his highlighted items *without comment.*

   (2) One at a time, each study group member considers what the First Turn speaker read aloud, and says what it means to her. *When a member is sharing, no one says anything at all.*

   (3) After every person has shared her response, the First Turn speaker now has the "Last Turn" by saying what the passage he read now means to him.

   (4) The next First Turn speaker is to the right of the person who just had the Last Turn. She reads aloud one of her highlighted items. After round-robin responses to this item, the First Turn speaker takes the Last Turn by sharing what the item now means to her.

   (5) Repeat this process until three or more different members have taken both the first and last turn.

d. Reflection for Learning. Invite all to write on a blank page in their CASL Notebook a response to the following questions:

- *How did listening to others' ideas influence your thinking about the passages that were read aloud?*
- *How might dialogue help us achieve our CASL goals?*

e. Sharing. Teachers share with their study group what they wrote.

Committed vs. Nonproductive Listening

a. Purpose. Explain that dialogue doesn't just happen. It requires us to monitor and sometimes change how we talk to one another. Show the communication skills and ask the recorder to list them on the right side of CASL Poster, as in Figure C.3, p. 132). Start with the skill of committed listening.

b. Committed Listening. Explain the directions and ask what questions teachers have before beginning.

    (1) Stand up and find a partner who is not sitting next to you. Remain standing.

    (2) In pairs, assign an "A" to one person and a "B" to the other person.

    (3) Person A reads aloud the section "Committed Listening" on pages 56–58.

    (4) When Person A reaches the end of her section, she stops and Person B summarizes two key ideas from the passage.

    (5) Person B reads "Judgmental Listening" (pp. 58–59), and Person A summarizes two key ideas.

    (6) Person A reads "Autobiographical Listening" and "Inquisitive Listening" (pp. 59–60), and Person B summarizes two key ideas.

    (7) Person B reads aloud "Solution Listening" (p. 60), and Person A summarizes two key ideas.

c. Reflection for Learning. Talk in study groups, *without interrupting one another*, about this question: *How might our ways of listening contribute to (or get in the way of) our dialogue as we pursue our CASL study group goals?*

Pausing

a. Transition. Explain that not all CASL dialogue is as structured as "First Turn, Last Turn" or as the reading activity that they just did. Those were for practice only, as is the next activity.

b. Purpose. Explain what pausing is and why it's important to pause. See Chapter 3 (pp. 60–62).

    c. Self-Assessment. Distribute the Committed Listening Self-Assessment (Figure C.4, p. 135), and ask each person to review it. They'll be using it for the next activity.

    d. Practice. The "Paired Verbal Fluency" Activity allows teachers to practice pausing and also to assess their own skills for committed listening.

    e. Directions. Give directions and ask what questions teachers have before beginning.

        (1) Form pairs with a person sitting at a different table.

        (2) Use "Paired Verbal Fluency" (Garmston & Wellman, 2009) to talk about this question, *How will dialogue, listening, and pausing support our group in pursuing, discovering, and applying responsive approaches for the success of students we struggle to reach and teach?*

        (3) Each pair decides who will be Partner 1 and Partner 2.

        (4) When one of the two is talking, the other is pausing and *must listen carefully* because when it's his turn, *he cannot repeat anything that was said by the other person.*

        (5) Partner 1 begins. After one minute elapses, facilitator says "Switch," and Partner 2 picks up right where Person 1 left off, *without repeating what Partner 1 has already said.*

        (6) After one minute, facilitator says, "Switch," and Partner 1 talks for 30 seconds without repeating anything said by Partner 2.

        (7) Facilitator says, "Switch" and allows Partner 2 to talk for 30 seconds, again, without repeating what has already been said. Invite reflections.

Self-Assessment of Committed Listening

    a. Self-Assessment. On Figure C.4, teachers place an X on each line to assess their own listening behavior.

    b. Reflections. They write on the bottom their reflections: *What was easiest for you? What was hard for you? What gets in the way of your own listening?*

    c. Goals. Ask teachers to circle the one(s) they want to be aware of in the future.

    d. Sharing. Ask for a few volunteers to share. Remind them that periodically they will self-assess their progress with the communication skills because they bring safety and power to the CASL inquiry.

    e. Notebook. Have the teachers place the self-assessment form in their CASL Notebook for the next session.

Figure C.4 Committed Listening Self-Assessment

Directions. Place an "X" on each line to indicate your current behavior.

Judgmental Listening and Responding

Listening with a desire to correct or judge the response in a negative way. Thinking about my disagreements with what is said rather than trying to understand it.

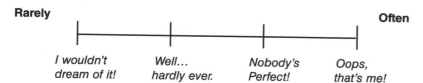

Rarely   Often

*I wouldn't   Well...   Nobody's   Oops,
dream of it!   hardly ever.   Perfect!   that's me!*

Autobiographical Listening and Responding

Shifting the focus from the speaker to myself when the topic being discussed triggers my own experiences or feelings.

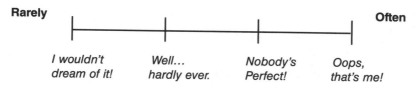

Rarely   Often

*I wouldn't   Well...   Nobody's   Oops,
dream of it!   hardly ever.   Perfect!   that's me!*

Inquisitive Listening and Responding

Listening from the perspective of my own self-serving curiosity.

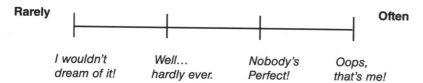

Rarely   Often

*I wouldn't   Well...   Nobody's   Oops,
dream of it!   hardly ever.   Perfect!   that's me!*

Solution Listening and Responding

Listening with the intention of providing answers, solving the speaker's problem, or offering advice.

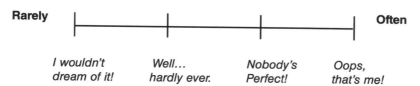

Rarely   Often

*I wouldn't   Well...   Nobody's   Oops,
dream of it!   hardly ever.   Perfect!   that's me!*

Write Your Reflections: What's easiest for me? Hardest for me? What gets in the way of my committed listening?

Communication Cue Card

a. Purpose. Explain the purpose for the card. Each teacher designs his own 5 × 7 card as a reminder of how he wants to communicate with other study group members. The cue card will be in front of him at every session.

b. Ask each teacher to write on his cue card the key ideas he wants to remember for *committed listening* and *pausing*.

Framework: Teacher as Collaborative Inquirer

a. Purpose (Why): Refer teachers to box to the left on Figure 1.1 (p. 14), labelled, "Framework . . . ." Explain that this framework describes the capacities developed in teachers as a result of CASL.

b. The Filtering System and Dispositions

  • Teachers jot down ideal characteristics of teachers who are able to accomplish the CASL goals: *What would they need to be like or believe?*
  • On the Framework Poster (p. 34), point to and explain each disposition as described in Chapter 2 (see pp. 45–47). Ask teachers to raise their hands if they had that item on their list and to explain why it's important to them.
  • Invite teachers to share other items on their lists. Some of these items may fit into another area of the framework (for example, the professional knowledge base). You can acknowledge that later.

c. Professional Knowledge Base

  • Ask teachers to think about and then call out what kinds of knowledge a teacher like Sue would need to have in order to succeed with students she has previously struggled to reach. *What would she need to know about and be able to do?* The recorder or facilitator lists them on chart paper or a sheet so that all can see the list.
  • Show the categories listed on the right side of the Framework Poster, and explain each briefly, using information from Chapter 2, pages 33–36. As you explain, show how these categories match the list generated by the group.

d. Collaborative Inquiry Cycle and Filtering System

  • Refer teachers' attention to the circle on the left side of the Framework Poster p. 34. Explain that the steps in the collaborative inquiry cycle slow things down so that teachers can understand why students might be struggling before planning the most appropriate interventions.

- Explain how this same cycle portrays the perennial skill of teacher reflection and decision-making. Share an example of how it works for a novice teacher (who sees something and jumps to action) and then an experienced one (who sees something and considers multiple interpretations before deciding what to do).
- Illustrate the use of the inquiry cycle in Sue's study group. Pairs take turns reading sections from Chapter 2 (pp. 36–42). After each section is read (e.g., "Share Background"), the listening teacher summarizes what was read. Then she reads the next section (e.g., "Observe"), and the listener summarizes. Continue through the "Act" section.
- Point to the filtering system in the middle and explain how sometimes, when teachers are trying to make sense of what is happening, their beliefs or feelings can cause them to draw the wrong conclusion. For example, early on in the Sue and Nika case, Sue had labelled Nika as a disengaged learner. Collaborative inquiry opened up her filters so she could find solutions rather than giving up.

e. Reflect on Learning. Teachers write about this question: *In what ways might collaborative inquiry benefit you and your colleagues?* As they share their ideas in their study groups, they listen and pause before responding.

CASL Features, Phases, and Benefits

a. Purpose (Why). Say something like, *Now we'll look at what you will be doing in your study groups—structured collaborative inquiry over time. In this way you can consider how the CASL phases might work for you and how much time to take with each one.*

b. Theory of Change. Refer to far left box in Figure 1.1: "CASL Design for Transformative Learning" on page 14. Explain each of the features briefly.

c. CASL Phases

- Teachers examine Figures C.1 and C.2 (pp. 124–126) and the examples of each phase from Sue's study group (Chapter 1, pp. 16–19).
- In pairs, they alternate explaining each phase as they understand it.
- Respond to teachers' questions.

d. Benefits of CASL

- One at a time, teachers share at their table(s) what they think the benefits of engaging in CASL might be. The recorder writes down the list on a sheet of paper or index card.

- Teachers compare their responses to the benefits listed in Figure 1.4 (p. 25).
- Explain how the "CASL Theory of Change" (Figure 1.1, p. 14) leads to these benefits.

Reflecting on Learning and Collaboration

- Purpose. Explain the importance of reflection on one's own professional learning (as described in Chapter 5, p. 114).
- Writing. Ask teachers to individually write their responses to the following questions:

  (1) *How might the collaborative analysis of student learning transform your practice and student learning?* Share their answers with the group.
  (2) *What concerns or questions do you have at this time?* If the questions or concerns cannot be addressed immediately, you may ask the teachers to write them on Post-it Notes and put them on the parking lot. Assure them that you will consider their ideas in depth and respond later in the day if possible.

Organizing for the Next Session

a. Scheduling. Create a schedule for engaging in the five CASL phases during the next several months (pp. 102–103). Allocate one or two months for Phase I and II, depending on the group's experience with classroom assessment design. Plan to spend three to five months in Phase III. Phases IV and V can be completed in one or two months.

b. Phase I Session Plans. Examine boxed Phase I Overview in Chapter 6 (pp. 141–142). Decide together how long to allocate for the completion of the tasks, including the design and administration of the Initial Assessment of the target learning area.

c. Materials. Make sure the group brings the necessary material by asking, *What information do we already have from tests and other sources that can help each study group identify their target learning area? What tools might be necessary to help each group design an initial assessment of the TLA for their own classrooms?*

d. Reading. Ask teachers to read Chapters 3 and 6 before the next session. Facilitators should also read Chapter 5.

e. Parking Lot. Teachers write on Post-it Notes any questions and concerns and leave them on the parking lot for the facilitator and leaders to read.

After this Introduction to CASL, it is time to begin Phase I, as described in Chapter 6.

HOW TO USE CHAPTERS 6–9

Each chapter contains the rationale, broad CASL goal, teacher learning outcomes, session outcomes, and purposes and directions for engaging in each step of the phase. Chapter 6 describes how to facilitate Phase I, Chapter 7 is dedicated to Phase II, Chapter 8 guides you in the analysis of focus student work samples, and Chapter 9 describes how to engage in Phases IV and V.

We have illustrated each phase with three different cases. Chapters 6 and 7 feature a teacher named Todd and his study group of fourth-grade teachers inquiring into their students' learning of mathematical problem solving. Chapter 8 illustrates Phase III with a case of early elementary teachers studying literacy development. Finally, Phases IV and V are depicted in Chapter 9 through a study group of high school teachers engaged in the analysis of their students' learning to write about science.

If you are the facilitator for a particular phase, we suggest that you prepare as follows.

- Read the relevant chapter, with special attention to the outcomes for that phase.
- Review Chapter 2 to reinforce the vision of the kind of teacher you are trying to develop. Use your understanding of the current needs and strengths of the group to set specific learning outcomes for the session.
- Consult Chapters 3 and 5 to tune up your own collaborative and facilitation skills. At this time, you might decide to set a personal goal for your own facilitation.
- Stay in contact with the administrator(s) in charge of professional learning and help them provide the appropriate support for CASL, as described in Chapter 4.
- Use your own style and the suggested ideas to make your own lesson plan to lead teachers toward the desired outcomes.
- Gather the most important materials for your own guidance, and use your intuition and facilitation tools to respond to the flow of the study group.

6 CASL Phase I

*Establishing a Focus
for CASL Inquiry*

The primary goal of CASL inquiry is to increase learning success for all students by improving the responsiveness of their teachers' practice. Since it is impossible to study in depth the learning of every content area at one time, teachers begin CASL by identifying the most important student learning outcomes on which to focus. We call this the *target learning area* (TLA).

Phase I leads teachers through a set of inquiry tasks to select, define, and assess their students' current proficiency in the target learning area (TLA). A final activity helps teachers to become aware of themselves as cultural beings.

In many schools, the school improvement team has analyzed significant data to identify areas for improvement. One of these areas may be selected as the target learning area for CASL. However, since data collection and analysis has become such a big part of teachers' work, there likely will be other sets of evidence that will inform the selection. These might include grade-level assessments from the prior year, reporting systems for specific standards assessed, and content-specific assessments designed by grade-level or content teams.

In cases in which school improvement plans are not available or in which they have not been derived from student performance data, we suggest that the school or district leaders provide relevant data summaries to groups of teachers for analysis. This can be done at a department meeting or at a separate session before the CASL phases begin. Wellman and Lipton (2009) provide an excellent inquiry-based process for this analysis.

To complete Phase I, teachers examine their student learning data and share the challenges they've frequently found in their own grade level and content areas. To select their TLA, they use a set of criteria to determine which area will yield the most learning for both students and teachers. Next, they draft a summative assessment task to measure students' ultimate attainment of proficiency, and unpack the learning outcomes—knowledge, reasoning, skills, and dispositions—to be developed within the TLA. Finally, teachers design an initial assessment to determine their students' current readiness and performance in the TLA.

As teachers examine the data, make observations, and compare their observations with their predictions, they begin to surface some of their own filters (See Figure 2.1, p. 34)— personal beliefs about why certain groups of students struggle with a particular set of learning outcomes. To continue this personal journey, teachers write about their own cultural background and add to it during the months of CASL inquiry. As they come to know themselves as cultural beings, teachers become more aware of how their own background (filters) influences their worldview and their professional practice.

PHASE I. ESTABLISHING A FOCUS FOR CASL INQUIRY: OVERVIEW

Goals

To collaboratively discover the most fruitful learning outcomes for study, assessment, and development. To examine one's own cultural background.

Inquiry Questions

- Within the areas determined by our school improvement committee, what do our students struggle with every year?
- Which target learning area (TLA) is most worthy of further inquiry?
- What will it look like and sound like when our students reach learning excellence (TLA)?
- What are the essential concepts, questions, and processes to develop in our students so they reach the TLA?
- How might we assess our students' current level of performance in the TLA?
- What is my own cultural identity, and how might it affect my teaching and learning?

Steps, Purposes, and Tasks

1. SHARING BACKGROUND: *To review data sources and raise awareness of teachers' predictions and assumptions.*

(Continued)

(Continued)

- Review student performance data sources.
- Share teachers' predictions and assumptions about areas in which their own students frequently struggle to learn.

2. OBSERVING: *To refine the content focus for inquiry.*

- Examine school improvement plans and grade-level test and other results.
- Identify grade-level content standards in need of improvement.

3. ANALYZING: *To select a content focus for maximum teacher and student learning.*

- Use the criteria for a powerful target learning area to select the TLA.
- Note other questions and puzzlements.

4. PLANNING: *To align the TLA with standards, define critical attributes of proficient performance, and design the initial classroom assessment.*

- List related standards.
- Define an end-of-year (summative) assessment task and proficiencies to be demonstrated.
- Design initial assessment of TLA, including prerequisite and enroute outcomes.
- Plan to address the group's questions.

5. REFLECTING: *To transfer learning from the study group to everyday practice, build collective responsibility for all students, and improve group productivity.*

- Share insights about new learning, collaboration, and group productivity.
- Consider needs for further professional learning.
- Begin the Teacher Cultural Autobiography.

6. ACTING: *To determine students' initial performance in the TLA and address the group's questions and needs.*

- Administer initial assessment of the TLA to each teacher's class.
- Address the group's questions and needs for further professional learning.
- Complete Teacher Cultural Autobiography.

PHASE I TEACHER LEARNING OUTCOMES

The inquiry tasks in this phase help teachers access and build upon their professional knowledge base, more specifically, their understanding of the content standards, the outcomes leading to accomplishment of those standards, and methods for measuring students' readiness and eventual proficiency in the TLA. Also, teachers begin to develop the inquiry and collaborative skills that will become part of their everyday professional practice. Finally, the examination of one's own cultural background sets the stage for examining personal filters—feelings and beliefs about oneself and students.

One of the main jobs of the facilitator is to assess teachers' capacities as described in the Framework: Teacher as Collaborative Inquirer, as described in Chapter 2. This evidence will guide how quickly to move through the inquiry tasks in this phase.

The activities in Phase I develop in teachers the following capacities:

Professional Knowledge Base

- Plan curriculum by starting with standards, outcomes, and summative assessments.
- Understand specific outcomes within content learning standards.
- Use assessment to identify learning needs.

Skills for Collaborative Inquiry

- Engage in productive dialogue.
- Follow the group's working agreements.

Filters and Dispositions

- Recognize how a teacher's filtering system influences the teacher's own practice.
- Take collective responsibility for overcoming learning challenges found among students.

PHASE I PREPARATION AND MATERIALS

The facilitator may lead teachers through Phase I in a large room with study groups sitting together at tables. Or, the facilitator may meet separately with study groups to complete the tasks. To make them easy to locate, the Phase I figures are provided at the end of this chapter.

Group Member Preparation

Well before the session, remind teachers to bring with them:

- This book and their CASL Notebook.
- Curriculum and assessment materials related to the school improvement goals for their grade level.

Materials

Post the following items in a location visible to all.

- CASL Poster (Figure C.3, p. 132)
- Framework Poster. Teacher as Collaborative Inquirer (Figure 2.1, p. 34)
- Parking Lot (See Chapter 5, pp. 109–110). With larger groups, the parking lot may be posted in the back of the room. With a single small study group, the parking lot may be a small sheet placed on the corner of the table.
- Phase I Recorder Sheet. Chart paper, electronic device, or computer screen that the every study group member can see, formatted as in Figure 6.4, p. 172).

Copy the following materials (Figure 6.1–6.4 are provided at the end of this chapter):

- Phase I Protocol (Figure 6.1). (One blank copy for each group member)
- One Study Group Log (Figure 6.2). (After study group meeting, recorder completes it and distributes it to group members and administrator[s].)
- Teacher Cultural Autobiography (Figure 6.3). (One blank copy for each group member)

GUIDING A STUDY GROUP THROUGH PHASE I

The Phase I Protocol (Figure 6.1) contains the purposes, tasks, and questions to be addressed in each step of the inquiry and serves as the study group's main guide during Phase I. To help you visualize how each step looks in practice, we provide examples from Todd's study group as they inquire into their fourth-grade students' math learning. The directions below are directed to both the group members and to the appointed facilitator.

Opening the Session

Begin by reviewing the five CASL phases so that teachers can see why it's important to select a powerful area of the curriculum as the CASL focus. Since the group is probably still learning to collaborate in ways that (a) deepen insights gained from dialogue and (b) maintain safety for risk-taking, take time to review *productive listening* and *pausing*. Then teach two new communication skills: *matching verbal and nonverbal cues* and *paraphrasing*.

To open the session, the facilitator leads the following activities. More detail about conducting opening activities is provided in Chapter 5 (p. 107).

a. Greeting. Ask teachers how things are going.

b. Grounding Activity

- Teachers write about these questions: (1) *How do you feel about being here today? (2) In what areas do many of your students struggle year and after year? (3) Which of these are crucial for their future success?*
- The groups share only the answer to the first question. Save the last two for later.

c. Framing the Session

- CASL Goal. Refer to it on the top of the CASL Poster (Figure C.3, p. 132). Review the CASL phases (Figures C.1 and C.2, pp. 124–126). Many learners need to see the big picture of how Phase I leads to the other phases.
- Session Outcomes. Pass out the Phase I Protocol (Figure 6.1) and draw attention to the Teacher Learning Outcomes on the cover sheet. Refer to the Framework Poster, Figure 2.1 (p. 34), to help explain the listed outcomes.
- Agenda. Teachers examine the steps on the protocol and the example of Todd's study group from this chapter to understand what they will be doing.
- Working Agreements. Teachers examine their group's working agreements as they listed them on the CASL Poster in the Introductory Session. Each group member identifies and then shares with the group one agreement that they want to pay special attention to during today's session. As each shares, the facilitator paraphrases and then probes for the reasons behind their choices.
- Parking Lot. Remind teachers of the purpose of the parking lot that is posted on the wall or table.

d. Distributing Materials. Pass out materials and remind teachers about the purpose of the parking lot that is posted on the wall or table. At any time, they can write a concern or question on it.

e. Identifying Roles

- Identify a recorder to use the headings in Figure 6.4 as she writes on the Recorder Sheet the group's ideas. Remind her that the group needs to be able to read the written information at the end of each protocol step.
- Give recorder (or another person) the CASL Study Group Log, and ask her to complete it after the session, and distribute it the next day to all group members and the relevant administrator(s).

Developing and Applying Communication Skills

a. Productive Listening and Pausing

- Cue Card. Teachers find the cue cards that they made during the last session.
- Review. Refer to the list of communication skills on the CASL Poster and ask pairs to share the notes on their cue cards for committed listening and pausing. If further review is needed, consult Chapter 3.

b. Matching Verbal/Nonverbal Cues and Paraphrasing

- Purpose. Explain the importance of developing rapport and trust in CASL.
- Reading. Form pairs and give directions.

   (1) One person reads aloud the section called "Matching Verbal and Nonverbal Cues" (pp. 62–63) and both partners make notes on their cue cards.

   (2) The other person reads aloud the section on "Paraphrasing" (pp. 63–65), and both partners make notes on their cue cards.

- Practice Passport Paraphrase Activity

   (1) Form groups of 5 or 6. Assign numbers to each person: Person 1, 2, 3, 4, 5.

   (2) Give directions and purpose. They will be talking about what they wrote earlier for questions 2 and 3. The goal is to practice all the communication skills learned so far using the "Passport Paraphrase" process.

   (3) Explain and demonstrate one round with a volunteer. Person 1 shares, and then Person 2 listens, pauses, matches the verbal/nonverbal cues, and paraphrases what Person 1 said. Then Person 2 shares his own ideas. Person 3 paraphrases what Person 2 said and then shares her own thoughts. Person 4 paraphrases what was just said, and shares. Keep going around the circle in this manner. By paraphrasing the prior speaker's idea first, each participant gains a "passport" to share her ideas.

   (4) As the teachers engage in the activity, monitor and clarify as needed.

c. Reflect on Learning. Ask the group members to use paraphrasing in a more natural way as they dialogue about these questions: *What did you notice as you did this activity? How might pausing and paraphrasing help us clarify our thinking and gain new insights?*

d. Cue Card. The teachers make notes on their cue cards for the two new communication skills. Suggest that they try pausing and paraphrasing with their students and families—they will be amazed at the results.

e. Personal Goals. Group members write their goals for collaboration on the front page of their protocol. Remind them that they will be reflecting on their use of the skills at the end of the session.

FACILITATION TIPS

Don't skip the practice with communication skills.

These ways of talking do not come naturally to many people—especially to teachers, who often feel rushed and "just want to get things done." Without thorough and careful communication, the wrong target learning area might be selected, or worse, trust may be lost, causing an individual to withhold her expertise from the group. These pose grave losses for the children under consideration.

Uphold the working agreement: Presume positive intent.

If you notice a lack of trust or negative comments among group members, you might suggest that they adopt an agreement called *presume positive intent:* To refrain from judging any group member as having consciously held harmful beliefs or actions. Instead, they assume that every teacher in the group shares a true desire to help students find success. This presumption of positive intent is especially important when sharing predictions and assumptions about students.

Protocol Step 1. Sharing Background

Purposes: To review data sources and to raise awareness of teachers' predictions and beliefs.

The first part of Step 1, *Data Context*, helps the group understand when and how test scores and other student performance data were collected and analyzed and what conclusions can be drawn.

If the CASL study group members were not involved in examining the data, a short report from those who did the analysis might include an overview of the data sources that were considered, without yet sharing the findings.

The second part of this step, *Predictions*, asks group members to reflect on the content outcomes that seem most difficult year after year—and for whom they are difficult These thoughts allow teachers to surface their thinking and beliefs (filtering system) about why certain groups struggle with certain outcomes.

Use the following activities to engage in this step.

Sharing Background: Data Context

a. Purpose. Examine Step 1 in the protocol and clarify the purpose.

b. Data Source. Review and record how the school improvement team came up with its current focus. You might ask, *What data sources are being (or have been) considered?* Also, probe to see what other evidence the group has that might be helpful in selecting their target learning area. Refrain from sharing results at this point.

Sharing Background: Predictions

a. Past Challenges. Begin by engaging teachers' curiosity and commitment. You might ask teachers to think or write about the following question: *In what content areas might your students struggle the most, year after year? Why do you think students might struggle so much in these areas?* Other helpful probes are, *Which one or two outcomes would you like to get better at helping your students learn? (Every year, you end up saying something like, "I sure wish I could figure out how to help kids learn [fill in the blank].")*

b. Share and Record. The recorder writes the responses on the posted sheet and places tally marks next to each idea to indicate the number of people who mentioned that area.

Protocol Step 2. Observing Patterns in Data

Purpose: To refine the content focus for inquiry.

This step asks teachers to observe the patterns found in the data they have before them. As they identify the areas for improvement and the characteristics of those students who are struggling, they can compare their predicted patterns (from Step 1) with what is seen in the data. The possible dissonance between teachers' impressions and the actual results can surface beliefs (filtering system) that may be helping or hindering student success.

For example, one school had engaged in significant professional learning to address "courageous conversations" of race (Singleton & Linton, 2005). During CASL Phase I, the third-through fifth-grade teams had examined achievement test results in writing. They predicted that both their white and minority students would achieve at about the same level. Then the principal distributed report card data showing that, in several areas, the African American students were achieving lower proficiency than were the white students. The teachers were shocked. The report card data created much dissonance, which was essential for creating the collective responsibility and moral stance that inspired the staff to find responsive approaches to help each and every student succeed.

Use the following activities to engage in this step.

a. Purpose. Examine Step 2 in the protocol and clarify the purpose. Refer teachers to Todd's group's example of Steps 1 and 2 below.

b. Observe. Ask the group questions similar to these: *Based on the data we have looked at, which learning outcomes are most in need of improvement? Which students are struggling the most, and how would you describe them as people and learners?* Use communication skills to note and clarify the patterns found in the data—content areas in need of growth and subgroups of students with low scores.

c. Recorder Sheet. The recorder writes the main content outcomes needing improvement, the student groups for whom these areas are a challenge, and any surprises or curiosities the group identified.

FACILITATION TIP

Listen for beliefs and assumptions.

As the study group members examine the achievement data for various student groups, are they surprised? What beliefs and/or assumptions do you hear? You might reinforce the teachers' commitment to equity by saying something like, "Yes, (paraphrase the gaps seen). That's a frustrating pattern. Let's hope our CASL inquiry will help us figure out how best to reach and teach these kids."

TODD'S STUDY GROUP: PHASE I, STEP 1 (SHARING BACKGROUND) AND STEP 2 (OBSERVING)

Step 1. Sharing Background

Data Context (sources considered)

- Fourth graders' state test data collected last spring

Predictions

- Our students have trouble transferring their understanding of one operation to a different context. They struggle with real-life problems that involve math processes we've just learned. They can't show their work or explain their reasoning. They just aren't motivated to persist when it gets too hard.

(Continued)

(Continued)

Step 2. Observing

Data shows: Outcomes in need of improvement

- Our students scored lowest in using mathematical processes and concepts to solve real-life problems and translating their explanations and rationales into words. Also knowing where to put decimals was a challenge.

Groups of students who struggled the most

- The students receiving free or reduced lunch and the Latino students scored much lower than did the white students.

Protocol Step 3. Analyzing the Power of the TLA as a Focus for Inquiry

Purpose: To select a content focus for maximum teacher and student learning.
Now is the time to critique each target learning area being considered and come to consensus on the TLA that the group will study for the next months. Recall that the ultimate purpose for CASL is to discover responsive approaches to improve the learning of those students who are not achieving proficiency in those content areas most in need of improvement.

For transformative teacher learning, we have suggested that the target learning area (TLA) should need improvement. But that is not all. It should also be *enduring*, should integrate a set of concepts and skills grounded in *complex learning*, and should be *developed over time* in a variety of contexts. Finally, it should tap into teachers' natural desire to improve those areas where they *feel most challenged* to help students succeed.

CRITERIA FOR A POWERFUL TARGET LEARNING AREA

Enduring

The TLA should have authentic value beyond school; that is, the students' accomplishments should have value throughout their lives. Students might express such outcomes in written and oral discourse, by making and repairing things, and/or in performances for audiences. Enduring learning is often applicable across multiple disciplines.

Complex

Complex outcomes require higher levels of reasoning, for example, analysis, synthesis, and evaluation. When selecting a complex TLA, consider the following principles based on theories of authentic learning (Newmann & Wehlage, 1993) and power standards (Reeves, 2002; Ainsworth & Viegut, 2006). Both approaches take steady aim at the vision of excellence with equity.

- Constructing rather than reproducing knowledge.
  Adults in diverse fields of endeavor face the primary challenge of constructing or producing, rather than reproducing, meaning or knowledge. They strive for in-depth understanding rather than superficial awareness.
- Development of prior knowledge and skills.
  One cannot engage in complex reasoning without the prerequisite knowledge and skills. Teachers understand how proficiency develops over time, and they deliberately scaffold the experiences leading up to fulfillment of the standard. They understand that such learning must be developed in a variety of contexts over a series of topics or units.

Developed Over Time

As anyone who has tried to develop complex skills in students knows, the task is not easy. It requires explicit instruction, repeated practice, application in a variety of topics or units, and continuous assessment with specific feedback. The dissonance created by students' struggles with such challenging complex outcomes often "shakes up" teachers' filtering systems (habitual beliefs); this dissonance can open the door for a gradual transformation in the teachers' outlook and the discovery of new responsive approaches.

Challenging to Teach

The TLA should be an area in which the data show that students need to improve *and* one that teachers are genuinely curious about learning to teach effectively. This is why, in Step 1, Sharing Background, teachers considered the content outcomes that they had consistently struggled to teach for success.

Examples of Powerful TLAs for CASL Inquiry

Examples of powerful TLAs for CASL inquiry include various types of writing (e.g., persuasive, narrative, expository, research); reading comprehension; scientific method; analyzing and critiquing cause and effect in social studies; using tables, charts, and graphs; musical interpretation; creating and following healthy eating guidelines; creating a skit in a foreign language; and using color and form to express emotions in art.

Note that such processes are difficult to pin down in behavioral terms. Yet that is what every learning standard requires—a precise definition of what it looks like when a student has achieved the standard. The purpose of Phase I is to define specifically the target learning area. But beware! As a result of this need to get so concrete, it is all too easy to reduce a complex skill into somewhat "mindless" outcomes that involve only lower-level learning.

Some examples of very specific learning outcomes that may *not* lend themselves to inquiry over time include isolated grammar mechanics and reciting factual knowledge about a particular topic (e.g., fossils), concept (e.g., evaporation), or process (e.g., the steps of the scientific method). In our experience, the study of such outcomes yields fewer insights about the learning-teaching process.

Many schools find it helpful to experience CASL for the first time by inquiring into writing, for example narrative or expository writing, in Language Arts or in other content areas. Some advantages to selecting writing as a TLA are that it often needs improvement, it is developed over several months in different units, it lends itself to authentic performance assessment, it crosses over many subject areas, and many excellent rubrics are available.

The goal of Step 3, Analyzing, is for each member in a study group to share the same TLA. Use the following activities to engage in this step:

a. Purpose. Explain the purpose listed on the protocol. Then ask teachers to read the criteria for a powerful TLA and to study the example of Todd's group's analysis of the TLA (pp. 153–54).

b. Share Possible TLAs. If the group members have different preferences for the TLA, they share them, one at a time, and explain why that area is so important. We sometimes ask, *"What area would you just hate to see students not master by the end of the year, and why is that so important to you?"* The recorder writes the ideas and circles those most frequently mentioned.

c. Analyze List. The group considers how well each TLA meets the four criteria for a powerful TLA. You might ask, *Which of the possible TLAs fits best with the criteria?*

d. Select a TLA. Make sure that (a) data show that this area is in need of improvement and (b) this area meets the four criteria. The recorder writes on the sheet the TLA and how well it fits the four criteria.

e. Questions. Ask, *What other questions might we explore to better understand the TLA and our students' learning?* Ask the recorder to write them on the record sheet.

FACILITATION TIPS

We often hear the following questions, and here is how we respond.

Is our TLA too narrow? Too broad? A broader area (e.g., narrative writing) allows the inquiry to be tailored to each teacher's curiosities and challenges. If the TLA is too narrow (e.g., adding detail in writing or fractions), the area may be confining to some whose students don't show that area as a challenge.

What if a committee has already selected the TLA? Ideally, teachers in a study group develop ownership of the TLA by looking at relevant data and selecting a TLA that is important to them and in the best interest of their students.

Do all teachers in the school need to have the same TLA, for example, the goals listed in the School Improvement Plan? Can some study groups have a different TLA from the others? Recall that each grade-level or content team examines their own data to determine the areas of the curriculum in need of greater student success. Then they apply the criteria for a powerful TLA to the observed areas needing improvement. The Phase I inquiry tasks might result in different study groups inquiring into different TLAs. When multiple teams study the same TLA, however, teachers gain valuable insights about curriculum integration across content areas and articulation across grade levels.

Must each teacher in the study group have the same TLA? The greatest benefit occurs when all teachers in a study group focus on the same TLA. As the teachers collaborate to examine standards, assessments, classroom assignments, and other student work, they come to a deeper understanding of the exact nature of the learning specified in the target learning area. They also share ideas about how to help students understand and use the related skills or concepts.

How long do we have to stay with the same TLA? Can we change it mid-year? Most study groups stay with the same TLA all year long. Exceptions might be when high school groups change students mid-year, when recent classroom assessments show that students have accomplished the TLA, or when mid-year evidence indicates a greater need or a more serious priority for inquiry. The bottom line is for the inquiry to yield insights that will promote the learning of those students who need it most in those areas most in need.

TODD'S STUDY GROUP: PHASE I, STEP 3 (ANALYZE THE TLA)

Our TLA

"Every student demonstrates application of mathematical problem solving in real-life situations."

Fit With Criteria

- Enduring: Yes. Math problem solving is a skill required in daily life and the workplace.
- Complex: Yes. Several skills and concepts are combined as students analyze and solve real-world problems.
- Developed Over Time: Yes. Students can't learn this in just one or two units; they need to practice this type of thinking within various contexts and mathematical operations.
- Challenging to Teach: Yes. This area has been a source of frustration for many of us (evidence: teacher comments on a survey). We often wonder why kids can't transfer their classroom learning to real situations.

(Continued)

(Continued)

Our Questions

- Fractions and Decimals: Where and how are these taught in our curriculum? Do they appear multiple times? When are they taught in terms of test dates?
- Problem Solving: How well are we teaching this? Is it too complex for their level of development? Does our curriculum include enough complex problems?

Protocol Step 4. Planning TLA Outcomes and Assessments

One major goal of CASL is to develop clarity about the learning targets for student achievement and to take charge of helping all students reach them. As teachers investigate the outcomes embedded within the TLA and design classroom assessments for them, they deepen their understanding of the kinds of learning they are trying to promote. Further, they refine their use of assessment tools to find out—at various points in the journey toward proficiency—how closely the students are coming to reaching the learning targets.

In this step, the group engages in two major activities: (1) Clarifying the essential outcomes and assessment tasks necessary to demonstrate students' ultimate proficiency in the TLA and (2) designing an initial assessment of the TLA to administer to each teacher's class before beginning the next CASL phase.

Plan the Outcomes and Summative Assessment

CASL offers an opportunity to bring the content standards "off the shelf" for deep consideration and analysis. As the group takes time to look at standards, en-route outcomes, work samples, and scoring guides they can visualize clearly the learning their students are to demonstrate.

Use the following activities to identify the learning outcomes that need to be mastered to achieve proficiency and to sort them into specific types of learning.

- Purpose. Teachers examine Step 4 in the protocol, clarify purposes, and study the example of Todd's study group on pages 159–160.
- TLA-Related Standards. Ask, *Which standards are integral to accomplishing your TLA?* The recorder writes on the sheet the district or state standards related to the selected target learning area.
- Summative Assessment. Consider the question, *How might students demonstrate excellence in the TLA at the end of the year?* Share ideas and

come to consensus on a summative assessment task and its general directions. The recorder writes the summative assessment on the posted sheet.

- Unpacking the TLA. Now imagine the outcomes leading to successful performance on the summative assessment. What would you look for? Ask, *What knowledge, reasoning, skills and dispositions are essential to reaching proficiency?*

  (1) Form pairs. Each pair divides a single sheet of paper into 4 columns: Knowledge, Reasoning, Skills, and Dispositions. If necessary, review with teachers Stiggins' Learning Targets system (Chappuis, Stiggins, Chappuis, & Arter, 2011) or Bloom's Taxonomy (Hunter, 2004).

  (2) Pairs fill in each column with the evidence they would see in a proficient performance.

  (3) Share each pair's ideas with the group. Begin with the first column. The recorder writes ideas under the area labeled "Knowledge."

  (4) Come to consensus on the main kinds of knowledge that need to be demonstrated in the summative assessment and ask the recorder to put a star by them.

  (5) Repeat the same process with "Reasoning," then with "Skills," and then with "Dispositions."

- Recording. Make sure the recorder writes down any questions that arise during this activity.

FACILITATION TIPS

Designing a truly "authentic" assessment

As teachers consider how students will eventually demonstrate proficiency in the TLA, recall that the best evidence will come from authentic performance (or extended response) assessments of the thinking and skills *applied in a new situation*. The summative assessment should require students to integrate and apply their learning in a real-life situation similar to, *but not the same as*, the ones used for practice in class. Merely repeating a memorized way of doing a "higher-level" task is not true authentic learning.

Confusion about types of outcomes

You may need to review the district's preferred framework for categorizing outcomes, either Stiggins' model (Chappuis, Stiggins, Chappuis, & Arter, 2011) or Bloom's Taxonomy

(Continued)

(Continued)

(Hunter, 2004). What is most important is to distinguish the lower-level knowledge and understanding outcomes from the higher-level reasoning (which requires application in a new situation or a new analysis or synthesis created from students' own knowledge). This is because lower-level learning and higher-level learning require different types of assessment tools.

Sticking to the protocol

Even if teachers already have a very detailed rubric for the TLA, be sure to fill in the four columns. This helps them check for other important aspects that may not be in the rubric. They will also find this breakdown useful in Phase III as they teach to the identified outcomes and analyze students' learning of them.

Moral stance and collective responsibility

Remind the group members that they are expected to hold all students to high standards. The study group will help teachers discover responsive approaches to achieve this goal. If you hear limiting language such as, "Some students will never get to this point," stay flexible and presume positive intent. You might say, "Up until now, that may have seemed true; we are here to do everything we can to help the students reach excellence. It is not that the child is not capable; it is that we—as a group—have not *yet* found equitable ways to reach her."

Specificity in language

As a facilitator, probe for clarity when you hear vague language (e.g., "When you say you want them 'to really understand,' what might you see or hear to indicate that?"). Such probes help everyone in the group to be more precise about the desired learning outcomes.

Plan the Initial Assessment and Scoring Rubric

Now that teachers have described the proficiencies to be demonstrated after a significant period of instruction in the TLA, it is time to develop an initial assessment to measure students' *current* proficiency in TLA, and a set of criteria (rubric) to score each student's performance.

To help understand where Phase I is heading, imagine that CASL's use of data analysis is shaped like a funnel. In Phase I, we begin at the top with broad *grade-level performance data* to select and define the TLA. At the end of Phase I, the focus gets narrower as each teacher assesses his own class's current performance in relation to the TLA proficiency criteria. In Phase II the analysis of this *classroom-level data* helps each teacher to select a student whose learning they will study during the next months. In Phase III, teachers analyze each *focus student's work samples (data)* to help them discover responsive approaches for those students they've had trouble reaching and teaching. Later in Phase IV, teachers will move back out to examine their entire class's progress from the initial assessment to the summative assessment.

As teachers design the *initial* (formative) *assessment* task, we suggest they consider the following guidelines.

GUIDELINES FOR DESIGNING CASL INITIAL ASSESSMENT

- Complex Tasks. Since the assessment task provides evidence of students' complex reasoning, short-answer and multiple-choice items will not be useful. The best assessment methods for CASL inquiry are extended-response items and performance assessments.
- Feasibility. Since the initial assessment is given well before students have had all the instruction necessary to reach full proficiency, the tasks and scoring criteria need to be feasible for the students' current knowledge and experience.
- Prerequisite Learning. The tasks should provide evidence of students' *prerequisite* knowledge and skills—those assumed to be mastered *before* the instruction toward the TLA begins. The assessment results should indicate which students might need re-teaching of essential prior skills or understandings. The foundational study by Bloom (1984) indicated that, with initial assessment and teaching to fill in the gaps found in students' in prior learning, those who would normally be near the average of the class can rise to achievement levels typical of the top 10%.
- Future Learning. The tasks should assess outcomes to be taught in future units but that *might have been mastered already* by some students. Some call these *en-route outcomes* because they lead to proficiency on the TLA summative assessment. It is not necessary to assess every single outcome that will be taught, as teachers likely have a good idea of which ones might have been learned already. Knowing which students have achieved them will help teachers to provide responsive approaches that challenge these students to move beyond the planned curriculum.
- Misconceptions. It might be important for the assessment to tap students' *prior or erroneous conceptions* regarding the content to be learned. In Todd's group's mathematical problem-solving example, a common misconception is that students think they need to use all the numbers provided; they don't stop to consider which numbers are irrelevant to the problem. To discover whether this is an issue for Todd's class, he might include a task that gives both important and irrelevant numbers and have students show their work.
- Analytic Rubric. Because these assessments measure multiple aspects of performance, they are best scored using an *"analytic" rubric* with more than one category of performance. For example, in writing, the rubric might require different scores for the categories of Organization, Voice, Supporting Detail, and Grammatical Conventions. The rubric then provides specific descriptors to illustrate three or four different levels of proficiency for each category. In contrast to an analytic rubric, holistic rubrics yield one score, with all categories to be evaluated lumped together into one large area. A holistic score makes it hard to pinpoint which parts of the student's performance are responsible for the score.

The following activities may be used to help the study group develop their initial assessment.

a. Purpose. Ask *How might you assess where your students are right now relative to these outcomes*? Explain that the next task is to design an assessment that every teacher will use in the next weeks to discover her own students' current learning in relation to the TLA outcomes. They will analyze the data from the assessment in Phase II to select each teacher's focus student.

b. Teachers examine Todd's study group's example of Step 4 on pages 159–160.

c. Guidelines for Initial Assessment. Teachers read and clarify the six guidelines presented on page 157.

d. Prerequisites. In pairs, consider which of the listed outcomes in the four columns are assumed to be already learned (prerequisites) and which ones are to be taught in the coming year (enroute outcomes). Place an asterisk (*) next to the prerequisites and an X next to the ones you plan to teach.

e. Essentials. Now circle the aspects that are most important to evaluate in the initial assessment. Add any others that seem essential, for example, common misconceptions that you see students bring with them from their prior learning.

f. Initial Assessment Task. Come to consensus on the initial assessment task and its directions. (Remember that a multiple-choice or fill-in-the-blank task won't be very helpful unless students write out their thinking or show their reasoning.)

g. Recording. The recorder writes down the task, directions, and scoring criteria.

h. Scoring Criteria. As teachers imagine themselves scoring the initial assessments, they develop their scoring criteria. In most cases this requires the design (or careful adaptation) of an analytic rubric.

i. Questions. Ask, *How might the group address the questions that surfaced today?* Look at the questions that the recorder wrote on the sheet and plan to address them either as a group or individually.

FACILITATION TIPS

Using an existing rubric.

If teachers want to use a rubric that they did not create, they will need to take time to see if it aligns with the learning outcomes discovered when unpacking the standards into the four types of outcomes for TLA proficiency.

The task and rubric are already designed.

Take time to check the task and the rubric for alignment with the listed outcomes, and revise them as necessary. If the group has not done so already, "pilot test" the new assessment with some work samples before doing the final scoring. You may need to plan a separate session to engage in "Rubric Calibrating" (see Online Resources).

Check for precision in language.

Probe for more clarity if vague language is heard (e.g., "You mentioned x; help me understand that"). Such probes help develop consciousness of group members' thinking and reasoning.

More time is needed for design.

Do not go on to Phase II if the group needs more time to design an initial assessment task and/or scoring criteria. If the group is inexperienced with rubrics (or any other aspect of assessment), you may take time out for further professional learning,

TODD'S STUDY GROUP: PHASE I, STEP 4 (PLANNING TLA OUTCOMES AND ASSESSMENTS)

TLA-Related Standards

CCSS.Math.Content.4.MD.A.2 Use the four operations to solve word problems involving distances, intervals of time, liquid volumes, masses of objects, and money, including problems involving simple fractions or decimals, and problems that require expressing measurements given in a larger unit in terms of a smaller unit. Represent measurement quantities using diagrams such as number line diagrams that feature a measurement scale.

CCSS.Math.Content.4.MD.A.3 Apply the area and perimeter formulas for rectangles in real world and mathematical problems.

CCSS.MATH.PRACTICE.MP3 Construct viable arguments and critique the reasoning of others. Mathematically proficient students understand and use stated assumptions, definitions, and previously established results in constructing arguments. They make conjectures and build a logical progression of statements to explore the truth of their conjectures. They are able to analyze situations by breaking them into cases, and can recognize and use counterexamples. They justify their conclusions, communicate them to others, and respond to the arguments of others.

Summative Assessment

The students will create a proposal for redecorating a room of their choice. They will measure the floors and walls; compute perimeter and area; and use fractions and decimals to calculate the amount of carpet, padding, border, and paint they will need. They have a $2000.00 budget.

(Continued)

(Continued)

They will write a letter to the person who will pay explaining how they determined their costs. They will present a poster or model that shows the proposed plan.

Unpacking the TLA

Knowledge (Understanding)	Reasoning (Thinking)	Skills (Doing)	Dispositions (Attitudes)
* Describes 4-step problem-solving process X Recites formulas for area and perimeter	* Translates problem into mathematical terms X Uses estimation appropriately X Draws conclusions and justifies proposal * Creates a strategy	* Measures using inches, feet, yards X Performs calculations with fractions and decimals * Creates a scale drawing of room — Presents report	— Persists when puzzled * Carefully checks work — Displays confidence and poise during oral presentation

(*) Prerequisites: Outcomes students should have developed prior to this year's instruction.

(X) To be taught: Outcomes to be taught en route to summative assessment and that some students may have already developed.

Initial Assessment Task and Procedures

Task: Students are given a picture of a room with the dimensions labeled. They are to figure out how much carpet to order for it. They must show their calculations and explain in writing their approach to solving the problem.

Procedures: Time allowed: 30 minutes. Completed independently in class. Students may use a calculator of any sort.

Initial Assessment Scoring Criteria (Beginning of rubric):

We will meet Thursday to examine examples of more and less proficient responses to help us complete the rubric.

The rubric has five categories with three levels of proficiency for each indicator (1 = beginning, 2 = developing, 3 = proficient). The five areas to be rated 1–3 are:

- Accuracy of mathematical concepts
- Accuracy of computations
- Logical approach to the problem
- Organization of letter
- Writing mechanics

Our Questions and Plans to Pursue Them

Lawanda and Joe will go through the textbook units and make a grid to show in which chapters both decimals and problem solving are taught (T) and/or practiced (P).

Protocol Step 5. Reflecting

Purpose: To transfer learning from the study group to teachers' practice, build collective responsibility for all students, and improve group productivity.

One of the most important parts of collaboration is to reflect upon what has been learned. First we ask teachers to share their insights about the assessment data considered and their selected TLA. We encourage them to consider how these insights might be used to benefit their own students' learning.

Next, they reflect on the quality of the group's collaboration and plan to make adjustments for the next time. This last piece is important because we want *every* teacher to contribute their expertise to the group. For example, if teachers are interrupting one another or if a personal conflict shuts down any teacher's participation, these difficulties need to be worked out as soon as possible, possibly through a privately facilitated conversation.

Finally, teachers consider whether the study group wants to take time to engage in further learning, for example, about assessment or curriculum outcomes.

Before teachers leave the session, ask them to complete (at home) the Teacher Cultural Autobiography. The goal here is for teachers to see how their life experiences and background influence what they value, their interpretations, and their behavior. This understanding will be important when they select a focus student in Phase II and as they seek to discover responsive approaches for those students during Phase III.

In the Step 5, Reflecting, the group engages in the following activities.

a. Purpose. Read Step 5 of the Phase I protocol and look at Todd's group's example on page 163.

b. Earlier Predictions. Ask, *How does what you learned today differ from or confirm your earlier predictions?* Refer back to the recorder's notes from Step 1. Predictions and ask the group to write or share their thoughts.

c. Remind the designated person to write on the Study Group Log (Figure 6.2) the rest of the group's reflections. He will complete it and distribute copies to the group members and administrator.

d. Ideas for Promoting Student Learning. Each group member shares how he can use his learning from the day's activities to help his own students' learning. The prompt might be, *What did you learn today that might help promote other students' learning?*

e. Collaboration and Teachers' Learning. Considering these last questions helps the group decide what to modify or continue to make it safe and powerful for future learning. These questions are

- *How consistently did the group follow the working agreements and communication skills?*
- *What influence did the collaborative process have on your learning today?*
- *How might we do better in the future?*

f. Further Professional Learning. Consider, *How might the group pursue further professional learning, if necessary?*

g. Teacher Cultural Autobiography (Figure 6.3). Pass it out. Explain how this tool will help raise awareness of teachers as cultural beings—those aspects of life experience that may be the same as or different from those of some of their students. Clarify how cultural factors influence teachers' practice by referring to the filtering system and dispositions as described in Chapter 2, pages 42–48. Ask teachers to respond to the questions for next time.

FACILITATION TIP

Don't skip the reflections.

Some people may be uncomfortable talking about how they communicate with others or about their own culture. In spite of these concerns, it is vitally important that teachers come to trust that the group is a safe place to explore what might be getting in the way of their students' learning. Therefore, we suggest that the facilitator acknowledge this discomfort and reiterate the purpose for the activities. Then go ahead and talk about the questions. Be patient. It may take some time for teachers to find their voices and contribute openly to the discussion. But make no mistake; these reflections are essential to discovering culturally responsive teaching approaches for those students who are not succeeding.

Protocol Step 6. Acting

Purpose: To determine students' initial performance in the TLA and address the group's questions and needs.

a. Actions. Teachers carry the planned activities into their daily work by

- completing the Teacher Cultural Autobiography,
- finishing the design of the initial assessment and rubric, if necessary,
- administering the initial assessment to their students and scoring each student's responses using the group's rubric, and
- reading Chapter 7 in this book.

b. Questions and Needs. The group pursues further professional learning as necessary to complete Phase I.

c. Study Group Log. The designated person copies the completed Study Group Log and on the next day distributes it to facilitator, all group members, and principal.

d. Notes. Be sure to save the notes the recorder wrote; these will be useful later when the group looks at students' progress over the year or semester during Phases IV and V.

TODD'S STUDY GROUP: PHASE I, STEP 5 (REFLECTING) AND STEP 6 (ACTING)

Step 5. Reflecting

Our Predictions and What We Found

- We did not anticipate the difficulties with decimals.
- No surprises with the problem solving.
- Scores are too low for our Latino and poor students!

Reflections on Student Learning

- We realized that we have not always considered each step and outcome leading to our students' mastery at the end of the year. This thinking may help us be more systematic in our teaching and assessing.

Reflections on Our Collaboration

- We still interrupt each other too much. One person said it made her want to sit back and not participate. The protocol structure kept us focused.

Our Questions and Professional Learning Needs

- We need to consult with the math resource person to help us finish our rubric.

Step 6. Acting

- We will give the initial assessment to our classes and score it, with assistance from our math resource person.
- We will begin our Cultural Autobiographies.
- We will read Chapter 7 in the book.

CASL NOTEBOOK CONTENTS FROM PHASE I

Study group members add the following items to their notebook under a tab for Phase I:

- Phase I Protocol with notes
- The group's target learning area

- The summative assessment task with the four boxes of outcomes
- Initial assessment design
- Teacher Cultural Autobiography
- Study Group Log

PHASE I: ADAPTATIONS

From time to time, the facilitator, or any group member, may engage the group in making decisions about the pacing of the CASL phases and tasks. This may involve taking more or less time with certain steps, or the group may decide to take time out for what we call *further professional learning*.

Here are some ways in which Phase I can be modified to align with the strengths and needs of the teachers.

Assessment Knowledge and Experience

We have found a wide variation in teachers' background when it comes to creating and using assessments, especially formative assessments like the initial one. In many groups, the teachers already have completed many of the tasks in Phase I as part of their curriculum or school improvement work. In this case, you may shorten or skip over some of the tasks.

In other groups, teachers have less experience with clarifying outcomes and assessments. In this case, you will need to work through all the tasks within this phase. You may even need to spend additional time teaching about assessment and rubrics. The Online Resources offer some activities for further learning about assessment.

Inconsistent Use of Scoring Criteria (Lack of Reliability)

For teachers who have had little opportunity to score papers with others and construct understanding of the rubric, we recommend that, after they have given the assessment, and before scoring their papers, you lead them through a one- or two-hour session we call "Rubric Calibrating" (described in Online Resources).

When teachers are designing a new rubric, this same activity is very helpful, provided that teachers have access to work samples at varying levels of proficiency. Many states provide these examples (sometimes called "anchor papers") online.

A Mandated Rubric

We are often asked if a state- or district-mandated rubric (e.g., the scoring rubric for a state writing assessment) can be modified. One of the strengths of CASL's long-term inquiry is that teachers come to understand deeply the required outcomes for success in the TLA. This often leads them to make suggestions for improving the rubric. This is especially true with holistic rubrics which are unwieldy for CASL student work analysis.

Early in the process, we would not encourage large modifications in a mandated rubric. We would, however, encourage teachers to add clarifying notes as they discover helpful interpretations of the language used in the rubric. Later in the year, before or soon after the summative assessment of the TLA, a teacher committee might propose rubric modifications to the school and other interested administrators.

No Test Data Available

Where no test data are available, teachers may bring local assessment results. When this is not possible, teams may begin by pooling their anecdotal recollections of areas in need of growth and use these as observation "data." In this case, you will need to bring and/or remind teachers to bring curriculum standards/outcomes, assessments, and other related curriculum materials.

Teachers New to District Content Outcomes or Curriculum

Make sure teachers have a copy of the relevant standards and outcomes with them at this session. Any material you can find (e.g., test items, tasks, rubrics, work samples) to help with defining the TLA should be duplicated and brought to the session as a reference. The Phase I tasks can be made easier by looking at scored work samples at various levels of proficiency, and exploring why they received the scores. Many states provide these examples (sometimes called "anchor papers") online.

If you find that the group has little experience with teaching the new curriculum, it can be very helpful to have them engage in the "Learning Pathway Activity" (Online Resources) to plan when to teach and assess each outcome leading to proficiency in the target learning area.

SUMMARY

Phase I sets up the group for the productive and transformative professional learning to come in the next phases. CASL aims its inquiry activities at an area of the curriculum most in need of improvement. But it doesn't stop there. The inquiry focuses both on the content and on culture—both that of the teachers and that of their students. At the end of Phase I, CASL teachers have defined the long-term learning targets and then have prepared to assess them in their classes. This information will be used in Phase II to select both the content and student cultural characteristics to investigate. In Phase III, as teachers study how their focus students construct understanding over time, teachers will identify the most responsive and equitable approaches to improve each and every student's learning.

Figure 6.1 CASL Phase I Protocol: Establishing a Focus for CASL Inquiry

Goal: *To collaboratively discover the most fruitful learning outcomes for study, assessment, and development. To examine one's own cultural background.*

- Within the areas determined by our school improvement committee, what do our students struggle with every year?
- Which target learning area (TLA) is most worthy of further inquiry?
- What will it look like and sound like when our students reach learning excellence (TLA)?
- What are the essential concepts, questions, and processes to develop in our students so they reach the TLA?
- How might we assess our students' current level of performance in the TLA?
- What is my own cultural identity and how might it affect my teaching and learning?

Teacher Learning Outcomes

- Plan curriculum by starting with standards, outcomes, and summative assessments.
- Understand specific outcomes within content learning standards.
- Use assessment to identify learning needs.
- Engage in productive dialogue.
- Follow the group's working agreements.
- Recognize how a teacher's filtering system influences the teacher's own practice.
- Take collective responsibility for overcoming learning challenges found among students.

Materials

Group members bring:

- This book
- CASL Notebook
- Curriculum materials related to school improvement goals: grade-level formative and summative assessment prompts, directions, and scoring rubrics

Posted in meeting room:

- CASL Poster (Figure C.3)
- Framework Poster (Figure 2.1)
- Parking lot

Facilitator brings:

- Phase I Recorder Sheet (Figure 6.4)
- Blank chart paper (2 for each group)
- Summaries of test or other assessment results (e.g., from School Improvement Plan)
- Study Group Log (Figure 6.2)

One blank copy for each teacher:

- Phase I Protocol (Figure 6.1)
- Teacher Cultural Autobiography (Figure 6.3)

Roles

Facilitator

- Teach, model, and monitor CASL working agreements and communication skills.
- Lead group members through the Phase I Protocol.
- Encourage multiple perspectives and interpretations.
- Paraphrase ideas offered and ask recorder to write them on sheet.

Recorder

- Take notes—visible to all—during each step of the protocol.
- Complete and distribute Study Group Log.

Study Group Guide for CASL Phase I Protocol

Establishing a Focus for CASL Inquiry

Opening the Session

- Greeting, Grounding, Framing the Session
- Review working agreements.
- Distribute materials and assign roles.
- Review, teach, and practice communication skills.

1. Sharing Background	
Purpose and Prompts	Notes

Data Context
 	
Purpose: To review data sources.
 	
   • What data sources are being (or have been) considered?
 	
Predictions
 	
Purpose: To raise awareness of teachers' predictions and assumptions.
 	
   • In what content areas might your students struggle the most, year after year?
   • Why do you think they might struggle in these areas?	

2. Observing	
Purpose and Prompts	Notes

Purpose: To refine the content focus for inquiry
 	
   • Based on the data, which learning outcomes are most in need of improvement?
   • Which students are struggling the most, and how would you describe them as people and learners?	

3. Analyzing/Interpreting	
Purpose and Prompts	Notes

Purpose: To select a content focus for maximum teacher and student learning.
   Based on your observations:
 	
   • How does your TLA fit with the suggested criteria:
 	
     o Enduring?
     o Complex?
     o Developed over time?
     o Challenging to teach?
 	
   • What other questions might you explore to better understand the TLA and your students' learning?	

4. Planning	
Purpose and Prompts	*Notes*
Purpose: To align the TLA with standards, define critical attributes of proficient performance, and design the initial classroom assessment • Which standards are integral to accomplishing your TLA? • How will your students demonstrate excellence in the TLA at the end of the year (summative assessment)? • What knowledge, reasoning, skills, and dispositions are essential to reaching proficiency? • How will you assess where your students are right now relative to these outcomes? • How might the group address the questions that surfaced today?	

5. Reflecting	
Purpose and Prompts	*Notes*
Purpose: To transfer learning from the study group to everyday practice, build collective responsibility for all students, and improve group productivity • How does what you learned today differ from or confirm your earlier predictions? • What did you learn today that might help promote student learning? • How consistently did the group follow the working agreements and communication skills? • What influence did the collaborative process have on your learning today? • How might the group pursue further professional learning, if necessary? • What is your cultural identity?	

6. Acting (Complete this step before the next meeting.)	
Purpose and Prompts	*Notes*
Purpose: To determine students' initial performance in the TLA, to address the group's questions and needs • Finish designing the Initial Assessment and check it with others before administering it to your class. • Collect and score a class set of student responses to the Initial Assessment task. • Complete the Teacher Cultural Autobiography. • Read Chapter 7. • Distribute Study Group Log to administrator and group members. • Take actions to address the group's questions and professional learning needs.	

Figure 6.2 Study Group Log

Directions. Please complete one form after each study group meeting. Distribute copies to your administrator and group members.

Date: _____   Time   Meeting   Started: _____   and   Ended: _____

Name of Group (Grade-Level and/or Content):

Group Members:

Today's Facilitator: Today's Recorder:

Tasks Accomplished:

How Our New Learning Will Help Our Students (from Step 5. Reflections):

Inquiry Questions We Want to Pursue:

Resources, Professional Learning, or Assistance Needed by our Study Group:

Figure 6.3 Teacher Cultural Autobiography (Cooper, He, & Levin, 2011)

Directions. Consider the following questions and create an autobiographical sketch of yourself as a cultural being.

Family Heritage and Origin

- Who were the first people in your family to come to the United States?
- Where were they from?
- What was the primary language, religion, ethnicity of your origin?
- What were some major holidays valued and celebrated by your family?
- Who named you in your family?
- Where did your name come from?
- What are some common sayings, folklore, or stories you learned from your parents, grandparents, or great grandparents?
- Do you remember some specific conversations at the dinner table? What were they about?

Neighborhood

- What do you remember about the neighborhood(s) in which you lived?
- Who are some neighbors you still remember?
- What cultural groups do you think they belong to?
- Has your neighborhood(s) changed over the years?
- What are some changes?

Schools

- What do you remember about the schools you attended?
- Who are some teachers or peers you still remember?
- What cultural groups do you think they belong to?
- How did you learn about cultural differences or cross-cultural communications during your schooling?
- Do you remember any particular incident that may have affected how you interact with people whose cultural backgrounds are different from yours?

Cultural Self-Description vs. Cultural Perceptions of Others

- How would you describe yourself as a cultural being?
- Which cultural groups do you think you belong to? Why?
- How do you think others (family members, neighbors, teachers, students, etc.) may perceive you as a cultural being? How do you know that?
- Why do you think they might have those perceptions? How is your self-description similar to or different from how others would describe you?

SOURCE: Cooper, J. E. , He, Y., & Levin, B. B. (2011).

Figure 6.4   Phase I Recorder Sheet

Directions. Using the following categories, write on a large sheet the group's ideas, so that all group members can see them. Add a second sheet as needed.

Step 1. Background

Data Context (sources considered)

Predictions

Step 2. Observing

Data shows: Outcomes in need of improvement

Groups of students who struggle the most

Step 3. Analyzing

Our TLA

How well the TLA fits criteria

- Enduring
- Complex
- Developed Over Time
- Challenging to Teach

Our questions

Step 4. Planning

TLA-related standards

Summative assessment task (end of year)

Unpacking TLA: Outcomes essential for proficiency

Knowledge   Reasoning   Skills   Dispositions

[*Prerequisites: Place stars next to outcomes that should have been learned in prior years.]

Initial assessment task and procedures

Initial assessment scoring criteria

Our questions and plans to pursue them

Step 5. Reflecting

(Record ideas onto Study Group Log to be copied for all members and administrator.)

Step 6. Acting

Who will do what?

7 CASL Phase II

*Defining Teachers'
Professional Learning Goals*

Phase II leads teachers through a series of tasks that set the stage for transformative learning. Whereas in Phase I teachers aimed to define the *content outcomes* most in need of improvement, Phase II adds another crucial ingredient of the inquiry: the *cultural backgrounds* of those *students* most in need of help.

To begin Phase II, each member brings to the group his class set of scored student responses to the initial assessment. The collaborative analysis of these work samples helps each teacher (a) frame a statement of her professional learning goals and (b) select a focus student who will help her reach these goals. The group will grow the most over the months of Phase III inquiry if each teacher selects a student who represents not only a common *content* learning challenge, but also a *student* whose cultural background is one in which the teacher acknowledges limited understanding.

The fact is that teachers find some students harder to teach than others—especially those who come from backgrounds very different from that of the teacher (Bacon, Totten, Bridges, & Jennings, 2010). These differences might arise from factors such as class, race, ancestry, ethnicity, gender, language, religion, exceptionalities, or physical characteristics.

Each teacher selects one focus student from her analysis to study over the next three to five months. Although in the first edition of this book (Langer, Colton, & Goff, 2003) we suggested selecting two focus students, our experience and research suggest that the process works just as well when each teacher studies one focus student.

Two realities have driven this decision: (1) The study of each teacher's focus student allows *every teacher in the group* to learn valuable lessons that can be applied to some of her own students, and (2) it is best to analyze each student's most current work sample at least once a month. Since it takes about 45 minutes for a single student-work analysis, having only one student per teacher makes the time-cost more feasible. Pages 100–101 in Chapter 5 provide more detail about scheduling time for CASL.

The final step in this phase is getting to know the focus student as both a person and as a learner. Over the next months, teachers collect information that is most relevant to unlocking the student's learning success and records these insights in the Focus Student Biography.

PHASE II. DEFINING TEACHERS' PROFESSIONAL LEARNING GOALS: OVERVIEW

Goals

To collaboratively discover areas for improvement in the TLA, to better understand the cultural backgrounds of struggling students, and to select focus students to successfully meet teachers' professional learning goals.

Inquiry Questions

- Which focus students will yield the most valuable learning for our study group as we strive to promote excellence in learning through equitable teaching approaches?
- What are our students' strengths and areas for improvement in the target learning area?
- What cultural characteristics do our struggling students have in common?
- What are my own cultural values, and how might they be influencing my interactions with students whose cultural experiences and languages differ from my own?
- How might we learn more about our focus students and the other questions we have?

Steps, Purposes, and Tasks

1. SHARING BACKGROUND: *To review data sources and make predictions.*

   - Share initial assessment context, predictions, and assumptions.
   - Complete Initial Student Performance Grid.

2. OBSERVING: *To identify patterns across student performances.*

   - Determine common areas for improvement on Initial Student Performance Grid.
   - Determine cultural and linguistic characteristics of students with lower performance on the grid.
   - Consider teachers' own cultural background in relation to that of their students.

(Continued)

(Continued)

3. ANALYZING: *To maximize teachers' professional learning and heighten their curiosity.*

- Use patterns and insights to engage curiosity for both

    a. content area for improvement, and
    b. student cultural characteristics.

- Consider teachers' own cultural backgrounds in relation to that of their students.
- Note other questions and puzzlements.

4. PLANNING: *To identify professional learning goals and next steps.*

- Set professional learning goals.
- Plan to address group's questions and to refine Initial Assessment for next use.

5. REFLECTING: *To transfer learning from the study group to everyday practice, build collective responsibility for all students, and improve group productivity.*

- Compare predictions (from Step 1) with observed performance patterns on grid.
- Build insights about new learning, collaboration, and group productivity.
- Consider needs for further professional learning.

6. ACTING: *To know the focus student as a person and a learner and to address the group's questions and needs.*

- Build the Focus Student Biography.
- Collect a recent TLA-related work sample from the focus student.
- Address the group's questions and needs for further professional learning.

PHASE II TEACHER LEARNING OUTCOMES

Through the activities in Phase II the facilitator and teachers monitor and develop the following capacities, described in greater detail in Chapter 2, Framework: Teacher as Collaborative Inquirer.

Professional Knowledge Base

- Use assessment to identify learning needs.
- Understand students' cultural backgrounds.
- Understand the teacher's own culture.
- Set professional learning goals.

Skills for Collaborative Inquiry

- Engage in productive dialogue.
- Follow the group's working agreements.

Filters and Dispositions

- Recognize how one's filtering system may influence one's own practice.
- Take collective responsibility for overcoming learning challenges found among students.

PHASE II PREPARATION AND MATERIALS

The group facilitator has important choices to make when arranging the space, materials, and tasks for Phase II. The effectiveness of the group inquiry is a function of the safe and productive nature of the learning environment. Chapter 5 elaborated on these decisions.

As mentioned earlier, Phases I and II may be facilitated in large groups, with teachers sitting with their own study groups to complete the inquiry tasks. As teachers compare their scoring and observations of each student's work, they refine their understanding of the key concepts and skills in the TLA and how to assess them.

To make them easy to locate, the Phase II figures are provided at the end of this chapter.

Group Member Preparation

Well before the session, remind teachers to administer to their class the Initial Assessment of the TLA and to bring to this session:

- Their class set of students' scored responses to the Initial Assessment
- A copy of the scoring criteria used for the assessment
- Their completed Teacher Cultural Autobiography (pp. 205–209)
- This book and their CASL Notebook

Materials

Post the following items in a location visible to all:

- CASL Poster: Goal, agreements, and communication skills (Figure C.3, p. 132).
- Framework Poster (Figure 2.1, p. 34).
- Parking Lot. With larger groups, the parking lot may be placed in the back. With a small study group, a small sheet on the table will do.
- Three colors of highlighters for each teacher.
- Phase II Recorder Sheet. A chart paper or electronic device formatted as in Figure 7.3, p. 204.

Copy the following materials found at the end of this chapter:

- Phase II Protocol (Figure 7.1, p. 200) (One blank copy for each group member)
- Initial Student Performance Grid (Figure 7.2, p. 203) (One blank copy for each group member)
- Focus Student Biography (Figure 7.4, p. 205) (One blank copy for each group member)
- Study Group Log (Figure 7.5, p. 210) (One blank copy for recorder)

GUIDING A STUDY GROUP THROUGH PHASE II

The Phase II Protocol contains the purposes, tasks, and questions to be addressed in each step of the inquiry and serves as teachers' main guide during Phase II. The directions below are directed to both the study group members and to the facilitator.

Opening the Session

When you reach Phase II, your group may still be learning how to collaborate in ways that (a) deepen insights gained from dialogue and (b) maintain safety for risk-taking. You will be taking two major risks during Phase II: (1) sharing concrete evidence of your students' low performance and (2) examining your own and your struggling students' cultural backgrounds. For these reasons, the *working agreements* and *communication skills* become even more important.

To open the session, the facilitator leads the following activities. More detail about conducting opening activities is provided in Chapter 5.

a. Greeting. Greet participants and ask how things are going.

b. Grounding. Write about these questions: *Within your target learning area, which areas do you anticipate will be most difficult for your students? Which students might struggle the most? How do you feel about being here today?* Share responses, one at a time, in study groups. Remind the group to pause and paraphrase as they talk about all three questions.

c. Framing the Session

- CASL Goal. Refer to the goal at the top of the CASL Poster (p. 132).
- Session Outcomes. Pass out Phase II Protocol, and draw attention to the Teacher Learning Outcomes on the front page. Refer to the Framework Poster, Figure 2.1, p. 4, to help explain the outcomes.

- Agenda. Review the CASL Phases (Figure C.1, pp. 124–125) so teachers can see the big picture of how Phase II fits with Phases III and IV. Share the steps listed in the Overview, pp. 175–176. You may use the examples of Todd's study group in this chapter to help teachers see how they'll be analyzing their Student Performance Grids and selecting their focus students.
- Working Agreements. Refer to group's CASL Poster and review their agreements. Ask each group member to identify one that they want to pay special attention to today.
- Parking Lot. Call teachers' attention to the sheet and remind them that they can write their concerns or questions on a Post-it Note and place it there.

d. Distributing Materials. Pass out the materials for Phase II.

e. Identifying Roles.

- Recorder. Identify a recorder to use the format in Figure 7.3 as she writes on the Recorder Sheet.
- Study Group Log (Figure 7.5). Give to the recorder (or another person) the Study Group Log, and ask her to complete and distribute it after the session.

Developing and Applying Communication Skills

a. Purpose. Refer to the list of communication skills on right side of the CASL Poster and remind teachers of the importance of intentional communication in accomplishing the goals of CASL.

b. Committed Listening, Pausing, Matching Verbal/Nonverbal Cues, Paraphrasing

- Teachers find the personal cue cards they made in the prior CASL sessions and join with a new partner.
- Teachers compare their cue cards for committed listening, pausing, matching verbal/nonverbal cues, and paraphrasing.
- Teachers share with the group how they have been practicing the skills with others and what effect their use had.

c. Probing for Clarity

- Purpose and Benefits. Clarify how probing helps group members delve deeply into their own thinking and dispositions. A *probe* usually follows a pause and a paraphrase. For example, listen, pause, paraphrase, probe, pause, listen, pause, paraphrase, probe.

- Reading. Teachers silently read pages 66–67 "Probing for Clarity" in Chapter 3 and make notes on their cue cards.
- Practice. To practice pausing, paraphrasing, and probing for clarity, engage in the following activity.

    (1) Give directions. For each statement, write a paraphrase and then craft a probe for clarity. Remind them to use their cue cards. Clarify that there are several possible responses that might prompt the teacher to think more deeply about what she has said.

    (2) Write on a poster and read aloud this statement: "These results are disappointing." Teachers work in pairs to create a paraphrase and a probe. As they share their answers, clarify any confusion.

    (3) Teachers work alone to create a paraphrase and probe for the next two statements (written so they can see them).

    - "These outcomes aren't realistic for our students."
    - "This unit in our curriculum is weak, and that's why so many kids struggle with this outcome."

    (4) In pairs, teachers compare their responses.

    (5) As a group, use the answers provided in the Online Resources to find examples of acceptable responses.

d. Reflecting for Learning. Ask the group to use pausing, paraphrasing, and probing as they dialogue about this question: *How might paraphrasing and probing for clarity help us clarify our thinking and yield new insights?*

e. Cue Card. Teachers make additional notes on their cue cards. Suggest they try paraphrasing, pausing, and probing for clarity with their families—they will be amazed at the results.

f. Personal Goal(s). Group members write their goals for collaboration on the front page of their protocol.

FACILITATION TIPS

The importance of confidentiality

Confidentiality is especially important in Phase II as personal information about particular students (and teachers) may arise in the conversations. Therefore, be sure to enlist each person's willingness to abide by this working agreement.

Re-teaching of Communication Skills

You may decide to review pausing and paraphrasing if necessary. For example, at the last CASL session you may have noticed that teachers were interrupting one another or skipping from one idea to another without pausing and probing to explore the meaning of the ideas presented by others in the group.

Presumption of positive intent

If you notice that the tone of communication is critical, you might suggest that the group consider the working agreement: Presume positive intent—i.e., presuming that every teacher in the group shares a true desire to help students find success. Therefore, each member refrains from judging any other member as having consciously held harmful beliefs or actions. This presumption of positive intent is especially important when sharing characteristics of students.

Balancing participation

During the initial study group sessions, old habits of group interaction (for example, interrupting others or dominating the conversation) may arise. For this reason, some groups temporarily adopt a "turn taking" strategy, whereby each group member shares, one at a time. Regardless of the structure that you use, be sure to monitor each person's "air time" and encourage teachers to respect others' voices and time.

Protocol Step 1. Sharing Background

Purposes: To review data source and raise awareness of predictions and assumptions. To prepare data for analysis.

Step 1 contains three discrete, but important tasks: sharing information about the initial assessment process, making predictions about what might be revealed in the data, and recording and displaying each teacher's assessment results on the Student Performance Grid.

Sharing Background: Data Context

If the study group members have used different prompts for the Initial Assessment, they will need time to explain their assessment to the others. Even when they've all used the same assessment, they should share how they administered it and anything they learned along the way.

Use the following activities to engage in this step:

a. Purpose. Examine Step 1 in the protocol and clarify the purposes.

b. Sharing. One at a time, teachers explain their prompt, directions, procedures, and scoring criteria. The following question may be useful: *What were your prompt, directions, procedures, and rubric for the Initial Assessment?*

c. Communication Skills. As each teacher shares, the others pause, paraphrase, and probe for clarity as necessary.

d. Recording. The recorder makes note of any new questions that arise on Recorder Sheet (Figure 7.3).

FACILITATION TIP

During the sharing, listen for understanding of the target learning area proficiencies. When vague language is used (for example, "This is right on target"), be sure to paraphrase and then probe for clarity so every member can check her own understanding of the attributes of various levels of performance.

Sharing Background: Predictions

Making predictions about expected patterns can illuminate *dispositions,* and *personal filters* about students' capacities to learn that may limit the mission of the group.

Professionals often rely on a "gut" impression of the patterns that they find in a set of student work. But these impressions may be limited by one's filtering system. Writing out one's hunches early in the inquiry and then comparing them later with the actual data can help teachers begin to question their first impressions and consider perspectives broader than their habitual ways of seeing.

To engage in this step, teachers engage in the following activities.

a. Predictions. Each teacher writes in the right column of the protocol the predictions about the common strengths and challenges they expect to find in their class set of student assessments. The following questions may be useful during this step:

- *Which groups of students might struggle the most?*
- *Which student learning outcomes may be most difficult for students?*

b. Sharing. As teachers share predictions, one at a time, be sure to listen, paraphrase, and probe for assumptions (i.e., the reasons underlying the predictions). You might ask, *What leads you to these predictions?*

c. Recorder. The recorder writes the predictions and assumptions in the "Background" section of the Recorder Sheet.

FACILITATION TIP

During this conversation, listen for group members' *filters, dispositions*, and enabling or limiting *assumptions*. For example, a teacher in Todd's group might say, "Oh, they won't be able to write about their thinking. Fourth graders never can."

The facilitator might first paraphrase that idea and ask the recorder to write it down. In an atmosphere of trust, someone might ask, "How many of you have this same prediction? What is your hunch about why this is so hard for them?" As the conversation proceeds, underlying assumptions might arise, for example, "They just don't care enough to put in the effort." The facilitator (or another group member) makes note of these often-stated ideas and waits until the moment is ripe to explore the possible reasons it appears that students "don't care."

It may be important at this point to acknowledge the purpose of CASL: that, while some students may not be reaching excellence, teachers are joining together in finding equitable ways to get them all there.

Present Background. Prepare Data: Initial Student Performance Grid

The Initial Student Performance Grid (Figure 7.2, p. 203) is a powerful tool for looking deeply into a class set of assessments. The grid requires a detailed description of each student's performance and thus presents an accurate picture of what patterns actually exist.

Most teachers score their students' work and then record the grades. As they do this, they might make note of the patterns found across the papers or in a particular student's work. But such informal notes don't always yield accurate information about what is really going on, partly because they are driven by teachers' personal filters and dispositions.

Another pitfall of the "score and grade" approach is the assumption that a single score tells the whole story. This brings us to our saying, "A score of 2 is not a 2 is not a 2." By this we mean that, although some students have the same score, the *reasons* for those scores are often different. And those reasons may call for *different teaching approaches*.

The confusion about what a score really means is especially true when the rubric is "holistic"—that is, when several categories (for example, organization, mechanics, voice) are combined into one score. In this case, it becomes difficult to determine which attribute earned the score. For example, Joe might have a low score because of lack of organization, whereas Sue earned the same score because of poor mechanics. For this reason, we prefer to use "analytical" rubrics in which students earn a different score for each attribute.

Teachers often ask us, "Isn't the rubric score enough? Why do I need to also describe the work on the grid?" The main value of the Student Performance Grid is the opportunity to look beyond the score to find evidence in the work of the student's specific misconceptions, strengths, and ways of learning.

We ask teachers to try out the Student Performance Grid for this activity so that they can experience the power of analyzing each student's performance *in detail*. As a result, they may choose to use this method for other important assessments that will inform the design or revision of their curriculum and instruction.

a. Purpose. Explain how the grid will be useful (or have teachers read the prior six paragraphs).

b. Student Performance Grid. Explain and demonstrate how to complete the grid. Teachers may consult the example grid presented in Todd's Step 2 on page 188. Note that Todd's grid uses symbols rather than colors. Also, the example grid does not show every student.

Use the following process to complete the Student Performance Grid.

- Sorting. Sort the papers (or data) into the number of scores on the rubric (e.g., three piles for a 3-level rubric). Take notes (to share later) about which parts of the rubric were hard to use or confusing.
- Description. Start with the pile with the lowest scores. Enter each student's name on the left side of the grid, record the score, and then write specific *details* you see in the paper—both the Strengths and the Areas for Improvement. *Important*: Use more detail than the rubric provides. Sometimes, crucial clues to student learning may appear in the work but may not appear in the rubric. For example, if a student drew an elaborate picture that shows mathematical understanding but did not write about that understanding, this might indicate a visual learner.
- Data. Enter every low-scoring paper onto the grid. Then go on to the next pile (middle scores) and do the same. Continue until all papers are entered, arranged from lowest performance to highest.

FACILITATION TIPS

When teachers are new to a curriculum or assessment tool

If some in the group are still learning about their grade-level content standards and the assessment of them, you may ask them to work in pairs as they score and sort the work samples. Encourage teachers to confer with others when they are unsure of or disagree on a score. Plan for enough time to hash out the participants' understanding of the scoring criteria. As they do this, they should bring to the group their notes and insights about how to best use and refine (if necessary) the assessment task and scoring criteria.

The Further Learning Activity called "Rubric Calibrating" in the Online Resources may be useful if teachers are struggling to use the rubric in a consistent way.

Recording detailed information about both areas for improvement and strengths

Some teachers may have a tendency to focus only on the flaws in a student's work. The grid serves the valuable purpose of also tracking each student's strengths; these strengths offer valuable clues to finding responsive approaches for a student.

TODD'S STUDY GROUP: PHASE II, STEP 1 SHARING BACKGROUND

Initial Assessment Used (Written on Recorder Sheet)

- Everyone used the task and criteria we designed last time.

Predictions and Assumptions (Written on Recorder Sheet)

- Students won't show their work. (Why? They are lazy, not motivated to do extra work.)
- Many students won't be able to do it. (Why? They hate writing.)

Prepare Data: Student Performance Grid (See Todd's Step 2. Observing, p. 188)

Protocol Step 2. Observing Patterns in Initial Assessment Data

Purposes: To identify patterns across student performances and understand students' and teachers' cultural backgrounds.

Public acknowledgement of the specific patterns found in teachers' classes creates a sense of shared responsibility and commitment to helping improve the learning of the struggling students. This energy will carry over into the selection of the focus students that teachers will study over the next months.

The patterns will help teachers select a focus student that (a) represents a skill or understanding that many students find difficult and (b) shares cultural characteristics that the teacher finds puzzling, especially in light of his own cultural background.

Observing: Learning Outcomes in Need of Improvement

To find the content-related patterns in the Student Performance Grid, engage in the following activities:

a. Purpose. Explain that they will use color-coding to find patterns in their grids, so they can discover the content outcomes that are most challenging to their students.

b. Directions. Give directions and draw attention to Todd's example grid for Step 2. Clarify any questions. Ask teachers to work alone.

- Highlight. On the grid's "Areas for Improvement" column, color-code common patterns. For example, highlight in yellow all of the struggles that are the same; then use pink to highlight all of the struggles of a different nature, and so on.
- Common Patterns. On the Performance Grid, place a star (*) next to the two or three most common color-coded areas.

c. Sharing. The group dialogues about the patterns found, using a question such as, *Based on the data, which learning outcomes are most in need of improvement?*

d. Recording. The recorder writes the top two areas for each teacher in the "Observe" section of the Recorder Sheet. The teachers also take notes on their copy of the Phase II Protocol.

FACILITATION TIPS

Stick with the protocol.

As teachers notice the patterns in their students' content challenges, they might be tempted to jump right past the "Analysis" step by sharing their favorite ideas for teaching these areas. This is only natural. They want to fix the problem. But please ask them to refrain—for now. Here's why: They may not yet know exactly *why* the problem exists.

For example, one of the most common areas seen in students' math writing is lack of use of mathematical terms. When analyzing individual writing samples, teachers may find different reasons for this. For example, some students lack the vocabulary to describe a mathematical process that they have used properly, while others use the term but don't understand the meaning underlying the mathematics. Clearly, different teaching strategies would be required for these two very different causes for the same "error."

**Using the Student Performance
Grid data in school improvement plans.**

The grid provides classroom-level data that can provide valuable insights for school improvement activities because the data are easily disaggregated by content outcomes and student characteristics.

While understanding such cross-classroom patterns is important, CASL's purpose is more specific than this. It addresses each teacher's natural desire to discover why her struggling students are not achieving and then to discover approaches that respond to those students' specific needs and strengths.

Observing: Characteristics of Students With Lower Scores

a. Purpose. Explain that the next task is to discover the common characteristics of the students with non-proficient performances. This information will be used when they select focus students.

b. Directions. Explain the directions below and show Todd's example of Step 2.

Clarify any confusion. Ask teachers to work alone.

- Description. In the "Student Characteristics" column, start at the top and write what you know about each student's cultural background. Consider the characteristics of class, race, ethnicity, gender, behaviors, language, religion, and exceptionality.
- Patterns. Circle the two or three most common cultural characteristics observed among the students with lower performance. Note these on your Phase II Protocol.

c. Sharing. The group discusses the patterns found, using questions similar to, *Which students are struggling the most? How would we describe them as people and learners?*

d. Recording. The recorder writes the top two characteristics found by each teacher in the "Observe" section on the Recorder Sheet.

FACILITATION TIP

Culture, ethnicity, and class can be sensitive subjects as they touch individuals' deeply held beliefs about diverse groups of people. Be sure to notice any inclusive or limiting statements while avoiding judgment or finger pointing.

If the trust level is high enough, you may use pausing, paraphrasing, and probing to bring limiting beliefs or assumptions to the conscious level, without necessarily labelling them as such to the group. Some of the most transformative insights are first acknowledged internally.

TODD'S STUDY GROUP: PHASE II, STEP 2 OBSERVING

Todd's Student Performance Grid

Student Name	Score	Areas of Strength	Areas for Improvement	Student Characteristics
Jose	2	Correct calculations Drew picture accurately	+ Confused formulas for perimeter and area ∧ Writing lacked mathematical terms	Hispanic Limited English Male Low-income family
Mary	2	Attempted to do calculations Drew own picture with dimensions	* No systematic approach to problem + Didn't use correct formula ∧ Hard to read written explanation	Artistic Hates writing Family is breaking up Female
Rima	2	Used correct formula for perimeter	* Didn't set up a diagram to solve the problem ∧ Writing includes only math terms. No sentences + Confused formula for area	Shy Little spoken language in class From Syria and is still learning English Female
Esteban	2	Calculated correctly in formulas for both area and perimeter Drew picture correctly	∧ Lacking a written explanation	Hispanic Male Trouble with English

Notes Written on Recorder Sheet

Our Common Areas for Improvement (Written on Recorder Sheet)

- Writing out their thinking (Symbol used: ∧)
- Confusing the formula for perimeter and area (Symbol used: +)

Our Struggling Students' Characteristics (Written on Recorder Sheet)

Many of the students with lower scores are in the process of learning to speak and write English.

Protocol Step 3. Analyzing Professional Learning Goals

Purpose: To maximize teachers' professional learning and heighten curiosity.

As the group thinks about the patterns that they have found, encourage them to consider the content outcomes and student cultural characteristics that they have frequently found challenging to teach.

To address these curiosities, engage in the following activities.

a. Areas for Improvement. Each teacher examines the color-coded patterns on his own grid and completes this statement: "I'd most like to discover new ways of helping students reach the content outcome(s), _____." The prompt for this writing might be, *Which of the learning outcomes that your own students struggle with are of most interest to you? Why is this important to you?*

b. Writing. Teachers write the statement in the right column (Step 3, "Analyzing") on the protocol. As they share, the recorder writes.

c. Student Cultural Characteristics. Each teacher refers to her own grid and completes this statement: "I'd most like to discover new ways of teaching kids who have the following cultural characteristics: _____." The prompt for this writing might be: *Which characteristics of your struggling students are you most curious about and why?*

d. Writing. Teachers write the statement on the right column (Step 3, "Analyzing") on the protocol. As they share, the recorder writes.

e. Teacher's Own Background. Ask each teacher to examine his own Cultural Autobiography (Figure 6.3 from Phase I), and then write about this question in the "Analyzing" section of the protocol: *How does your own cultural background compare with the cultural characteristics of the students who struggle most in your classroom?*

f. Sharing. Teachers share their thoughts with the group, or perhaps with another trusted person in their group.

g. Questions. Ask teachers to consider, *What other questions might you explore to better understand the TLA standards/outcomes, assessment, students, or yourself?*

h. Recording. As teachers share their curiosities and questions (one at a time), ask the recorder to write them down in the lower left corner of Record Sheet.

FACILITATION TIPS

Selecting a content area for improvement

Be sure the selected area is not too discrete or rule-based, for example, using periods or reciting a set of facts. These skills usually can be developed in one or two lessons, and therefore they don't lend themselves well to long-term study. The inquiry will be most fruitful when the outcome is a complex understanding or process that is *developed over time.*

Trust level

Gauge the trust level in the group to decide whether to ask the members to delve more deeply into details about students' and their families' cultural groups. You may even wait until teachers analyze their focus students' work samples in Phase III to investigate these areas.

> **TODD'S STUDY GROUP:**
> **PHASE II, STEP 3 ANALYZE**
>
> *We're Curious About These Areas for Improvement.* (Written on Recorder Sheet)
>
> - We have trouble reaching students who struggle to write out their mathematical thinking.
>
> *We're Curious About These Struggling Students' Characteristics.* (Written on Recorder Sheet)
>
> - We have always struggled to reach immigrant students who are learning to speak and write English.
>
> *Our Questions* (Written on Recorder Sheet)
>
> - We need to know more about English-language learners: how they develop their skills in English and how they make sense of math concepts.

Protocol Step 4. Planning for Professional Learning

Purpose: To identify professional inquiry goal(s) and select focus students to fulfill the goals.

Because teachers will be spending at least three months analyzing the work of their own and other team members' focus students, it's important that the students who are selected help everyone reach the professional learning goals that they most want to address. That is why, at this point, each teacher will write out their own learning goal and share it with the group.

Next, the group will check that the various areas of content struggles and cultural characteristics of interest that are shared across the members of the group. The CASL inquiry will yield the most growth when each teacher has a professional learning goal that benefits not only his own learning but also that of the other group members.

Next, each teacher will finalize her selection of a focus student. While the student should represent the learning challenges and characteristics found on the teacher's Performance Grid, the student should also (1) attend school regularly and (2) not be so idiosyncratic or special that what is learned from this case won't easily translate to other similar students' needs.

Finally, teachers begin an intensive Focus Student Biography (Figure 7.4) for the selected student. The Biography, adapted from Herrera (2010), is a tool for creating a detailed case study of the focus student. As teachers seek more information and experiment with various approaches, they discover valuable clues about the culture, perceptions, and learning strengths of that student. The Biography is where these insights can be documented;

it also prompts teachers to consider all aspects of the student's culture and ways of learning.

The final activities in this step involve revising the assessment and completing the Study Group Log for the administrator.

To engage in the Planning Step, use the following activities.

a. Professional Learning Goal. Teachers complete this statement and write it on their protocol (right column, under Step 4 Plan): "*Studying* (fill in focus student name) *will help me develop responsive approaches for students who are* (fill in a cultural characteristic), *and struggle to learn* (fill in content outcomes) *within the target learning area of* (fill in target learning area)."

b. Focus Student Selection.

- Teachers share (one at a time) the student(s) they are considering selecting and explain why. Others listen, paraphrase, and probe for clarity.
- The group makes sure the focus students represent a variety of challenges. A useful prompt for this conversation is, *Which focus students might each teacher select, and how might that promote the learning of the other study group members?*
- The recorder writes on the Recorder Sheet the names of each focus student selected and why each was selected.

c. Focus Student Biography (Figure 7.4, pp. 205–209).

- Pass out the Biography form and explain its purpose. The facilitator may ask, *How might you learn more about your focus student?*
- They begin completing the Biography and make plans to add more information before the next session.

d. Assessment Revision. The group members and recorder have been keeping notes about the quality of the assessment task and scoring rubric. A useful question at this stage is, *What changes might you want to make to your assessment for the next time you use it?* Decide, as a group, which revisions need to be made, and appoint a person to do that. Then make a plan to distribute the new version.

e. Questions and Curiosities: Refer to the area labelled "Our Questions" on the Recorder Sheet, and make plans to pursue any questions that came up about content (e.g., standards, curriculum materials), students (e.g., cultural backgrounds), or other curiosities or gaps in knowledge. The facilitator might ask, *How might the study group address the questions that surfaced today?*

f. Study Group Log. Assign a group member to complete the Study Group Log for the administrator and other group members (Figure 7.5).

FACILITATION TIPS

Selecting a focus student for maximum professional learning

We sometimes encounter teachers who choose a student characteristic or content area that is not sufficiently challenging. It is the facilitator's job to ask questions like, "What is it about this student that you are seeking to understand?" "How does the student's background compare with yours?" or "How will studying this student benefit other students you've struggled to teach?" If the teacher can justify his reasoning by using the patterns found in his Student Performance Grid and his Autobiography, then he may decide to stay with that student.

For example, Todd might initially select a shy Latino student as his focus student. Then, the facilitator asks Todd to consider his own cultural background and how studying this student over time might inform his practice. Todd realizes that this student is from an upper middle-class family similar to Todd's own family. With prompting from his group members, he ultimately decides that this student may not provide the challenge he needs to truly grow. He then selects Jose, who also struggles to explain his calculations but represents an economic background different from Todd's own.

Selecting the most challenging student

Some teachers are drawn to a student who is "driving them crazy" but whose needs are only rarely encountered. In this case, the in-depth study of that child may not yield insights that will help many other students.

One exception is when a teacher has selected a student who is being evaluated for special services. For example, the Response to Intervention model (www.rtinetwork.org) requires documentation of "tiered levels" of interventions. The work samples and reflections generated during Phases II and III are especially useful in providing such evidence.

Distributing student challenges across teachers

Study group members grow from studying both their own student *and* those chosen by the other group members. Therefore, before making the final selection of their focus student, teachers might want to check that the student shares cultural characteristics or content-learning challenges that showed up in other group members' Student Performance Grids.

Changing focus students during the months of inquiry

Teachers often ask, "Must I stay with this student the entire time?" We respond by saying, "As long as the study of a particular student helps you fulfill your professional learning goal, then stick with this student. If you've achieved your goal and need a different student to address your new goal, then let's talk about it." Some good reasons for changing the focus student are that the student is no longer a member of the class, the student has achieved a satisfactory performance and no longer poses a challenge, or the student has been assigned to a different teacher (e.g., Special Education) for instruction in the target learning area being studied.

If a teacher does select a new focus student, we suggest that he use the exact same procedure described in Phase II: finding patterns on a recently created Student Performance Grid and forming a new professional learning goal. This switch may also require a new look at the Teacher Cultural Autobiography.

TODD'S STUDY GROUP: PHASE II, STEP 4 PLANNING

Todd's Professional Learning Goal (Written on Todd's protocol)

Studying Jose will help me develop responsive approaches for poor students who are learning English and struggle to explain formulas and calculations within Math problem solving.

Focus Students Selected and Why (Written on Recorder Sheet)

- Todd selected Jose, who is from a low income immigrant family and couldn't explain his thinking in math.
- Clara selected Mary, who has foster parents and who often makes problem-solving errors.
- Paul chose Rima, a second-language learner from Syria who couldn't write out her math thinking.

Assessment Revision (Written under "Plan" on Recorder Sheet)

We clarified the language in our rubric to make it easier to use. Paul will make the changes and give copies to us.

Our Questions (Written on Recorder Sheet)

- Why can some kids can talk about their thinking but can't write about it? (We will check with the math specialist.)
- We need to understand what it means to come from poverty so we can reach students like Jose.

Protocol Step 5. Reflecting

Purposes: To transfer learning from the study group to teachers' practice, build collective responsibility for all students, and improve group productivity.

As stated earlier, it is important to reflect in writing to solidify teachers' learning. We encourage study group members to reflect on three major areas: their earlier predictions, the group's collaborative functioning, and their professional learning needs.

Comparing the group's earlier predictions with what was learned about the students' actual performance can show the value of using concrete evidence to check out one's assumptions. Further, this comparison may illuminate beliefs (filters) about students' capacities to learn that could interfere with the group's efforts to reach them.

Sharing insights about teaching and learning may help the group members find ways to respond to their own students who are similar to the focus students studied that day.

Next, teachers reflect on the quality of the group's collaboration and plan to make adjustments for the next time. This piece is important because we want *every* teacher to contribute their expertise to the group. Finally, the group considers whether they want to take time out to engage in further professional learning (for example, to revise the assessment tool or learn more about a cultural group).

The facilitator asks the group to write and share as follows:

a. Predictions versus Data. Privately, teachers compare their initial predictions (Recorded in Step 1, "Share Background") with the patterns found in their grids: the areas needing improvement and the struggling students. A useful question to consider is, *Look back at the recorder's notes from Step 1. How does what you learned today differ from or confirm your initial predictions and assumptions?* Teachers may choose to keep their insights private or share them with the others, depending on the trust level of the group.

b. Recording. Remind the recorder to write on the Study Group Log (Figure 7.5) the reflections that are shared in the next three activities.

c. Ideas for Promoting Student Learning. Each group member shares how he can use his learning from Phase II to respond to his students in the future. The prompt might be, *What did you learn about students and yourself today that might help promote other students' learning?*

d. Collaboration and Teacher Learning. Considering these last questions helps the group decide what to modify or continue to make the group safe and powerful for future learning. These questions are,

- *How consistently did the group follow the established working agreements and communication skills?*
- *What influence did the collaborative process have on your learning today?*
- *What might we do better next time?*

e. Further Professional Learning. Ask the group members to look at "Our Questions" on the record sheet. Ask them what resources or additional professional learning they might need. Have the recorder write them on the Study Group Log. The prompt might be, *How might the group pursue further professional learning if necessary?*

f. Recorder Tasks. Remind the recorder to copy the completed CASL Study Group Log and distribute it to the facilitator, all group members, and the principal by the end of the next day.

FACILITATION TIPS

Reflecting on what teachers are learning about students and themselves

Some people are uncomfortable with the idea of sharing their reflections, especially when it comes to talking about their personal insights about themselves as cultural beings. Still, as we have said before, it is in just such conversations that many of the most powerful insights to benefit student learning are gained.

Reflecting on collaboration

Some teachers might be hesitant to talk about how they felt about the group's interactions. In spite of this concern, it is vitally important that teachers come to trust that the group is a safe place to explore what might be getting in the way of their students' learning. Therefore, we suggest that the facilitator acknowledge this discomfort and reiterate the purpose for the discussion.

Development of collaboration

As teachers progress through Phase II, they come to value one another as important resources for professional learning. Teachers begin to turn to one another for insights rather than just to the facilitator. The facilitator can highlight this growth to make it more conscious for teachers.

TODD'S STUDY GROUP: PHASE II, STEP 5 REFLECTING

How Our Learning Can Help Our Students (Written on Study Group Log)

- We can build on the success of students' calculations to develop their confidence in showing and explaining their thinking.

Our Collaboration (Summary of conversation)

- We interrupted one another too much and we forgot to paraphrase. One person was frustrated by this, so we made a goal to practice paraphrasing at our next meeting. It helped having a recorder who could review the ideas that we shared at each step. The facilitator and protocol kept us organized.

Our Questions (Written on Study Group Log)

- We are curious about English language learners (ELL) and the demonstration of their mathematical thinking.

Our Professional Learning Needs (Written on Study Group Log)

- We are going to invite the ELL specialist to our next meeting.

Protocol Step 6. Acting

Purposes: To know the focus student as a person and a learner, and to address the group's questions and needs.

Teachers carry the study group's activities into their daily teaching by seeking to understand the focus student more deeply, gathering a new work sample, and pursuing other curiosities that have surfaced during the study group session.

The facilitator helps the group agree on the agenda, time, and place for the next session. Then be sure to complete the following actions before the next session.

a. Focus Student Biography (Figure 7.4). Teachers may choose to put a photo of the student in the upper right-hand corner, and continue to complete the description. Bring one copy for each group member. Sharing these Biographies develops a heartfelt commitment to each and every student studied in the group. As successive work samples are analyzed, teachers add to each Focus Student Biography the insights gained.

b. Planning. Teachers who are presenting their own focus student's work at the next session (Phase III) will collect a recent TLA-related work sample and make copies of it for each group member. If not too much time has passed since completing the Initial Assessment, this piece of work may come from the Initial Assessment.

c. Questions and Needs. Take actions to address the group's questions and professional learning needs.

d. Study Group Log. Recorder copies the completed log and on the next day and distributes it to the facilitator, all group members, and principal.

e. Preparation. Teachers read Chapter 8 in this book.

CASL NOTEBOOK CONTENTS FROM PHASE II

Study group members add the following items to their notebook under the tab for Phase II:

- Phase II Protocol with notes
- Initial Assessment task, directions, and scoring rubric
- Initial Student Performance Grid
- Professional Learning Goal (written on protocol)
- Focus Student Biography (will be placed in Phase III Section)
- Study Group Log

PHASE II ADAPTATIONS

In the early CASL sessions, the facilitator guides the group to follow the working agreements, communication skills, and protocol. The greatest facilitator responsibility, however, is to *read the individuals and the group* and *to modify or supplement the tasks as necessary*. The facilitator will use the framework described in Chapter 2 as the target for teachers' development.

From time to time, the facilitator's observations of the group may warrant a brief change of direction. At this point, he may engage the group in making decisions about the pacing of the CASL phases and activities. This may involve taking more or less time with certain steps or taking time for further professional learning.

Here are some ways in which Phase II can be modified to align with the strengths and needs of the teachers.

Curriculum Revision

If teachers are learning to use a new unit or curriculum, the Student Performance Grid can provide valuable direction for revisions and improvements. After teachers aggregate their findings with others in the same grade or content, they can easily see the students' strengths and weaknesses in the content just taught. They can then analyze the possible reasons for the patterns found and revise the curriculum as necessary.

If teachers decide to do this, be sure to complete all steps in Phase II *before* engaging in the curriculum revision. Also, avoid getting side-tracked for too long. Some teachers may find working on the curriculum more comfortable than looking at their own teaching and its effects on individual students' learning. Because of this tendency, we suggest that you complete Phase II, move briskly through the curriculum revision activities, and then go on to Phase III.

Lack of Experience With Assessment

If teachers are still developing their understanding of the indicators of various levels of proficiency in the TLA, or if the rubric is new, consider using the "Rubric Calibrating Activity" presented in the Online Resources *before* completing the Student Performance Grid.

Considerable Experience With Assessment

If teachers already have done a lot of scoring with the rubric and you've seen evidence of this expertise during Phase I, you may ask them to complete the Student Performance Grid on their own before the Phase II session. That said, there is still much to be learned—especially for teachers new to the curriculum—from sharing and resolving dilemmas that arise while scoring the performances.

Hesitation to Share Student Work

If little trust or comfort exists, consider devoting some time to sharing just the strengths in the student performances and then inquiring into how teachers have contributed to developing these strengths. This activity builds confidence in those teachers who may be discouraged by their students' learning results.

Such sharing also creates a safe environment for practicing listening, paraphrasing, and probing questions and develops trust among the group members before the more challenging steps of this phase—inquiring into which students are not achieving.

Limited Time

If time is short, you may have teachers record onto the Student Performance Grid only the information from the less-proficient papers during the session. In this case, be sure to have the teachers also acknowledge the more successful performances and clarify how their teaching influenced this success. Invite the teachers to complete the grid outside of the session because much can be learned from the performances of the more proficient students.

Multiple Scores for Each Student (Multiple-Trait Rubric)

Teachers may create a grid that has each trait listed across the top and the students' names down the side. First, enter the score for each trait. Next, color-code the common patterns (one color for lower scores, another color for higher scores). When it is clear which traits need the most improvement, select eight to ten of the lowest-scoring papers in that area and record onto the Student Performance Grid the information required for each column. Finally, look for the common characteristics of the students with lower overall scores.

Mandated Assessment or Scoring Rubric

Although we have suggested that you take time to reflect on changes that would improve the assessment used, we understand that some assessments are mandated and cannot be modified. In this case, you can still note valuable details for using such instruments. These ideas will improve the assessment the next time you use it. For example, you can write on Post-it Notes examples or hints to clarify those areas of a rubric the group found difficult to understand. In this case, it's important to compare notes to aid in consistency of scoring.

SUMMARY

Phase II of CASL is crucial for setting the stage for productive inquiry that results in teachers' responsive teaching. Although the steps require several tasks, each one helps the members of the study group to focus their inquiry on students who will help them discover equitable approaches for those students they've struggled to reach in the past.

Finally, we hope that you are finding that each and every person in your study group is a powerful and helpful resource for interpreting assessment results and analyzing individual students' strengths and needs. It is now time to begin analyzing in detail your focus students' work samples so you can discover responsive equitable approaches that benefit their success.

Figure 7.1 CASL Phase II Protocol: Defining Teachers' Professional Learning Goals

Goal: To collaboratively discover areas for improvement in the TLA, cultural backgrounds of struggling students, and to select focus students to successfully meet teachers' professional learning goals.

- Which focus students will yield the most valuable learning for me and my study group as we strive for excellence through equitable teaching approaches?
- What are my students' strengths and areas for growth in the target learning area?
- What are the common cultural characteristics of my struggling students?
- What are my own cultural values and how might they be influencing my interaction with students with experiences and languages different from my own?
- How might we learn more about our focus students and other questions we have?

Teacher Learning Outcomes

- Use assessment to identify learning needs.
- Understand students' cultural backgrounds.
- Understand the teacher's own culture.
- Engage in productive dialogue.
- Follow the group's working agreements.
- Set professional learning goals.
- Recognize how personal filters and dispositions influence teachers' own practice.
- Take collective responsibility for overcoming learning challenges found among students.

Materials

Group members bring:

- This book
- CASL Notebook
- Class set of scored Initial Assessments, with rubric
- Cultural Autobiography (Figure 6.3)

Facilitator brings:

- One Phase II Recorder Sheet
- Chart paper (for recorder)
- One Study Group Log (Figure 7.5)

Posted in meeting room:

- CASL Poster (Figure C.1)
- Framework Poster (Figure 2.1)
- Parking lot

Facilitator brings one blank copy for each teacher:

- Phase II Protocol (Figure 7.1)
- Initial Student Performance Grid (Figure 7.2)
- Focus Student Biography (Figure 7.4)

Roles

Facilitator

- Teach, model, and monitor CASL working agreements and communication skills.
- Lead group members through the Phase II Protocol.
- Encourage multiple perspectives and interpretations.
- Paraphrase ideas offered and ask recorder to write them on sheet.

Recorder

- Take notes—visible to all—during each step of the protocol.
- Complete and distribute Study Group Log.

Study Group Guide for CASL Phase I Protocol

Opening the Session

- Greeting, Grounding, Framing the Session
- Review working agreements.
- Distribute materials and assign roles.
- Review and teach and practice communication skills.

1. Sharing Background	
Purpose and Prompts	*Notes*
Data Context Purpose: To review data sources • What were your prompt, directions, procedures, and rubric for the Initial Assessment? **Predictions** Purpose: To raise awareness of predictions and assumptions • Which students might struggle the most? • Which student learning outcomes may be most difficult for students? • What leads you to these predictions? **Prepare Data** Complete Student Performance Grid.	

2. Observing	
Purpose and Prompts	*Notes*
Purpose: To identify patterns across student performances. To understand students' and teachers' cultural backgrounds • Based on the data, which learning outcomes are most in need of improvement? • Which students are struggling the most, and how would you describe them as people and learners?	

3. Analyzing/Interpreting	
Purpose and Prompts	*Notes*
Purpose: To maximize teachers' professional learning and heighten curiosity. Based on your observations: • Which of the learning outcomes that students struggle with are of most interest to you? • Which characteristics of your struggling students are you most curious about and why? • How does your own cultural background compare with the cultural characteristics of the students who struggle most in your classroom? • What other questions might you explore to better understand the TLA and your students' learning?	

4. Planning	
Purpose and Prompts	*Notes*
Purpose: To identify professional learning goal(s) and select focus students to fulfil the goals • What is your professional learning goal? • Which focus students will each teacher select, and how might that promote the learning of study group members? • How might you learn more about your focus student (for the Biography)? • What changes might you want to make to your assessment for the next time you use it? • How might the study group address the questions that surfaced today?	

5. Reflecting	
Purpose and Prompts	*Notes*
Purpose: To transfer learning from the study group to everyday practice, build collective responsibility for all students, and improve group productivity • Look back at the recorder's notes from Step 1. How does what you learned today differ from or confirm your initial predictions and assumptions? • What did you learn about students and yourself today that might help promote student learning? • How consistently did the group follow the established working agreements and communication skills? • What influence did the collaborative process have on your learning today? • How might the group pursue further professional learning, if necessary?	

6. Acting (Complete these before the next study group meeting.)	
Purpose and Prompts	*Notes*
Purpose: To become acquainted with the Focus Student as a person and a learner; and to address the group's questions and needs • Complete the Focus Student Biography and make copies for group members. • Collect a recent TLA-related work sample from each teacher's focus student. • Take actions to address the group's questions and professional learning needs. • Read Chapter 8 in this book. • Recorder distributes Study Group Log to administrator and group members.	

Figure 7.2 CASL Initial Student Performance Grid

Phase II INITIAL STUDENT PERFORMANCE GRID

Directions. Sort your students' assessment products into the number of scores on the rubric (e.g., three piles for a 3-level rubric). Begin with the lower-scoring papers. Record the information below for each student's work. Be sure to look for and record detailed evidence of strengths and needs *beyond* those described in the rubric.

Student Name	Score	Strengths	Areas For Improvement	Student Characteristics

Figure 7.3 Recorder Sheet for CASL Phase II Refining Teachers' Inquiry Focus

Directions. Use this format to write group's ideas on chart paper or electronic device so that all can see it.

1. **Background:** Initial Assessment Used:
   Predictions and Assumptions:

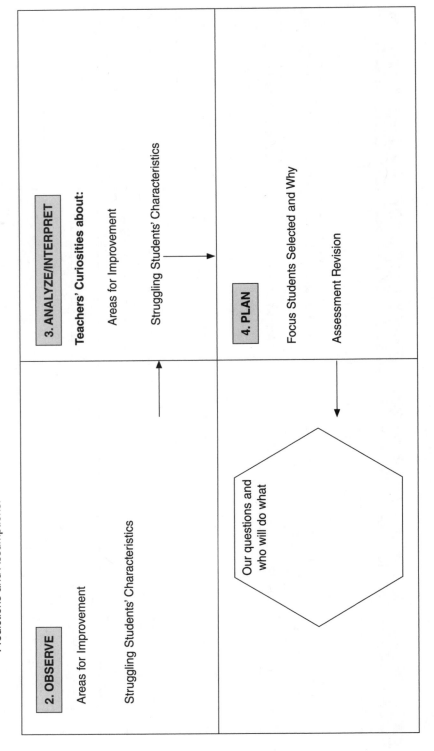

Figure 7.4 CASL Focus Student Biography

Directions. Use this tool to get to know your focus student as a cultural being, as a person, and as a learner. You may add new relevant categories if they don't appear here. Continue adding useful information and insights as you experiment with responsive approaches and analyze the results in your study group.

Basic Knowledge	Insert Student Picture Here (Optional)
Focus student name: Name likes to be called:	
Date of birth: Place of birth:	
Parent or guardian's names:	
Any siblings? What ages? Do they live with your student?	
Others who live in the household with your student?	
Who would your student like to have you tell when he/she does something especially well?	
What language is spoken at your student's house?	
Is your student new to this school? Where was he/she before?	
Grade/Subject:	

Country of origin:	
Length of time in the United States:	
Race: Ethnicity:	
Physical features:	

Activities and Interests
What time does your student usually get up in the morning?
How does your student get to school? How long does it take?
When does your student usually go to bed?
What brings your student pleasure, laughter, and comfort?
What interests does your student have?

What cultural groups did/does your student belong to, and how might participation in those groups influence how he/she learns?

What might your student imagine him/herself doing ten years from now? What are his/her aspirations?

What cultural groups did/does your student belong to and how might his/her participation in those groups influence how he/she learns?

What experiences has your student had that you might draw upon to promote learning and the transfer of learning?

The Way the Student Learns

How does your student process information/learn best (e.g., solve problems, organize information)?

What configuration is your student most comfortable in (e.g., pairs, large group, independent).

What kind of help might your student appreciate from you?

What is your student's preferred learning style and what strategies might be most responsive to that style?

What does your student want to learn from your class?

How does your student feel about the subject you teach?

What about your class is going to be particularly difficult for your student?

Academic Background Information
What are your student's strengths in the content area?
What areas of the content does your student need to improve?
What factors might be helping or hindering your student's access to equitable educational approaches, engagement in learning, and hope for the success in the future (e.g., interests, motivation)?
What was your student's last school like? What kinds of things did he/she study?

What language does the student speak at home?
For English Language Learners, what is the level of English and writing proficiency?
Current language support, if receiving it.

Adapted from: Herrera, S. (2010). *Biography-driven culturally relevant teaching.* New York: Teachers College, Columbia University and from Cushman, K. (2003). *Fires in the bathroom: Advice for teachers from high school students.* New York, NY: The New Press.

Figure 7.5 Study Group Log

Directions. Please complete one form after each study group meeting. Distribute copies to your administrator and group members.

Date: _____   Time Meeting Started: _____   and Ended: _____

Name of Group (Grade-Level and/or Content):

Group Members:

Today's Facilitator: Today's Recorder:

Tasks Accomplished:

How Our New Learning Will Help Our Students (from Step 5. Reflections):

Inquiry Questions We Want to Pursue:

Resources, Professional Learning, or Assistance Needed by Our Study Group:

8 CASL Phase III

Inquiring Into Teaching for Learning

Now that the group has selected focus students to maximize their professional learning for equity and excellence, it is time to delve into the connections between teachers' actions and their students' learning. The purpose of Phase III is to discover what hinders and facilitates each focus student's learning in the target learning area (TLA) and then to tailor the teaching approaches accordingly. The catalyst for this inquiry is the students' own recent work samples.

The work brought to the study group includes any data or evidence that reveals information about the students' learning in the TLA, for example, writing samples, projects, pictures, videotapes, recorded observations, oral responses, or other products from classroom activities or assessments. These samples are most enlightening when they are completed by the student without outside help. We discourage the use of multiple-choice or single-answer responses because such tasks mask the thinking underlying the student's responses. When such responses are called for, we encourage teachers to ask students to explain their reasoning.

The first work sample analyzed is usually the focus student's work gathered from the Initial Assessment completed in Phase II. When meeting to analyze a student's work, the group follows the steps in the collaborative inquiry cycle. They begin by *sharing background* information about the student and the sample. Then they carefully *observe* the work and describe what they see. Next they *analyze* multiple explanations for why the student is performing as she is. They consider causes such as the student's cultural background, motivation, reading level, visual processing, language development, prior knowledge, content misconceptions; teaching and assessment methods; the teacher's personal filters (feelings and beliefs); and the context surrounding the learning. Next the group uses their insights to *plan* responsive teaching approaches. Finally the group members *reflect* on their own learning and collaboration.

As the teachers engage in these steps, they identify their own *curiosities and questions*. For example, if a paper has inconsistent use of punctuation, they wonder if the errors mean that the student has misconceptions about punctuation or if she is just being careless. Such questions are addressed by *finding more information*, for example, in conversations with the student. Other questions may require *further professional learning* or outside resources. Teachers might ask, for example, "How important is punctuation at this student's stage of writing development?" or "How do I improve my student's reading comprehension?"

Between the study group sessions, the presenting teacher *acts* on the plan by using the responsive strategies that the group identified. After using these approaches for a while, each teacher collects the next work sample and brings it to the group as evidence of how well the plan worked.

As the group members analyze the work of their focus students, they uphold their working agreements and use communication skills to maintain trust and to enrich each member's professional knowledge, dispositions, and inquiry skills.

When thinking about Phase III, new CASL participants may worry that by studying only one student so closely, the others in the class may not benefit. We have not found this to be true. CASL teachers report that they can tailor the study group's ideas to the needs of other similar students and, as a result, they see great improvements in their learning.

What do teachers discover when they look this deeply and consistently into their own impact on a student's learning? They gain insights into how the student makes sense of the content and skills being taught. The continuation of the Focus Student's Biography helps teachers understand how the student's cultural background, experiences, and characteristics influence his performance in school. Finally, teachers look closely at their own personal Teacher Cultural Autobiographies and consider how their own filters (beliefs and feelings) might be facilitating or hindering their attempts to reach their selected student.

Phase III is a most powerful vehicle for transforming teachers' assumptions that may be limiting their success. Often in the privacy of their own reflections, they come to realize, for example, that they

- are tempted to give up too early on a student by blaming his background, only to realize that these assumptions were caused by mismatched cultural factors;
- typically consider only a limited number of explanations for a given performance;

- rarely delve into a thorough analysis of a given student's learning;
- need to develop a broader repertoire of strategies and resources to respond to the specific needs of their struggling students; or
- hold low expectations that limit their efforts with certain students.

These are uncomfortable realizations, and CASL is designed to allow teachers to acknowledge such shortcomings at their own pace. The truth is, however, that each teacher has agreed to the CASL goal: to relentlessly pursue, discover, and apply responsive approaches for the learning so that each and every student reaches excellence. The mere act of sitting in a group of teachers who demonstrate the dispositions of moral stance, cultural competency, collective responsibility, and efficacy has a positive "rub-off effect"—even on those who have shied away from such tough issues as the influence of class, race, economic status, and family structure on teachers' professional practice.

PHASE III OVERVIEW

Goal

To collaboratively discover which teaching approaches are most responsive to individual students' cultural backgrounds, strengths, and learning needs so that each one reaches proficiency in the target learning area.

Inquiry Questions

- How do specific students construct understanding of complex academic content?
- What teaching approaches are most responsive to the cultural backgrounds, strengths, and needs of our focus students and others in the target learning area?
- How are our feelings, beliefs, values, and dispositions influencing our practice?

Steps, Purposes, and Tasks

1. SHARING BACKGROUND: *To reveal the teachers' current understanding of the student as a person and learner and to provide information about the work sample.*

   - Presenting teacher shares information about the student from the biography.
   - Presenting teacher describes desired learning outcomes, teaching approaches, and conditions for the work sample.

2. OBSERVING: *To expand what teachers look for as evidence of students' cultural background, learning strengths, needs, experiences, and interests.*

(Continued)

(Continued)

- Share initial observations with supporting evidence; avoid explanations for what is observed.
- Presenting Teacher selects two or three observations to analyze in next step.

3. ANALYZING: *To consider multiple explanations for what influenced the student's learning.*

- Share and explore explanations for selected observations.
- Presenting Teacher selects one or two explanations to guide the planning step.
- Note other questions and puzzlements.

4. PLANNING: *To broaden teachers' repertoire and intentionally respond to students' specific cultural background, strengths, interests, and learning needs.*

- Select the next (short-term) learning outcome(s) for the student.
- Consider which teaching approaches might be most responsive for the student.
- Presenting teacher selects specific actions and approaches to use in the next weeks.
- Group plans to address questions and needs for more information.

5. REFLECTING: *To transfer learning from the study group to everyday practice, build collective responsibility , and improve group productivity.*

- Share insights that might help other learners.
- Evaluate group's collaboration and productivity.
- Consider needs for additional professional learning.

6. ACTING: *To implement responsive approaches, gather evidence of results, and pursue additional professional learning if warranted.*

- Try out plan and collect focus student's next work sample.
- Add to Focus Student Biography and teacher's own Cultural Autobiography.
- Address the group's questions and needs for further professional learning.

PHASE III TEACHER LEARNING OUTCOMES

The activities in Phase III develop in teachers the following capacities, described more fully in the framework presented in Chapter 2. The capacities are listed here and on the protocol to help the group focus on their intended learning.

Professional Knowledge Base

- Understand themselves and their students as people and learners so that teachers can provide culturally and linguistically responsive instruction and thus increase their students' learning and success.

- Develop the professional knowledge base required for responsive teaching approaches.
- Determine their needs for additional professional learning.

Collaborative Inquiry

- Engage in productive dialogue using working agreements and communication skills to inquire deeply into dilemmas of student learning.
- Use the collaborative inquiry cycle to systematically study students' learning to discover approaches that foster each student's success.

Filters and Dispositions

- Consider and restructure (as needed) the influence of personal filters (feelings, beliefs) on their own practice.
- Be guided by the dispositions of cultural competency, moral purpose, efficacy, and collective responsibility.

PHASE III PREPARATION AND MATERIALS

Phase III is best conducted with individual study groups facilitated by a person who has experience with the protocol and procedures. To prepare the space for maximum learning, place the chairs so that each person can see the Recorder Sheet. A round table or horseshoe is best. If the table is rectangular, cluster the group around one end.

By now, the study group members automatically bring this book and their CASL Notebook to every session. As in Chapters 6 and 7, all the figures are provided at the end of this chapter.

Other suggestions for preparation are provided next.

Presenting Teacher Preparation

A week before the session, remind the teachers who are bringing their focus student's work sample to bring:

- A copy for each group member of the *focus student's most recent work sample*, with the scoring guide. This is *very important*. If only one copy is available for the group to look at, it hinders participation, and thus, the depth of analysis.
- A copy for each group member of the Focus Student Biography (Figure 7.4) (unless teachers already have it from a prior session).

- The teacher's own Cultural Autobiography (in CASL Notebook).
- A single copy of the presenting teacher's notes and the Recorder Sheet from the last analysis of this student's work. This information will be used during Step 1. Sharing Background.

Materials

Post in a location visible to all (and provide copies to teachers to place in notebook):

- CASL Poster (Figure C.3, p. 132).
- Framework Poster (Figure 2.1, p. 34).
- Phase III Recorder Sheet (one for each student to be presented). Use a chart paper or electronic device formatted as in Figure 8.2, page 251, so that *every group member can see the information.*
- Parking Lot (may be a small sheet on the corner of the table).

Copy the following materials (found at the end of the chapter):

- Phase III Protocol (Figure 8.1) (One blank copy for each group member)
- Study Group Log (Figure 8.3) to give to administrator(s) and group members after study group meeting.

GUIDING A STUDY GROUP THROUGH PHASE III

In this phase, your study group will begin analyzing work samples from each teacher's focus students. Since it usually takes a period of time to develop your students' proficiency in a complex TLA, we suggest that the study groups meet for 3–5 months. This will allow for multiple rounds of analyzing each student's work, trying out strategies, and checking the results by examining the next work sample. Ideally, a group would spend 3–5 months in Phase III.

For a typical session, allocate about 5 minutes for the opening, about 45 minutes for each student whose work will be analyzed, and 5 minutes for the wrap-up. When the work samples are short (e.g., writing in first grade), less time may be appropriate. The schedule should allow each focus student's latest work sample to be analyzed every 2–4 weeks. Note that the first two Phase III sessions include an extra 10–15 minutes to teach three new communication skills.

The Phase III Protocol contains the purposes, logistics, and specific tasks to be addressed in each inquiry step. Here we provide specific directions and suggest questions and probes to ask during each step. To illustrate Phase III, we introduce a new study group who is investigating first graders' acquisition of oral reading fluency. Our teacher, Lila, has selected Dana as her focus student because her Initial Assessment results showed that Dana and several other students did not use word-attack strategies when faced with unknown words. They either skipped the word or substituted ones that didn't make sense.

Dana is of interest to Lila for another reason, though. Dana receives a free lunch and comes from a single-parent home. Her mother doesn't come to parent-teacher conferences and is hard to reach on the phone. Lila has often struggled to help students whose parents don't actively support their child's reading and learning.

As Lila ponders her professional learning goal and her own cultural background, she realizes that her upbringing was very different than was Dana's. Lila grew up in a two-parent home, with a mother who worked part-time, so she still had time to volunteer in her daughter's school. Lila acknowledges that she gets extremely frustrated with students whose skills are low and whose parents don't support their student's learning. She hopes that her study of Dana will help her develop a better understanding of these parents and ways to provide support for students like Dana.

We illustrate each step of the Phase III Protocol as Lila's group analyzes Dana's second work sample. At the end of this example, we summarize the group's analysis of Dana's third work sample. By seeing the two study group sessions together, you can appreciate the power of analyzing samples from each focus student every few weeks.

Opening the Session

Begin each study group meeting using the following activities.

a. Presenting Teacher(s) Preparation. As teachers arrive, clarify who will be presenting student work and make sure they have brought *multiple copies of the work sample*. If the presenting teachers have only one copy, ask them to go duplicate it. Make sure they also brought multiple copies of the scoring criteria for the work sample and the Focus Student Biography. (*NOTE: Do not pass out copies of the student work samples until the beginning of the* Observing Step).

b. Greeting. Greet participants and ask how things are going.

c. Grounding. Ask the group to write and share about questions such as (a) *What did you learn about the questions that you planned to address after the last session?* and/or (b) *What ideas have you been pondering about your students' learning?* and/or (c) *How do you feel about being here?* Ask the group to share anything they want to about the three questions. Do this one at a time with no interruptions.

   d. Framing the Session

- CASL Goal. Refer to the goal at the top of the CASL Poster.
- Session Outcomes. Pass out the Phase III Protocol, and draw attention to the Teacher Learning Outcomes on the cover sheet. To help explain them, refer to the Framework Poster (Figure 2.1).
- Agenda. Go through the protocol to explain the tasks for the day. Use the example of Lila's study group in this chapter to help teachers visualize how they'll be analyzing their focus students' work samples.
- Working Agreements. Refer to the CASL Poster and review the group's working agreements. Each group member identifies one agreement to which he needs to pay special attention during today's session.
- Parking Lot. Remind group members that they can write a question or concern on a Post-it Note at any time and place it in the middle of the table. It will be read and addressed later.

   e. Distributing Materials. Be sure the presenting teachers don't pass out the student work yet.

   f. Identifying Roles. Identify a recorder to take notes on Phase III Recorder Sheet (remind her that she will be showing and summarizing the recorded information at the end of each protocol step). Give her the CASL Study Group Log, and ask her to complete it after the session and distribute it the next day to all group members and the principal.

Developing and Applying Communication Skills

Up until now, we have emphasized the communication skills of listening, matching verbal and nonverbal cues, pausing, paraphrasing, and probing for clarity. These skills make sure that each person's ideas are heard, understood, and explored. Now we move on to the skills that help the group dig more deeply into teachers' professional thinking to discover both how the student learns best and which teaching approaches might be most responsive. These skills include *empowering probes, putting ideas on the table* (taught in the first Phase III session), and *probing for beliefs and feelings* (taught in the second Phase III session).

Use the following activities to develop teachers' use of the communication skills.

a. Purpose. Remind teachers of the importance of the communication skills to both maintain safety and to deepen thinking.

b. Review.

- Refer to list on the right side of CASL Poster and ask teachers to quickly read the cue cards that they made in the prior CASL sessions.
- In pairs, teachers use pausing, paraphrasing, and probing as they share the impact they've noticed as they use the skills in their daily lives.

c. New Communication Skill Taught at First Phase III Session. Empowering probes (presuppositions).

- Purposes and Benefits. Clarify how probing raises efficacy, one of the key dispositions in the framework. Refer to Chapters 3 and 5 for a review of the key ideas.
- Mini-Lecture. Summarize pages 67–69 (Chapter 3), "Empowering Probes." Refer teachers to page 69 for the summary box and examples.
- Practice. In pairs, group members write an empowering probe to substitute for the following statements.

  1. "I wish I could find a way to motivate Larry!"
  2. "Why don't you try a graphic organizer?"

- Ask them to share their answers with the group. Then refer to the empowering probes provided in the Online Resources, "Responses to Communication Skills Exercises in Chapters 7–8."
- Ask teachers to add this new skill to their cue card with reminder notes.

d. New Communication Skill Taught at First Phase III Session: Putting Ideas on the Table

- Purposes and Benefits. Clarify how putting ideas on the table encourages the group to consider ideas by offering them in an open and tentative way.
- Reading. In pairs, read pages 72–73 (Chapter 3), "Putting Ideas on the Table" and make notes on the cue cards. Refer teachers to page 73 for the summary box and examples.
- Practice. In pairs, group members write *a more tentative way* of putting the following ideas on the table.

  1. "Why don't you try a graphic organizer?"
  2. "I know what it is! He's confused!"

- Ask them to share their answers with the group. Then refer to the ways of putting these ideas on the table as provided in the Online Resources, "Responses to Communication Skills Exercises in Chapters 7–8."
- Ask teachers to add this new skill to their cue card with reminder notes.

e. New Skill Taught at Second Phase III Session. Teach probing for beliefs and feelings.

- Purposes and Benefits. Clarify how probing for beliefs and feelings relates to the filtering system in the middle of the Framework Poster. You might say, *A key to unlocking the cases that stump us is examining our own interpretations and considering a different perspective.*
- Mini-Lecture. Summarize pages 69–71 (Chapter 3), "Probing for Beliefs and Feelings." Refer teachers to page 71 for the summary box and examples.
- Practice. In pairs, group members read each statement and say a paraphrase and a probe for beliefs and feelings.

  1. "I'm stumped. No matter what I do, it doesn't seem to work."
  2. "Mary just doesn't care."

- Ask them to share their answers with the group. Then refer to the probes for beliefs and feelings provided in the Online Resources, "Responses to Communication Skills Exercises in Chapters 7–8."
- Ask teachers to add this new skill to their cue card with reminder notes.

FACILITATION TIPS

Confidentiality

At this point in the CASL inquiry, very detailed information about specific students is shared, along with concrete evidence of their work. It may be tempting for some teachers to share with others outside the group sensitive information that would best be kept private. Have a conversation about the potential problems that could result with the parents and/or community if such information were shared.

Working Agreements and Communication Skills

At the end of the last session, the group reflected on how their ways of interacting helped or hindered their group purpose. Keep track of these insights and bring them forward to the next session to improve the power of their collaborative inquiry.

Practice With Communication Skills

Don't skip the activities where you teach and practice the communication skills. While some teachers may be uncomfortable with such a deep level of personal interaction, intentional use of the communication skills helps the group maintain trust and explore one another's best thinking. This is especially true in Phase III when considering multiple interpretations for specific aspects of each student's performance. Therefore, before every protocol step, be sure to remind teachers to use the communication skills they have been learning.

Protocol Step 1. Sharing Background

Purposes: To reveal the teachers' current understanding of the student as a person and learner and to provide information about the work sample.

Let us take a moment to clarify the importance of biographical information throughout Phase III. The personal information and the student's picture on the biography build your group's connection to each focus student studied. As one teacher said, "He really began to hold a special place in my heart . . . . This child benefited from the collaborative effort focused on his needs as a writer."

After developing a first draft of a group member's Focus Student's Biography, she will give a copy to each group member when she presents that student's first work sample. During the next weeks and months, each teacher will add to the biography any new understandings about the cultural, personal, and cognitive worlds of that focus student.

The teacher's own personal autobiography serves as a mirror to help her determine her own cultural background and proficiency with people and students of other cultures. The autobiography invites group members to explore and record insights about their own life experiences and world view. This information, considered in conjunction with the Focus Student Biography, may help soften hearts and attitudes toward the life experiences of the focus students. As empathy and understanding is reached, the teaching approaches often become more responsive to the needs and strengths of the child.

When beginning Step 1. Sharing Background, make sure *the copies of the work sample have not yet been passed out.* The group members are more likely to focus on the student and background if they don't have the work sample in front of them.

During this step, the presenting teacher refers to the Focus Student Biography, her own Cultural Autobiography, and the notes taken the last time the student's work was analyzed. The study group members or the facilitator use the questions on the Phase III Protocol (also listed below) to elicit the relevant information about the student and the work sample.

Note that the group *does not have to follow the exact order of questions listed in the protocol.* By the end of this step, however, each element of the background should have been explained to the group.

Use the following questions for Step 1. Sharing Background. As you interact with the presenting teacher, be sure to listen, paraphrase, and probe to make sure everyone understands the relevant information.

a. Purpose. Teachers examine Step 1, Background on the protocol. Explain why this step is so important.

b. Student Information. Study group members add details to their copy of this student's Biography.

- Professional Learning Goal: *Remind us why you selected this focus student. What were you hoping to learn?*
- Focus Student Biography: *What new information from your Focus Student's Biography would you like to share with the group?* Group members add this information to their copy of the Biography. They may add information from their own experiences with the student.

c. Work Sample Information. The recorder writes this information on the "Background" section of the Recorder Sheet. The teachers also make notes on their protocols.

- Learning Outcome(s): *What learning outcomes did you hope to see displayed in today's work sample? (refer to scoring criteria)*
- Approaches (Strategies) Used: *In the weeks leading up to the work sample, what approaches did you use to facilitate the students' learning?*
- Assignment or Assessment: *What were the assigned task(s) and directions for this work sample? Under what conditions was this work generated (e.g., done individually or as a group, time provided)?*

After you have all of the necessary information about the work sample, move on to the Observing Step. If more background information is needed later, you can ask for it at that time.

FACILITATION TIPS

Facilitator role

For the first few times your group uses the Phase III Protocol, the facilitator will do much of the explaining and modeling of the process. After the first few sessions, however, teachers begin to follow the protocol on their own with less guidance. At this point, the facilitator can be less directive, while still monitoring—and adjusting as necessary—how the group follows the protocol and uses the collaborative skills.

Sticking with the protocol

When the presenting teacher explains the assignment, she may point to the work sample to clarify it. It will be tempting for teachers to start reading it. The facilitator may refocus the group by saying, *"When we get to the Observing Step, you will have some time to look at the work on your own. For now, let's stay with the background information."*

Communication skills

As teachers share their ideas, be sure to *pause, paraphrase, probe,* and *put ideas on the table.* You might choose to label what you are doing for the others. One person we know puts these labels on a card and holds them up as she uses the skills. Also point out when others use these communication skills.

Assumptions

As the teacher shares, listen for sweeping generalizations (e.g., "There is no support at home."). At the appropriate time, you may choose to paraphrase a general statement and probe for beliefs and feelings (e.g., *"You said . . . ; help me understand how the support at home plays into this . . . . How might the mother see this situation?"*)

Professional knowledge base

Listen for teachers' understanding of the TLA-related concepts, skills, outcomes, assessment, and pedagogy. If you note confusion, for example, about the assessment, you might say, *"You mentioned that this task taps the student's understanding of the story; help us to see that connection."*

Background: Not too long

The facilitator and/or timekeeper will need to keep the pace going. Sometimes, groups spend so much time sharing the background information that too little time is left for the rest of the work analysis steps.

LILA'S STUDY GROUP:
PHASE III, STEP 1 SHARING BACKGROUND

Dana's Work Sample #2. October Study Group Session. (Lila's responses to the group's questions)

Student Information

"I selected Dana to help improve my ability to reach low-income first-graders who have little support at home and who use few word-attack skills when they are stumped by a word."

(Continued)

(Continued)

After Lila reminds the group to find Dana's Biography in their notebooks, she says, "Since the last study group session, I have learned that, in kindergarten, Dana was very shy and spoke little with other children. It's the beginning of the year and I'm still getting to know Dana. She lives in the apartment complex on the poorer side of town. Dana's mother doesn't seem to care much about Lila's learning." Study group members add this new information to their copy of Dana's Biography.

Work Sample Information

Learning Outcomes

"After the last session, we decided that Dana lacked confidence and relied too much on help from others when she was stumped by a word. I was hoping to see her try to use word-attack skills in her reading group instead of skipping a word or substituting a meaningless one."

Approaches Used With Dana

"In her reading group, when Dana stopped, skipped a word, or made an error, I tried to help her figure it out without giving her the answer or sounding it out for her. When she hesitated, I waited for her to try to say the word and made sure that the other children did not give her the answer. I asked, 'What do you think it might be?' I also asked her if her answer sounded right. Sometimes I asked her to reread it. I also tried asking her what other word might fit into that spot."

Task, Directions, Conditions

"I asked Dana to read aloud a passage from *My Dog Willy* (Reading Level C). She did this during reading group. I used a modified running record to assess Dana's ability to use word-attack skills when faced with unknown words. I coded Dana's miscues, self-corrections, and also how long she hesitated before either trying to say the word or asking for help. I kept track of the prompts I gave her when she looked to me for help. Where possible, I tried to observe her body language and expression when she was stumped by a word."

Protocol Step 2. Observing

To expand what teachers look for as evidence of students' cultural background, learning, strengths and needs, experiences, and interests.

It might seem obvious that teachers need to closely examine their students' work. But our experience has taught us that when any of us first looks at a student's work, we often miss important clues to unlocking a student's pathway to progress. This is partly because we all fall into the habit of looking for only those things that have meaning for us. For example, some teachers may focus on punctuation or spelling errors and miss the fact that the student has demonstrated a deep understanding of the concept about which he was writing.

We sometimes call these our "hot buttons"—aspects in a students' work that are hard for us to look beyond. By observing with others, you will find your own hot buttons, and you will begin to see beyond them. When your colleagues notice things that you missed, you begin to look for those aspects too.

When reading the sample, take time to notice everything that might help you understand how the student learns—including *both the strengths and the errors*. The strengths offer clues to interventions that you may be able to capitalize on. For example, in one writing sample that we analyzed, the student's language lacked expressive words. But in the part in which he wrote about animals, his language became quite detailed. This clue came in handy later during the Planning Step, when the teacher capitalized on this strength by asking the student to focus on animals in his next written assignments.

It is for these reasons that we have isolated the first step of the inquiry cycle to observing, and *only* observing. As you share what you see, we ask you to point to the place in the sample and then say, "I see . . . " without offering any interpretations or explanations for what is observed.

We also ask you to refrain from suggesting strategies to fix the problems you see in the work. That will come later after the most noteworthy observations are analyzed to understand why the patterns exist. As we often ask, "Without understanding *why* a student performs a certain way, how can we possibly design a strategy that is responsive to that student's needs?"

Note that we begin each step by asking the presenting teacher to share her ideas first. This is in contrast to the Tuning Protocol (Blythe, Allen, & Powell, 1999) which asks the teacher to remain quiet throughout the work analysis. We believe that the presenting teacher gains efficacy, respect, and self-awareness by sharing her professional thinking before the other group members jump in with their ideas.

In your early sessions, the facilitator will guide you through each activity below. As your group gains more familiarity with the protocol, however, you will begin to guide yourselves through some of the steps. In this case, the facilitator still has an important role: to remind the group when the conversation strays off-topic or when the group has skipped a step in the protocol.

To engage in the Observing Step, use the following activities. Remember: *Don't pass out the work sample* until everyone has read the purpose and directions for Step 2. Having the work in front of them may distract them from important information about this step.

a. Purpose. Group members read Step 2. Observing on the protocol. Explain the purpose—that hearing the observations of others can open our eyes to aspects of the work we had not previously noticed.

b. Directions. Explain the difference between an *observation* ("I see x..") and an *interpretation* ("He did x because . . . "). Clarify that this step is for observation only; the analysis, interpretation, and suggestions will take place later.

c. Distributing Work Sample and Rubric. The presenting teacher gives each group member a copy of the student work and the related scoring criteria or rubric.

d. Outcomes. The presenting teacher reminds the group what to focus on. You might ask, *What would you like us to look for in the work?* Also remind everyone to look for both strengths and areas for improvement.

e. Reading the Work Sample. All group members *silently* read the work sample with the rubric beside it and write what they observe in the margin. They also note any questions or hunches, and save these for a later step. Be sure teachers don't talk about what they are seeing in the work (e.g., by whispering). Such sharing can reduce the sense of safety for the presenting teacher.

f. Background. Note that anyone may ask for more background information at any time; this is fine, as long as it isn't a hidden suggestion (e.g., "Have you tried . . . ?") Be sure to return promptly to the Observing Step.

g. Presenting Teacher Begins. Remind the presenting teacher that no explanations or interpretations are necessary at this time. Ask, *What strengths or areas for improvement do you see (or not see)?* (Probe for Clarity: *Where specifically do you see that?*)

h. Recording. The recorder lists all ideas shared on the "Observe" section of the Recorder Sheet, in two separate columns, the observed "Strengths" and the observed "Areas for Improvement." The teachers may also make notes on their protocols.

i. Group Member and Presenting Teacher Observations. When the presenting teacher is running out of ideas, ask, *Are you ready to hear some other observations from the group?* Then ask the group, *What other strengths or areas for improvement do we see (or not see)? Where specifically do you see that? What else do you see that may be a clue to what the student does or does not understand, and how the student learns?*

j. Our Questions. As questions or curiosities arise, ask the recorder to write them under "Our Questions" on the Recorder Sheet.

k. Selection. The presenting teacher selects two or three observations for analysis in the next step. Ask the presenting teacher, *Which two or three observations do you wish to analyze further? What puzzles you about these areas?*

- The recorder shows and/or reads aloud all the recorded observations on Recorder Sheet.
- As the presenting teacher selects two or three observations, the recorder circles them.

FACILITATION TIPS

Specificity in language

Be sure to point to specific evidence in the work sample to support your observation. If this hasn't happened, a group member might say, "You mentioned [x]; show us where you see that in the paper." Probe for clarity if vague language is heard. For example, if you hear, "He needs to get better at his spacing," you might probe for clarity, "What might a better performance look like? What don't you see? What would you want to see?" Such probes help develop precision in thinking and language.

Focus on both strengths and areas for improvement.

If you are hearing only observations of "Areas for Improvement," then ask the group to look also for the "Strengths." Remember that sometimes an important observation is to notice what is not in the work, but that should be there.

Skipping ahead to the analyzing step

If the teacher or group member offers an explanation or reason ("He is just too unfocused to do this!"), prompt the recorder to put that in the "Analyze" section and gently remind the group to stay with observations only. If an interpretation does come out ("Oh, this is better because he's writing about animals and he loves them,") just probe for clarity by saying, *"What do you see that indicates it is better?"* and record the observation. In this case, you may might ask the recorder to add the enthusiasm about animals in the "Analyze" section.

Skipping ahead to the planning step

Beware of questions like, "Did you try . . . . ?" This is a not-so-hidden suggestion (solution listening) which may put the teacher on the defensive. In this case, you might say, *"Let's hold on to the ideas for interventions until we get to the Planning Step."* You may also direct the recorder to write that idea in the "Plan" section, and then come back to the Observing Step by asking, *"What other observations do we have?"*

Facilitator participation

As facilitator, you may add an observation, but wait until all others have added theirs.

Multiple perspectives

During the first few sessions of Phase III, some group members may not understand that taking time for so many observations helps them see more. Therefore, before you go on to the next step, you might ask everyone to look at his own initial observations and then identify one on the Recorder Sheet that he didn't see at first. Point out how people may

(Continued)

(Continued)

see the same thing differently and that this is one of the main strengths of collaboration: the value of multiple eyes and perspectives.

If the student already has met proficiency in the target learning area

Occasionally, you will find that partway through the months of Phase III, the focus student has achieved the outcomes stated in the target learning area. In this case, be sure to seek out the evidence of proficiency in the work and go on to analyze explanations for the success. Then you may proceed to identify other aspects of the student's performance that may need improvement. If the student no longer poses a challenge, the teacher may identify a new professional learning goal and a different focus student, using the steps suggested in Chapter 7.

Rubric understanding

If the group members are still learning about the content outcomes and how to assess them, you might ask them to share how they would score the work sample: *How does the work stack up against the rubric? What evidence do you see of proficiency? What is missing?* If there is vagueness or disagreement about the fit of the work with the rubric, come to consensus on specific indicators of varying degrees of proficiency. Take notes for rubric revisions. Being explicit about which aspects of a rubric are seen in the student work develops a common understanding of the desired outcomes (content knowledge).

LILA'S STUDY GROUP: PHASE III, STEP 2 OBSERVING

Dana's Work Sample #2. October Study Group Session.

The evidence of Lila's reading performance is in the form of notes taken by Lila during Dana's reading. Lila shared her observations first, then the others added their own observations. The only observations listed in this example are the ones that Lila asked the group to examine more deeply in Step 3.

Recorder Sheet "OBSERVE" Section (Partial List)	
Strengths	**Areas for Improvement**
"My dog Willy likes to [wake WALK] me up in the morning." Read "morning" correctly.	*"WALK me up"* instead of "Wake me up." Kept on reading; didn't seem to notice the meaning changed.
	I asked her to go back to see if it made sense. She got quiet, so we went on.
My dog Willy AWAY . . . pauses, says both words, and corrects *"all . . . . . ways . . always" goes shopping with us."* I was silent as she self-corrected.	*My dog Willy likes to take a bath BALL.* Long hesitation, looked at me for help.
	I waited and asked "What other word might make sense there?" No self-correction.
She read the word "shopping" with no hesitation..	*My dog Willy likes to make new SOME friends.* No hesitation. No correction after I asked her to read it again.

Protocol Step 3. Analyzing

Purpose: To consider multiple explanations for what influenced the student's learning.

As we stated before, the essence of responsive teaching is to craft approaches tailored to the needs, strengths, and cultural backgrounds of the student. We call the Analyzing Step "the pause that refreshes" because it slows things down so teachers can examine them carefully.

Now that all the evidence (Background and Observations) is in front of the group, it is time to figure out *why* those patterns exist. In this step, the group tries to crawl inside the head and heart of the learner to understand what influenced the observed patterns. When they think they understand how the student is thinking and feeling, then they can plan teaching approaches to address those strengths and needs.

When seeking explanations for the specific patterns found, you will want to consider a wide variety of perspectives. The listed questions prompt you to search your professional knowledge base, as portrayed in the framework described in Chapter 2 (pp. 33–36). The actual causes for the observed patterns might come from the student, content, assessment, pedagogy, or context.

As in the Observing Step, you will begin with the presenting teacher. It is she, after all, who knows the student best. Please note that it isn't necessary to ask the teacher each and every question. We are merely trying to elicit her initial hunches about what is going on with the student. After she has shared her thoughts, then all of the group members dedicate their own knowledge and experience to understanding this student.

Also, you *do not have to follow the exact order of questions as posed on the protocol*. By the end of this step, however, each element should have been considered carefully through group dialogue. The facilitator will check off each area as it is discussed, and, if any one area is missed, the facilitator will bring the group back to that question.

After a question is posed, one of you will put an idea on the table. The recorder will write it on the sheet, and then you will use the communication skills to check the explanatory power of that one idea. Then another person might put an idea on the table, and the process continues.

Use the following activities to engage in the Analyzing Step.

a. Purpose. Teachers read Protocol Step 3, Analyzing. Explain the purpose—to consider multiple explanations for what influenced the student's learning.

b. Directions. Explain the difference between a possible *explanation* ("It could be . . ") and a *strategy* ("Try this idea . . . "). Clarify that this step is for analyzing possible explanations only; the planning of strategies will take place in the next step.

    c. Recording. Ask the recorder to write the ideas on the "Plan" area of the Recorder Sheet. The teachers also make notes on their protocols.

    d. Presenting Teacher's Interpretations. Ask, *As you look at your selected observations, what reasons come to mind about why the student is performing this way?*

    e. Exploring Each Idea. All use communication skills to explore each idea. For example, ask, *Tell us what evidence in the work or biography led you to think this might be the cause? What other explanations might there be?*

    f. Group Member and Presenting Teacher Analysis. When the presenting teacher is running out of ideas, ask her if she is ready to hear some ideas from the group. At some point in the group's dialogue, use the following questions to explore the six areas of the professional knowledge base (see Framework Poster):

- Content (outcomes, concepts, skills). *What does this student understand well about the content? What misconceptions are demonstrated? What might be the cause?*
- Student (biography, culture, learning, and performance). *What does the student's performance suggest about how he/she learns? What cultural characteristics listed in the Focus Student Biography might be influencing the student's performance? What does the work reveal about the student's cultural background?*
- Pedagogy (teaching approaches and resources). *What influence might the teaching strategies or resources have had on the student's performance? Why might that be?*
- Assessment (fit with student and/or outcomes). *How well did the assigned task (or assessment) measure the student's progress? What is the reason for that?*
- Context (conditions in room, school, or community). *What contextual factors in or outside the class may have influenced the student's performance? Why might they have had that effect?*
- Filtering System. *How might your own background, beliefs, or feelings have influenced this student's performance?*

    g. Our Questions. Ask, *What other questions might we explore to better understand the students' learning or other areas?* Recorder writes these under "Our Questions" on the sheet.

    h. Selection. The presenting teacher selects two or three explanations to guide the planning of strategies. Ask, *Which of the listed explanations seem most plausible? What puzzles you about these areas?*

- Recorder shows and/or reads aloud all explanations on the "Analyze" section of the Recorder Sheet.
- As the presenting teacher selects two or three explanations, the recorder circles them.

FACILITATION TIPS

Natural flow of dialogue

Chapter 5 explains the importance of facilitating the conversation in a way that balances the group's natural curiosities with the structure of the protocol. When you notice that the group has strayed from the protocol, stop to summarize what the group has been talking about, and then engage the group in a decision about what to do. You all might choose to continue exploring the ideas right then, or you might ask the recorder to write the ideas on the Record Sheet, for later consideration . As soon as possible, return to the protocol steps that remain to be completed.

Multiple perspectives and causes

Don't stop before you discover the gold. By considering all aspects and perspectives, you may unearth a key to the student's success. Therefore, we suggest that you spend a significant amount of time in the Analyzing Step to explore and select the most likely explanations for the observed performance. Empowering probes and probes for beliefs and feelings will be important in this dialogue.

Inquiring into successes

For both the presenting teacher and the group, it's important to acknowledge successes and discover what prompted them. This builds the teacher's sense of efficacy and provides valuable clues to understanding the learner. For example, the group delved into the moment when Dana hesitated before the word "always," said "away," and then corrected herself. They inquired into how Lila's actions—waiting patiently without saying anything—might have contributed to this success. As they analyzed further, they realized that Dana had been able to read an unfamiliar word when she saw that it was composed of two distinct words that she knew. This insight prompted Lila to trust that, given enough time to divide the word into smaller parts, and without constant questioning, Dana might be able to figure new words out. She also began to wonder about Lila's use of visual cues.

Playing nice

It is tempting to "play nice" by engaging in polite conversation that only scratches the surface of the problem. But don't forget your group's stated purpose: to relentlessly pursue and discover responsive ways to help the student succeed. This may require asking one another some hard questions, for example, this probe for beliefs. "Earlier you said the mother doesn't value learning. What might be some other reasons for her not reading to Dana?" Other tough questions might look like the following empowering probes: "How

(Continued)

(Continued)

well do you think this assignment worked to get at the skill you were hoping to see?" or "You said you modelled the substitution of words on the board; explain how you did that and help us see how that might have affected the quality of Dana's work." The challenge for your study group is to dig below the initial assumptions and generalities so that you can think analytically and from multiple points of view.

Finding more information

Often during the work analysis, the group members find that they can't come up with a reasonable explanation without gathering more information. For example, Lila realized that Dana's mother might be able to tell her how Dana handles frustration during reading at home. So, she decided to consult with the mother before using strategies that respond to this need. She's also not sure how much Dana actually reads at home, either with the mother or without her. The recorder writes these questions on the sheet for consideration when making the plan for action.

LILA'S STUDY GROUP:
PHASE III, STEP 3 ANALYZING

Dana's Work Sample #2. October Study Group Session. Here's a part of the study group transcript wherein Lila begins with some information she needs to find about her student. Then the group moves on to analyzing how well the strategies worked with Dana and why.

Lila:	I still don't know how much reading actually goes on in the home.
Facilitator to Recorder:	Why don't you write that question down under "Our Questions" on the sheet?
Group Member:	Let's think about the effect of the *strategies* that we came up with last month....How well do you think those worked in helping Dana catch and correct her errors?
Lila:	Well, I did try stopping her after an error and asking her if that sounded right. I also asked her to reread it. Sometimes I asked her what other word might fit into that spot. When I think about how well that worked, I'd say not so well. She's still making errors. I'm kind of stumped.
Facilitator:	So, let's figure out what was going on there . . . you mentioned that she's a rather shy and anxious child. How might that play into this?
Lila:	Hmmm....I'm not so sure. I thought I was being supportive.
Group Member:	Here's an idea. Perhaps when you prompted her in the group, she started to feel self-conscious and her anxiety went up? (The recorder writes this idea down on the sheet.)
Lila:	Well, every time I did that, she *did* look more uncomfortable. So, maybe she *gets really tense* and it shuts down her thinking? That might be true. I'll have to think about it.

Group Member:	Hmmm . . . her frustration level. That's interesting. Tell us what you've observed in another context—math, for example—when she gets stumped. What happens?
Lila:	Well, in math she does pretty well, actually. But she is usually working alone. But when I send her up to the front to show her work to the class, she tends to shut down. So, maybe it *is* an issue of *anxiety when she's in front of other students*? (Recorder writes this idea on the sheet.)
Group Member:	I had a student like that once and I asked her to read into a tape recorder. How might that work?
Facilitator:	So you're thinking that might be a way to check out her fear of public reading? Let's write that idea under "Plan" and come back to it after we've considered some other hunches about the causes for Dana's reading problems.
Group Member:	I'm interested in this idea that she *feels embarrassed* when she hesitates too long. Maybe that *causes her to hastily guess* at the word without using any word-attack skills. (Recorder writes this idea on sheet.)
Lila:	Yes . . . you could be right. I'm thinking about how she squirmed when I asked her, "What do you think it might be?" and then I told the other children not to give her the answer. But later, when I waited and said nothing, she was able to figure out the word "always."
Group Member:	So when she had that success, what might have been going on in her head?
Lila:	Well, I did *give her more time than usual* because I could see that she was covering up one part of the word, and then another, and reading the two parts separately. Then she looked up with a big smile and said, "always."
Group Member:	You said she was covering up parts of the word . . . . that's interesting. What's your hunch about how that helped her?
Lila:	I think that's the first time I saw her persist in using a strategy. Seeing the two words seemed to help her. Maybe she was visualizing each smaller word before combining them. Maybe *she's a more visual learner*? (Recorder writes this idea on sheet.) That gives me an idea. Maybe tuning into the picture clues might help her.
Facilitator:	Let's put that idea down under "Plan" and come back to it. So, you think she might be more of a visual learner. What other ideas occur to us? [The group considers more interpretations and then Lila selects a few explanations that seem to be the most reasonable ones. These will guide the selection of responsive strategies.]
Lila:	Ok, I want to focus on the anxiety thing. I think her miscues might be due to the public nature of reading in front of a group. I also think that when I prompted her, she just got more tense and embarrassed. So, that didn't help much. I'm also wondering about the strength she showed when she visualized those two words and came up with "always."
Lila:	Let's circle these explanations to guide my plan for strategies to try in the next few weeks.

Protocol Step 4. Planning

Purpose: To broaden teachers' repertoire and intentionally respond to students' specific cultural background, strengths, interests, and learning needs.

Now that the presenting teacher has selected a few reasonable explanations for the student's performance, it is time to devise the next learning outcome for the student and the teaching strategies that best fit the student's ways of learning. This is the moment you have been waiting for, and you will want to offer your best ideas right away. Again, however, honor the expertise of the presenting teacher by giving her the first say.

First, the facilitator prompts the presenting teacher to consider the specific indicators of success she would like to see demonstrated in the next work sample. These outcomes will guide the plan. If, for example, Lila sets a goal of having Dana use visual cues to correct her errors in the text, then her strategies will need to match this outcome.

Next it's time to make a two-part plan: (1) finding more information to inform the proposed explanations and (2) developing strategies that are responsive to the student's strengths and needs. For example, while analyzing, the group wondered if anxiety is a consistent issue for Dana. So the first part of Lila's plan is to ask the mother what happens at home when Dana gets stumped on a word. Lila will use what she learns (about Dana's anxiety) to decide which of the proposed strategies might be most responsive. If anxiety is not the issue, she might use some of the other strategies generated by her group, for example, visual cues.

When the teacher or a group member puts a possible strategy on the table, it's important to check how well this approach might work, given what has been learned so far about the student, the next learning outcome, and the classroom context. This might include a paraphrase and then a probe to find out what leads the person to think this might be a useful strategy.

At the end of this step, after the teacher has selected her planned actions, be sure she considers the details involved in putting the plan into action. This is where probes for clarity come in handy—for example, "So you're going to try out a recording device to see if privacy would ease Dana's anxiety. Tell us more about how you're going to make that happen. What logistics might you consider?"

To engage the group in the Planning Step, engage in the following activities. Remember that the items don't have to follow this exact order, as long as the topics are all covered at some point.

a. Purpose. Ask teachers to read the purpose for Step 4. Planning on the protocol.

b. Learning Outcome. The presenting teacher identifies the next short-term learning outcome. *Given what we now understand about the student, what is the next appropriate learning outcome you want him to achieve before our next session?* If necessary, probe for clarification—for example, *What specifically would you like to see her do? Why is that the next right outcome for her?*

c. Recording. The recorder writes the group's ideas on the sheet. The teachers also make notes on their protocols.

d. Presenting Teacher's Approaches. Ask the presenting teacher to share her initial thoughts about teaching approaches that might meet the student's learning needs and to explain why the approach might support the student's learning—for example, *What strategies might you use to reach this goal, and why might they be helpful?* Ask for clarification of the teacher's thinking.

e. Explore Each Idea. Ask the group members to use communication skills to explore the presenting teacher's ideas—for example, *Tell us what evidence in the work or Focus Student Biography led you to think this might work?*

f. Group Members' and Presenting Teacher's Approaches. When the presenting teacher is running out of ideas, ask her if she is ready to hear some ideas from the group—for example,

What other strategies might we use to reach this outcome, and why might they be helpful?

g. Selection. The presenting teacher selects two or three strategies to try. The questions might be, *Which of the strategies will you use with this student? Why do you think they might be helpful?* The recorder shows and/or reads aloud all explanations on Recorder Sheet. As the presenting teacher selects strategies, the recorder circles them.

h. Planning. Ask the teacher to rehearse the details involved in using the planned strategies. *What specifically will you do next? What might that look like? What support might you desire?* If time is running out, make sure the teacher will consult with the person suggesting the strategy to work out the details.

i. Next Work Sample. Ask the teacher to specify what evidence (i.e., next work sample) will show the student's learning progress. Ask, *After using these approaches, what evidence (i.e., next work sample) will you gather to show the student's progress?*

j. Questions and Finding More Information. Direct the group's attention to section labelled "Our Questions" on the Recorder Sheet. Decide who, if anyone, will pursue the answers.

- Ask the teacher, *What more do you want to learn about your focus student? How might you gain that understanding?* The teacher writes down her questions and how she will address them.
- Ask, *How might the group address the listed questions?* The group decides who will pursue answers to the listed questions.

FACILITATION TIPS

The next learning outcome

Quite often, the group members get so involved in planning the strategies that they forget to clarify the learning outcome the strategies are designed to produce. Don't forget to begin by clarifying what kinds of performance you hope to see in the next work sample.

Finding information to address the listed questions

As we've said, the group members may want to jump ahead to strategies without realizing that they are missing some crucial information. Be sure that the plan includes key questions to be investigated *before* implementing the plan. The information may significantly alter the teacher's decisions about which strategies will be most responsive.

Rationale for strategies

We often see teachers share ideas with one another without considering how responsive the ideas might be for the specific strengths, cultural backgrounds, and needs of the students. CASL thinking always involves probes for *how* a proposed idea might be responsive to the students' needs. Nothing slips by without being looked at a second time from a different angle.

Rehearsing the plan

How many times have you thought that you understood the specifics of a particular strategy, only to find that when it comes to using it in your classroom, you end up with some pretty significant questions? This reality guides our suggestion that you ask the presenting teacher to mentally rehearse the specifics of the planned strategies. If the teacher is unclear, you could suggest resources or support to consult after leaving the group. To illustrate this point, let's consider the strategy of cooperative learning. The teacher might say, "Oh, yes, I'll use cooperative learning groups for Dana's reading." Don't let the teacher stop there. You might encourage her to address the details of this complex strategy by using empowering probes and probing for clarity: *How big will you want the groups to be? How will you decide whom to put together? How will you make sure you're not needed by every group at once? How will you teach them to get along?* If the group time is too short to answer all these questions, you can offer resources such as an online example of cooperative learning, with an interview of the teacher explaining the decisions she made before and during the lesson. Or the presenting teacher might observe how a group member introduces cooperative learning in his class.

LILA'S STUDY GROUP: PHASE III, STEP 4 PLANNING

Dana's Work Sample #2. October Study Group Session.

Learning Outcome for Next Work Sample (Written on Recorder Sheet)

- Dana will relax and show more self-corrections when reading to me and in group. She will take time to figure out the word by using self-questioning and visual cues in the word and pictures.

Possible Strategies and Why They Might Help Dana (Written on Recorder Sheet)

- Have her read into a recording device. (This may reduce anxiety about having an audience.)
- Ask her to breathe deeply before starting to read. (Doing so may help to decrease her anxiety.)
- Teach her how to use picture clues. (If she is visualizing words, maybe the pictures will help.)
- Give her a self-checking strategy: to read the sentence silently (to see if it made sense the way she read it aloud).
- Give her more praise when she persists and figures out a word correctly. (This may build confidence.)
- After an error, wait, and then ask her to look at the pictures and say another word that might work. (A visual cue might help.)
- Give her time to figure out a word, without urging her. (This may reduce anxiety.)
- Give her the part she will read aloud before reading group starts and ask her to circle the words that stump her. (This gives her time to prepare and may reduce anxiety.)

Information to Seek About Dana (Written on Recorder Sheet)

- How anxious is she in various situations? How does that affect her performance?
- Talk to mother about Dana's anxiety when stumped. Also, how much reading at home?
- Try having Dana read into a recorder to check if errors are only in public.

Strategies I'll Try and Support Needed (Written on Lila's Protocol or a sheet of paper)

1. I'll have Dana *read into a recorder* a passage at the same reading level (C). Afterward, I'll listen to it to see how she performs. If it's pretty accurate, I'll move up one reading level when she reads to me again.

   Support needed: I'll need help with rigging up the recorder and how to teach Dana to use it.

2. Next, I'll ask Dana to *read to me alone*. After a miscue, I'll try two things: (a) prompt her to see if her anxiety remains or escalates and (b) withhold prompts and wait to see what strategies she uses. If she isn't making self-corrections, I will teach and practice with her some self-questioning strategies, how to use picture clues, and give

(Continued)

(Continued)

her positive and specific feedback when she succeeds. If she seems agitated about reading to the group next, I'll teach her to take two deep breaths to settle herself.

Support needed: I need to talk to Larry about how to teach self-questioning strategies.

3. Finally, During *the reading group*, I'll give Dana a nonverbal reminder to use her new strategies. She and I will work these out after our individual sessions.

Evidence I Will Gather for Next Work Sample (Written on Lila's Protocol or a separate sheet)

After talking to the mother, and using that information to guide my plan, I will try out the responsive strategies for a week or two. Then I will collect a modified running record when Dana reads in the group. I will note body language (squirming, deep breaths), miscues, and self-corrections.

Our Questions and Who Will Do What (Written on the Recorder Sheet)

- What are good ways to calm a student's anxiety? (Joe is going to find resources to bring next time.)
- Why is it so hard for some students to self-monitor? (We might need further professional learning—outside resources—for this one.)

To illustrate the full power of Phase III's student work analysis, let's take a peek at some highlights from the next study group session (three weeks later) when the group analyzes Dana's next work sample. For economy of space, we have provided only Lila's responses and reflections.

LILA'S STUDY GROUP PHASE III. ALL PROTOCOL STEPS FOR DANA'S WORK SAMPLE #3. NOVEMBER

Sharing

Background: Student Information

The mother said that Dana seems to read silently at home but hesitates to read aloud to her mother. She also said that Dana hates it when she makes mistakes, even when playing a game. She gets very quiet and hides.

I must admit that I had assumed that the mother doesn't care about language or reading. Well, since our last session, I learned that the mother works long hours. Dana's father doesn't pay child support, so her mother is under a lot of financial stress to pay the bills. She has even taken on a second part-time job but feels guilty about that because it takes time away from Dana. All of this has added to the mother's stress, and she said she isn't always as patient as she'd like to be. So, perhaps she just doesn't have the time or energy to read or talk much with Dana.

In contrast to Dana, I grew up in a two-parent family that actively supported my learning. I kind of assumed that every parent should and could do that. Now I can't even imagine how hard it must be for Dana's mother to come home from two jobs and try to read with Dana. We may have to find some other ways for Dana to read aloud.

Sharing Background: Work Sample Information

- **Learning Outcomes**

  I was hoping to see Dana reduce her anxiety and use the strategies I had taught her when she got stuck on a word (taking a deep breath, picture clues, and self-checking). I wanted to see her make fewer errors or miscues when reading aloud in her group.

- **Strategies I Used**

  1. When I had Dana read into the *recorder*, she hesitated a long time when she was stumped by a word, but then she would come up with a word that, even if it wasn't the right word, made sense. This told me that perhaps anxiety about others watching her *was* a significant issue. So, I taught her how to take a deep breath and started giving her positive and specific feedback when she figured out a word on her own.

  2. When Dana *read to me aloud*, I used a passage one level higher in reading difficulty. I again saw Dana use some of the word-attack strategies that I had taught (for example, looking at the picture clue). But, when she hesitated on a hard word, she did get tense and stopped trying. I reminded her to breathe and taught her to self-check. We practiced the self-check a few times, and I reinforced her effort. With me there to encourage her, she did better.

  3. Finally, I asked Dana to read aloud *in her reading group* and collected a modified running record as my work sample to bring to the group.

- **Task, Directions, Conditions**

  Dana read part of a story aloud to her reading group. The passage was at the same difficulty level as when she read to me alone. I coded her miscues, time of hesitation, and which strategies she appeared to be using.

Observing (Partial Recorder Sheet)

- Strengths: Only three miscues, less hesitation. Evidence of using the picture clue, breathing when stumped, self-checking.
- Areas for Improvement: Instead of reading "Meow, I like this," she read, "Meow, I EAT this." Instead of reading "Said the hungry little kitty," she substituted "ANGRY" for "hungry." Saying words that don't make sense.

Analyzing (Lila's thoughts after the session)

It was nice to see that my interventions helped Dana figure out more words. But she is still substituting words that don't make sense. As we talked about this, a group member

(Continued)

(Continued)

asked me, "How well do you think she's understanding the story itself?" That made me wonder: When Dana substitutes a word that doesn't make sense, does she lose the meaning of the story? For example, Dana read aloud, "Meow, I EAT this" rather than "Meow, I like this" (with a picture of cat looking at a glass of milk). Later in the story, after being shooed away, the kitty sneaks up and drinks the little girl's milk. Would this make sense to Dana if she had read that the cat had already "eaten" it?

As we talked about word recognition and its relationship to comprehension, I saw that I had no idea how well Dana understood the story. So, we wrote that on the Recorder Sheet in the "Our Questions" area. I had to admit to myself that I usually allowed the more vocal students in Dana's reading group to tell the meaning. This was because I had been trying to protect Dana from embarrassment by not calling on her.

I was a little frustrated at myself for allowing my discomfort with Dana's anxiety to get in the way of requiring her to demonstrate her comprehension. I had to ask myself, "Would I rather help Dana be more successful in life or would I rather live with the fact that I didn't push Dana (and myself) to improve her reading comprehension?" It was hard to see that I'd done this with a few other shy kids, too. These insights really motivated me to figure this out!

Planning (Lila's Notes on Her Protocol)

We decided that I would find more information by asking Dana to tell me the meaning of a story she had just read silently. Then I will decide whether to check her comprehension of oral reading either with me alone (if she shows anxiety) or in the group (if she shows little anxiety).

If she is still making similar miscues and has lost the meaning of the story, I will use the idea that my study group gave me: Put the sentence up on the board and show the two substitutions that many students had made. Explain how it changed the meaning. Then give them practice at reading a sentence and saying what it meant. Then move on to a story.

I might even rearrange the groups for a week or two so that those students who struggle with comprehension are all in the same group with Dana.

Given what I learned from the mother, we may have to find some other ways for Dana to read aloud. Mary told me about the reading initiatives that they have at the apartment complex's community center. I will check it out and get back to the group on that.

Protocol Step 5. Reflecting

Purposes: To transfer learning from the study group to teachers' practice, build collective responsibility for all students, and improve group productivity. To consider if additional professional learning is needed.

As stated earlier, reflecting on our experiences solidifies our learning. We encourage you to reflect on three major areas: your own learning, your group's collaborative functioning, and what you still want to learn more about. Before you share your thoughts with the group, take time to review your notes and jot down your thoughts.

Sharing your insights about teaching and learning may help you find ways to respond to your own students who are similar to the focus students studied that day. Reflecting on the quality of your group's collaboration and making adjustments for the next time is important because we want *every* teacher to contribute her expertise to the group. As important, we want every teacher to feel comfortable posing questions and dilemmas. Finally, considering the group's questions and curiosities may lead to additional professional learning to fill gaps in the group's Professional Knowledge Base.

Engage in the following activities:

a. Purpose. Direct teachers to the purpose for Step 5 of the protocol. Explain why reflecting is so important.

b. What Was Learned Today. Say something like, *I'm going to give you a minute to look over the notes from today and write about your insights on your protocol. What did you learn about students and yourself today that might help promote other students' learning? What influenced your insights? How specifically might that apply to the student you have in mind?* Share insights, one at a time.

c. Recording Reflections on Log. Remind the recorder to write the group's reflections on the Study Group Log (Figure 8.3).

d. Collaboration. Ask group to write on their protocol (and provide evidence of) how their use of the working agreements and communication skills influenced the group's ability to meet its purpose: *How consistently did we follow the Agreements and Communication Skills today? What influence did they have on our learning? What might we do better next time?*

e. Further Professional Learning. Ask the group members to look at "Our Questions" on the Recorder Sheet. Ask them what resources or additional professional learning they might need. Have the recorder write them on the Study Group Log. Ask, *How might the group address the listed questions? What time and resources might be necessary?*

f. Preparing for Next Meeting. Clarify who will present student work next time. Encourage the group members to read Chapter 8 of this book to clarify the Phase III process.

g. Recorder Tasks. Remind the recorder to copy the completed CASL Study Group Log and distribute it to facilitator, all group members, and the principal on the next day.

FACILITATION TIPS

The power of writing

Writing out the responses to the reflection questions helps build and reshape teachers' professional knowledge, filters, dispositions, and collaborative inquiry capacities. It is a way of making conscious and solidifying new learning and curiosities. For this reason, we suggest you reserve 5 or 10 minutes at the end of each session for writing and sharing new learning and lingering questions.

Sharing reflections

Some groups may feel that talking about their interactions may be too "touchy-feely." However, it is vitally important that they do so, especially in the early CASL sessions. It may take some time for each of you to find your voice and contribute openly, but it is worth continued effort. You want each member to trust that this is a safe place to explore what might be getting in the way of students' learning.

Development of collaboration

As you progress through Phase III, you will come to value one another as important resources for professional learning. You will likely begin to turn to one another more often for insights about your everyday work.

LILA'S STUDY GROUP: PHASE III, STEP 5 REFLECTING

How Our Learning Can Help Our Students (Written on Study Group Log)

We learned several ideas to try with our shy and anxiety-prone students. We also realized that just because a single parent doesn't read to a child at home, it doesn't mean that she doesn't care. We need to check our cultural lenses before making assumptions about others who are living a very different life from our own.

Our Collaboration (Summary of Study Group Dialogue)

Two members felt their ideas had not been given enough attention. The group decided to remedy this by using paraphrases and probes, and by carefully putting their own ideas on the table. Lila said that the questions, probes, and others' ideas were helpful to her in reframing her assumptions and in finding ways to approach Dana and students like her.

Our Questions and Further Professional Learning (Written on Study Group Log)

Our group is intrigued about the relationship between comprehension and fluency. We decided to take the next session to consult with the county reading specialist and two other resources. Then we will apply what we learned as we return to analyzing the work of our students.

Protocol Step 6. Acting

Purpose: To implement responsive approaches, gather evidence of results, and pursue additional professional learning if warranted.

   a. Action. The presenting teacher carries the plans out in the next few weeks and adds to the focus student's biography as she learns more about her culture and learning. The teacher then collects the next work sample from the focus student to bring to a later study group session.

   b. Questions. Selected group members (or the group as a whole) may pursue more information or further professional learning as needed.

   c. Next Meeting. The group decides who will bring their focus students' work samples next time.

   d. Study Group Log. The recorder copies the completed CASL Study Group Log and on the next day distributes it to facilitator, all group members, and principal.

   e. Preparation. After the last Phase III study group session, the group members prepare for Phase IV by reading Chapter 9.

CASL NOTEBOOK CONTENTS FROM PHASE III

Study Group members add the following items to their CASL Notebook, Section III:

- Updated Teacher Cultural Autobiography
- In a separate section for each focus student

   o Updated Focus Student Biography
   o Each work sample with its scoring criteria
   o Protocol Notes and Recorder Sheet for each work sample
   o Study Group Log for each study group session

PHASE III ADAPTATIONS

Phase III in a Single Semester

If the group engaging in CASL has the same group of students for only a single semester, you may have fewer months for the student work analysis sessions. In this case, try to analyze each focus student's work sample every two weeks.

Changing the Focus Student

A teacher might choose to change his focus student part way through Phase III if the student has moved or is no longer a challenge to reach. In this case, the teacher may select another student who might benefit the learning of the teacher and the group. If this occurs, the teacher needs to write another professional learning goal and begin a new Focus Student Biography, as described in Chapter 7. This switch may also require a new look at the teacher's Cultural Autobiography.

Changing the Target Learning Area

A teacher or group might change the TLA when they find that all their students have achieved the outcomes within the TLA.

New Curriculum and/or Teaching Methods

The collaborative analysis of students' work samples can be extremely illuminating when pilot-testing or implementing new teaching strategies or curriculums. For example, take the case of Todd's study group featured in Chapter 6. These math teachers had a new curriculum that required students to solve complex real-life problems. Since few of the teachers had experience with helping students succeed on such tasks, the teachers had skipped these tasks and assessments. When they picked math problem solving as their TLA, the months of student work sample analysis helped them understand which strategies were most helpful in developing complex thinking for specific student characteristics. As they clarified how various students developed these skills, they discovered new teaching strategies that were responsive to individual students' strengths, needs, and ways of learning. As a result, they grew in their efficacy; they felt more confident and able to help their students reach these complex learning outcomes.

SUMMARY

The analysis of student work during Phase III can be the most powerful aspect of CASL. It is here that you will come to understand your puzzling cases of learning and discover approaches that will best fit the strengths, needs, and cultures of these students. This is the essence of culturally responsive teaching.

During Phase III, the conversations go so deep that you may begin to surface some of your own limiting beliefs or feelings. The study group becomes a safe place to do this—either privately in one's own conscience or by talking it out with the group. Nothing needs to be forced; no one needs to be confronted. The process itself, when followed with commitment to unlocking paths to students' success, helps enhance teachers' moral commitment, cultural competence, efficacy, and collective responsibility.

In our experience, the extent to which a study group follows the protocol and uses the communication skills determines the depth of professional learning, both for the teachers and the student. The growth for teachers is portrayed in the framework (Chapter 2) and in our research results (Chapter 1). The students' growth is apparent every time the work samples come to the table. By the end of the year, it is rare that the group has failed to find the key to the success of their most challenging students.

Figure 8.1	Phase III Protocol: Inquiring Into Teaching for Learning

Goal: *To collaboratively discover which teaching approaches are most responsive to individual student's cultural background, strengths, and learning needs so that each one reaches proficiency in the TLA.*

- How do specific students construct understanding of complex academic content in our TLA?
- What teaching approaches are most responsive to the strengths and needs of our focus students and others in the Target Learning Area?
- How are our feelings, beliefs, values, and dispositions influencing our practice?

Teacher Learning Outcomes

- Understand themselves and their students as people and learners so that they can provide culturally and linguistically responsive instruction and thus increase their students' learning and success.
- Engage in productive dialogue using working agreements and communication skills to inquire deeply into dilemmas of student learning.
- Develop the professional knowledge base required for responsive teaching approaches.
- Use the collaborative inquiry cycle to systematically study students' learning to discover approaches that foster each student's success.
- Consider and restructure (as needed) the influence of personal filters (feelings, beliefs, values) on their own practice.
- Be guided by the dispositions of cultural proficiency, moral stance, efficacy, and collective responsibility.
- Determine their needs for additional professional learning.

Materials

Presenting teacher brings:

- Student work sample, with scoring criteria (one copy for each group member)
- Focus Student Biography (one copy for each group member unless they already have it)
- Notes from focus student's most recent work analysis

Facilitator brings:

- CASL Poster (Figure C.1)
- Framework Poster (Figure 2.1)
- Phase III Protocol (Figure 8.1) (one for each participant)
- Phase III Recorder Sheet (Figure 8.2) (one for each student work analysis)
- Study Group Log (Figure 8.3)

Group members bring:

- This book and CASL Notebook
- Teacher Cultural Autobiography

Roles

Facilitator

- Teach, model, and monitor CASL working agreements and communication skills.
- Lead group through Phase III Protocol.
- Encourage multiple perspectives and interpretations.
- Paraphrase ideas offered and ask recorder to write them on sheet.

Recorder

- Take notes—visible to all—during each step of the protocol.
- Complete and distribute Study Group Log.

**Study Group Guide for CASL Phase III Protocol.
Inquiring Into Teaching for Learning**

Opening the Session

- Greeting, grounding, framing the session
- Review working agreements.
- Distribute materials and assign roles.
- Review and teach and practice communication skills.

1. Sharing Background	
Purpose and Prompts	*Notes*
Data Context *To reveal the teacher's current understanding of the student as a person and learner, and to provide information about the work sample* **Student Information** • Why did you select this focus student? What were you hoping to learn? • What new information from your focus student's Biography would you like to share with the group? **Work Sample Information** • What learning outcomes did you hope to see displayed in today's work sample (refer to scoring criteria)? • What approaches did you use to facilitate the student's learning? • What were the assigned task(s) and directions for this work sample? • Under what conditions was this work generated (e.g., time provided, completed independently)?	*Teacher does not pass out student work until after this step.*

2. Observing	
Purpose and Prompts	*Notes*
To expand what teachers look for as evidence of students' cultural background, learning, strengths, learning needs, experiences, and interests Make sure all have read the work sample. Presenting teacher responds first. When teacher is ready, others add observations. Recorder writes them. • What strengths or areas for improvement do you see? Where specifically do you see that? After all observations are recorded, ask presenting teacher: • Which 2 or 3 observations do you wish to analyze further? Recorder circles the selected observations.	• *Presenting Teacher passes out the work sample and restates the learning outcome(s).* • *Study Group members silently read the work and highlight significant evidence.* ***Tip:*** *Avoid explaining why.*

(Continued)

(Continued)

3. Analyzing/Interpreting	
Purpose and Prompts	*Notes*
To consider multiple explanations for what influenced the student's learning. Presenting teacher shares first. • As you look at your selected observations, what reasons come to mind about why the student is performing this way? What evidence in the work or Biography supports this interpretation? When ready, others add ideas. Recorder takes notes. • What does this student understand well about the content? What misconceptions are demonstrated? Why might that be? • What does the student's performance suggest about how he/she learns? • How might the student's cultural background be influencing his performance? • What influence might the teaching or use of resources have had on the student's performance? Why might that be? • How well did the assigned task (assessment) measure the student's progress? • What contextual factors in or outside the class may have influenced the student's performance? • How might your own cultural background, feelings, or beliefs influence this student's performance? • What other questions might we explore to better understand the students' learning or other areas? Presenting teacher narrows focus. • Which of the listed explanations seem most plausible? Recorder circles the selected observations.	*Tips:* • *Focus on the "Why" of what was observed. Avoid suggesting "what to do about it" (strategies).* • *Offer evidence from the work sample or Biography to support the proposed interpretation.* • *Pause, Paraphrase, and Probe to explore the "fit" of a proposed explanation before moving on another one.*
4. Planning	
Purpose and Prompts	*Notes*
To broaden teachers' repertoire, and intentionally respond to students' cultural background, specific strengths, interests, and learning needs. Presenting teacher shares first. When ready, others add ideas. Recorder takes notes. • What is the next appropriate learning outcome for this student? • What strategies might you use, and why might they be helpful?	*Tip: When an idea is put on the table, encourage others to pause, paraphrase, and probe to explore how reasonable each idea is for meeting the learning outcome before moving on to another idea.*

Presenting teacher selects next steps.

- What more do you want to learn about your focus student? How might you gain that understanding?
- Which of the strategies will you use with this student? Why have you selected them? What support might you desire?
- What evidence (i.e., next work sample) will you gather to show the student's progress?

Facilitator asks

- How might the group address the listed questions?
- Who will present student work next time?

5. Reflecting

Purpose and Prompts	*Notes*

To transfer learning from Study Group to everyday practice, build collective responsibility, and improve group productivity.
  All members share:

- What did you learn about students and yourself today that might help promote other students' learning? What influenced these insights?
- How consistently did the group follow the CASL agreements and communication skills?
- What influence did the skills of collaboration and the process have on your learning?
- How might the group pursue further professional learning, if necessary?

6. Acting

Purpose and Prompts	*Notes*

To implement responsive approaches, gather evidence of results, and pursue additional professional learning if warranted.
  Presenting Teacher

- Adds to Student Biography and Autobiography
- Addresses other questions
- Tries out plan and collects next work sample

Recorder distributes Log to administrator and group members.

  Group may pursue additional learning.
  Teachers read Chapter 9.

Figure 8.2 Recorder Sheet for CASL Phase III: Inquiring Into Teaching for Learning

Directions. Use this format to write group's ideas on chart paper or electronic device so that all can see the information.

Focus Student: _____ **Date:** _____

1. Background: (a) Student Information (add to the Focus Student Biography). (b) Work Sample Outcomes, Approaches, Task (list here):

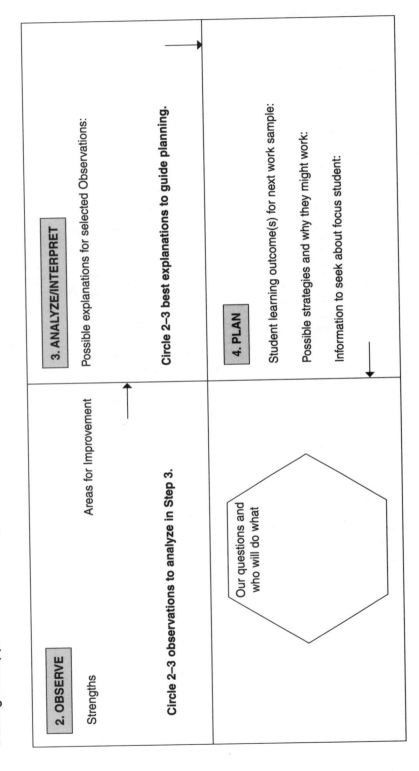

2. OBSERVE

Strengths

Areas for Improvement

Circle 2–3 observations to analyze in Step 3.

Our questions and
who will do what

3. ANALYZE/INTERPRET

Possible explanations for selected Observations:

Circle 2–3 best explanations to guide planning.

4. PLAN

Student learning outcome(s) for next work sample:

Possible strategies and why they might work:

Information to seek about focus student:

Figure 8.3 Study Group Log

Directions. Please complete one form after each study group meeting. Distribute copies to your administrator and group members.

Date: _____ Time Meeting Started: _____ and Ended: _____

Name of Group (Grade Level and/or Content):

Group Members:

Today's Facilitator: Today's Recorder:

Tasks Accomplished:

How Our New Learning Will Help Our Students (from Step 5. Reflections):

Inquiry Questions We Want to Pursue:

Resources, Professional Learning, or Assistance Needed by Our Study Group:

9 CASL Phases IV and V

Assessing Learning Progress and Integrating Learning Into Teachers' Professional Practice

Now that the group has spent several months analyzing each focus student's work samples, it is time to step back and look at the entire class's progress in meeting the target learning area's (TLA's) complex outcomes. This inquiry allows teachers to look more broadly at the connections between their instructional actions over the prior months and their students' learning progress.

We recognize that teachers have been measuring their students' learning all along through benchmark assessments and unit tests. These other assessments, however, likely included a wide array of knowledge and skills. Now is the time to look specifically at the attainment of the learning outcomes involved in the TLA.

In Phase IV, teachers finalize their design of the Final Whole-Class Assessment, similar to the one used earlier in the year, to measure each student's growth in the TLA. If possible, the assessment is "parallel" to the first assessment; that is, it measures the same outcomes, but in a new context. It is considered parallel if it can be scored by the most of the same scoring criteria that were used for the Initial Assessment.

Teachers analyze the results using the same process described in Phase II. They score the work, and describe each student's performance on the Final Student Performance Grid. For the students who have not reached proficiency, teachers color-code the common challenges and describe the backgrounds of these students. Finally, they analyze what may be hindering these students' progress and plan responsive approaches to help them move forward. These approaches might also include special resources or programs outside of the regular classroom activities.

If the assessment used earlier in the year is parallel to the one used in Phase IV, teachers can examine the learning gains made by each student over the months of CASL. To do this, they compare each student's Initial Assessment score(s) with the Final Assessment score(s) and analyze the growth of each student.

Many teachers new to CASL say that they have rarely gathered concrete evidence of their students' progress from the fall to the spring *in a specific complex outcome*. Such evidence can be a powerful element in developing a sense of collective responsibility for learning, teacher self-efficacy, and moral commitment. This information also can be used for school improvement data; during conferences with students, teachers, parents, and supervisors; and for personal insights.

Sometimes teachers find that they have seriously misjudged the extent of their students' progress. They thought that their students were growing as planned, but the hard numbers challenge that assumption. While this cognitive dissonance is uncomfortable, it is a crucial element in prompting a teacher to reconsider how he works with students. When this level of awareness is reached, the teacher is often willing to pursue additional professional learning specific to the areas he has found challenging to develop.

In Phase V, teachers reflect on and write about their learning during the months of CASL and set their own professional learning goals. Finally, the teachers publicly display and celebrate the progress that they and their students have made during the year.

PHASE IV. ASSESSING LEARNING PROGRESS: OVERVIEW

Goals

To analyze student progress in the TLA, determine characteristics of struggling students, and pursue responsive approaches for those students.

Inquiry Questions

- What progress have our students made toward the target learning area?
- What areas of learning have improved and for which students?
- How did we contribute to our students' success?
- What areas still need improvement and for which students? What might explain the lack of progress?

- How can we develop responsive approaches for these students?
- What additional professional learning might we need?

Steps, Purposes, and Tasks

1. **SHARING BACKGROUND:** *To clarify data sources, raise awareness of teachers' predictions and assumptions, and prepare data for analysis*

   - Share Final Assessment context, predictions, and assumptions
   - Complete Final Student Performance Grid
   - Complete Phase IV Teacher T-Chart

2. **OBSERVING AND ANALYZING PROFICIENT PERFORMANCE:** *To identify patterns of success and discover influences on students' learning*

   - Determine strengths and areas of proficient performance on Final Performance Grid
   - Compare proficiencies achieved between Initial and Final Assessments
   - Analyze the influences on satisfactory student learning progress

3. **OBSERVING AND ANALYZING NON-PROFICIENT PERFORMANCE:** *To identify patterns of non-proficient performance and discover influences on student learning.*

   - Find areas still in need of improvement on Final Performance Grid
   - Determine characteristics of students not meeting proficiency
   - Analyze what might have hindered the learning. Note other questions and puzzlements

4. **PLANNING:** *To identify next steps for improving the learning of those students not achieving proficient performance.*

   - Select responsive actions to raise performance of students not reaching proficiency
   - Plan to address group's questions and refine assessments as needed

5. **REFLECTING:** *To transfer learning from the study group to everyday practice, build collective responsibility for all students, and improve group productivity.*

   - Compare predictions (from Step 1) with observed performance in Final Performance Grid
   - Build insights about new learning, collaboration, and group productivity
   - Address the group's questions and needs for further professional learning

6. **ACTING:** *To implement the planned actions.*

   - Address the group's questions and needs for further professional learning

PHASE IV TEACHER LEARNING OUTCOMES

The activities in Phase IV develop in teachers the following capacities, described more fully in the framework presented in Chapter 2.

Professional Knowledge Base

- Develop the professional knowledge base required for responsive teaching approaches.
- Understand themselves and their students as people and learners so that they can provide culturally and linguistically responsive instruction and thus increase their students' learning and success.
- Determine their needs for additional professional learning.

Skills for Collaborative Inquiry

- Engage in dialogue using the working agreements and communication skills to inquire deeply into dilemmas of student learning.
- Use the collaborative inquiry cycle to systematically study students' learning to discover approaches that foster each student's success.

Filters and Dispositions

- Consider and restructure (as needed) the influence of personal filters (feelings and beliefs) on their own practice.
- Be guided by the dispositions of cultural proficiency, moral purpose, efficacy, and collective responsibility.

PHASE IV PREPARATION AND MATERIALS

To prepare for Phase IV, design and administer to your class a Final Assessment for the target learning area. The assessment should require independently developed (not multiple-choice or short-answer) responses that provide evidence of the attainment of the TLA-related learning outcomes. The TLA knowledge, skills, and reasoning should be applied in a new situation, one not previously practiced by the students.

In many cases, the Final Assessment involves a more complex task than did the Initial Assessment. After all, in the fall, most students would not be expected to reach this level of proficiency. If necessary, additional categories may be added to the rubric to score the attainment of the skills not included in the Initial Assessment. You will see an example of this later in this chapter.

Most study groups already have designed the Final Assessment and have been aiming their TLA-related instruction toward it over the months of CASL inquiry. In this case, your group needs to review the task, decide when to administer it, and review the scoring criteria (rubric) to be used.

If your study group has not yet designed the common assessment for the TLA, you will want to meet to do so. Use the directions in Chapter 7 for designing an assessment. To refine the scoring criteria (rubric), you may use the "Calibrating Activity" provided in the Online Resources. As you score the responses to a new assessment task, be sure to keep track of improvements you want to make to both the task and the scoring of it.

You will find that we depart from the typical protocol format for Phase IV. Teachers first describe their students' learning on the Initial Assessment on their own Teacher T-Chart. Then they prepare the data by completing the Final Performance Grid and (Figures 9.2 and 9.3, pp. 285 and 286, respectively). Then the group observes and analyzes explanations for the positive performance of their students. In Step 3, they will focus on those students who have *not* reached proficiency by describing and then seeking interpretations for the lack of success. Step 4, Planning, is reserved for seeking ways to support the learning of those students who did not reach proficiency.

Phase IV may be conducted in a large meeting with study groups sitting together or with individual groups. As in Chapters 6, 7, and 8, the Phase IV figures are provided at the end of this chapter. Other suggestions for preparation are described below.

Group Member Preparation

Well before the session, ask group members to do the following:

- Administer the Final Assessment to their classrooms.
- Bring a class set of scored Final Assessments, with the scoring rubric.
- Bring their CASL Notebook and this book.

Materials

Post in a location visible to all:

- CASL Poster (Figure C.3)
- Framework Poster (Figure 2.1)
- Parking Lot
- Phase IV Recorder Sheet (A chart paper or electronic device, formatted as in Figure 9.4, p. 287)

Copy the following materials (found at end of this chapter):

- Phase IV Protocol (Figure 9.1. One blank copy for each group member)
- Final Student Performance Grid (Figure 9.2. One blank copy for each group member)

- Teacher T-Chart (Figure 9.3. One blank copy for each group member)
- Study Group Log (Figure 9.5)

GUIDING A STUDY GROUP THROUGH PHASE IV

The Phase IV Protocol contains the purposes, logistics, and specific tasks to be addressed in each inquiry step. Here we provide directions, suggested probes, and tips for group members to follow during each step.

To illustrate Phase IV, we introduce you to Bill's study group, who is investigating tenth-graders' acquisition of the TLA "Integration of knowledge and ideas in science by constructing explanations and designing solutions in writing."

After Bill analyzed the patterns in his Initial Student Performance Grid, he selected Janelle as his focus student because she fit into a color-coded cluster of students who struggled to write coherent paragraphs and to develop ideas using scientific terms correctly. Janell is of interest to Bill because she seems to be smart but she is very distracted by her own popularity. She doesn't seem to believe that science is important and puts very little effort into the class. Janell is African American and comes from a family of professionals on the more affluent side of town.

Bill is Caucasian and was raised in a lower-middle class home in which getting ahead was very important. He can't imagine not taking education seriously. To him, it's the main vehicle for getting ahead in this society. Bill has often wondered how he can help students like Janell to take learning more seriously.

His *professional learning goal* is: "Studying Janelle will help me develop responsive approaches for African American girls with low motivation and who struggle to use scientific terms accurately in written essays in science."

Opening the Session

Make sure every teacher has brought the class set of responses to the Final Assessment (preferably already scored), along with the scoring criteria or rubric.

a. Greeting and Grounding. Greet participants and ask how things are going. Engage the group in a grounding activity, for example, teachers might share what progress they expect to see in their assessment results.

b. Framing the Session

- CASL Goal. Refer to the goal at the top of the CASL Poster.
- Teacher Outcomes. Pass out the Phase IV Protocol and refer to the list on the front page. Use the Framework poster (Figure 2.1) to explain the capacities to be developed.
- Agenda. Draw the group's attention to the tasks listed on the protocol and the examples of Bill's study group provided in this chapter.
- Working Agreements. Refer to the CASL Poster (Figure C.1) and engage teachers in the consideration of the CASL Purpose, working agreements. Ask if any working agreements need to be honored more fully or modified. If yes, make changes as needed.
- Parking Lot. Remind the group of its purpose and point it out.

c. Distributing Materials. Pass out other materials.
d. Identifying Roles. Ask for a volunteer to be the recorder and give him the Recorder Sheet to copy onto a piece of chart paper. Also give him the Study Group Log to complete at the end of the session.

Developing and Applying Communication Skills

a. Cue Cards. Teachers review on their cue cards the Communication skills of committed listening, pausing, matching verbal/nonverbal cues, paraphrasing, probing (three types), and putting ideas on the table.
b. Goal Setting. Ask each teacher to silently identify at least one skill to work on today. Remind the group members that, at the end of the session, they will be reflecting on how well their ways of collaborating supported the group's purpose.

FACILITATION TIPS

Confidentiality

At this point in the CASL inquiry, very detailed information about specific students and teachers is shared. It may be tempting for some in the group to repeat to others outside of the group sensitive information that would best be kept private. Remind one another the harm that could be done if such information were communicated.

Working agreements and communication skills

At the end of the last session, the group reflected on how their ways of interacting helped or hindered their group purpose. Keep track of these insights, and bring them forward to this session to help the group set goals for improving the power of their collaborative inquiry.

Protocol Step 1. Sharing Background

Purposes: To clarify the data sources, raise awareness of teachers' predictions and assumptions, and prepare data for analysis.

Step 1 contains three discrete, but important tasks: sharing the data context for the final assessment process, making predictions about what might be revealed in the data, and displaying each teacher's results from her Initial and Final Performance Assessments.

Data Context

If your study group members have used different prompts for the Final Assessment, you will need time to explain them to the others. If you've all used the same assessment, you will still want to explain how you administered it and anything you learned along the way.

The facilitator leads the following activities:

a. T-Chart. Each teacher writes under the appropriate heading on her own Phase IV T-Chart a description of both her Initial and Final Assessment Tasks (Figure 9.3, p. 286).

b. Sharing. One at a time, each group member explains the prompt, directions, procedures, and scoring criteria. The following question may be useful: *What were your prompt, directions, procedures, and rubric for both the Initial and Final Assessments?* As each teacher shares, the others pause, paraphrase, and probe as necessary.

c. Recording. The recorder writes only the new questions that arise (on lower left corner of the Recorder Sheet, Figure 9.4, p. 287) .

Predictions and Assumptions

Writing out your hunches about what you will find in the data and then comparing them later with the actual results can help you to consider perspectives and beliefs beyond your habitual ways of seeing. To engage in this step, use the following activities.

a. Purpose. Examine Step 1 in the protocol, clarify purposes, and consult Bill's study group example, (pp. 263–264).

b. Predictions. Write on your own Phase IV Protocol (not on Recorder Sheet) your predictions about the strengths and challenges you expect to find in the class set you brought. The following questions may be useful during this step:

   • *What predictions are you making about the Final Assessment Results?*
   • *In which areas do you expect most students to reach proficient performance?*

- *Which groups of students might be most successful?*
- *Which student learning outcomes might be most difficult for students?*
- *Which students might struggle the most? What are these students like?*
- *What leads you to these predictions?*

c. Save your notes to examine later during the Reflection Step.

Prepare Data: Teacher T-Chart and Final Student Performance Grid

The purpose of the Individual Teacher T-Chart is to display the results of both the Initial and the Final Assessment. After transferring the information from your Initial Assessment Student Performance Grid onto the T-Chart, it is time to prepare the Final Assessment Student Performance Grid (Figure 9.2, p. 285). To prepare the data for further analysis, engage in the following activities.

a. Purpose. The data display will allow you to gauge your students' learning progress over the year.

b. Teacher T-Chart. Enter the results from your Initial Assessment into the left column of the chart.

c. The Final Student Performace Grid. Complete the Final Grid using the same process you used for the Initial Performance Grid.

(1) Sort Data. Sort the papers (or data) into the number of scores on the rubric (e.g., three piles for a 3-level rubric). Take notes (to share later) about which parts of the rubric were hard to use or confusing. If you have two or three scoring categories, record the score for each category. You may need to sort and describe lower-scoring performances two or three times. For example, Bill described two categories—writing and the use of scientific language—on his grid. Since the two scores are different, he might need to sort them twice.

(2) Describe on the Grid the Student Performance. Start with the pile with the lowest scores. Enter each student's name on the left side of the Grid, record the Initial score(s), the Final score(s), and then describe *in detail both* the Strengths and the Areas for Improvement seen in the Final Assessment papers. Then go on to the next pile and do the same. Continue until all papers are entered, from lowest performance to highest.

(3) Describe on the Grid the Student Characteristics. Finally, enter information about the lower-performing students in the Student Characteristics column. Describe what you know about each student's cultural background, including class, race, ethnicity, gender, behaviors, language, religion, and exceptionality.

FACILITATION TIPS

Predictions and assumptions

During the conversation about predictions, listen for group members' limiting assumptions. For example, a teacher in Bill's group might say, "Oh, they won't be able to write correctly. My students are horrible writers!" A group member might first paraphrase that idea and then ask, "How many of us have this same prediction? What is our hunch about why this is so hard for them?" As the conversation proceeds, underlying assumptions might arise, for example, "They just don't care enough to put in the effort." Then the group can explore the possible reasons it appears that students "don't care."

Matching the initial and final outcomes assessed

We are not necessarily advocates of pre- and post-tests that are exactly the same. Why have a student try to answer (in a pre-assessment) questions for advanced content that you would not expect them to know? We *do* find it possible, however, to design matching Initial and Final Assessments that tap many of *the same TLA-related outcomes that appear in multiple units*. That is why we suggested that you select a powerful TLA that is developed over time—the thinking, writing, problem solving, analyzing, evaluating, and other processes that appear in several units. In Bill's case, he had been developing and assessing his students' ability to write paragraphs and essays in each science unit he had taught.

Adding a new category to the scoring rubric

Sometimes the Final Assessment task includes a higher-level outcome that may not have been tapped in the Initial Assessment. For example, in Bill's case, the Final Assessment scoring rubric included a new row labelled "Developing an Argument With Scientific Evidence." Bill used this new category when grading his students' in-class essays and used his notes about the patterns to revise his teaching of this skill the following year. We have not included this third category in our examples here.

District-created assessments

Using a standard assessment can save you valuable time. If you use such an assessment, however, make sure that (a) it aligns with the outcomes included in the TLA, (b) every teacher in the group understands how the assessment works and how to score it, and (c) it is *not a multiple-choice or a single-answer test*. If you do use multiple-choice items, you might ask for a written explanation of the student's thinking behind his selected response.

When teachers are new to a curriculum

If some in your group are still learning about your grade-level content standards, the assessment of the standards, or a new curriculum, you may wish to score and sort the assessment products (e.g., papers) in small groups. The dialogue will allow you to hash out your understanding of the scoring criteria, and, thus, of the outcomes themselves. Be sure that the recorder makes notes on what is learned at this time, for example, changes in the assessment task or clarification of the language used in the rubric. The further learning activity called "Rubric Calibrating" in the Online Resources may be useful for teachers who are struggling to use the rubric in a consistent way.

BILL'S STUDY GROUP:
PHASE IV, STEP 1 SHARING BACKGROUND

Bill's T-Chart: Initial Assessment Column

Description of Initial Assessment (from Phase II, October)

During the unit on Structure and Function, students were given an article that they had never seen before. The article included a diagram and an explanation of a cellular system that they were about to study. They were asked to read the article, use their preferred way of highlighting important ideas, and then write a three-paragraph summary, using the key terms and their own language to explain how the systems of cells function together.

The responses were scored using a 4-point writing rubric, which included two scores: (1) use of scientific terms and processes and (2) organization of ideas with conventions.

Strengths

Bill's students completed three paragraphs. About half of the students appeared to understand the content, even though their explanations were weak.

Number Reaching Proficiency

Less than half had a score of 3 or 4 on the Initial Assessment.

Focus Student Performance

Janell struggled to write coherent paragraphs, and she used scientific terms incorrectly.

Areas Needing Improvement

Color-coded patterns indicated that many students struggled to organize their ideas in a logical sequence and that they failed to use the scientific terms accurately in their explanations.

(Continued)

(Continued)

Number Not Reaching Proficiency

Over half had a score of 1 or 2 on the Initial Assessment.

Characteristics of Students Not Reaching Proficiency

A group of lower-scoring students shared the characteristics of being unmotivated, popular African American girls.

Bill's T-Chart Final Assessment Column (Phase IV, April)

The Final Assessment was administered after a unit on Interdependent Relationships in Ecosystems in which students had completed a group research paper that required them to "Design, evaluate, and refine a solution for reducing the impacts of human activities on the environment and biodiversity." The assessment required students to draw on their research to write (in class with the aid of a 3 × 5 card of notes, turned in with the work) a policy brief for a local agency that was about to design legislation to protect the environment. Students were to provide a statement of the problem, supported by data, as well as two proposed solutions, with the pros and cons of each supported by scientific justification. The writing was scored using the same rubric that had been used in the fall. One score was given for the science understanding demonstrated, and another score reflected the quality of the writing. Bill's group added a third score for "developing an argument with scientific evidence." Bill's completed Final Student Performance Grid is in the next section. (The example does not include the third score.)

Protocol Step 2. Observing and Analyzing Proficient Performance

Purpose: To identify patterns of success and discover influences on student learning.

Finding these patterns will help you discover what areas were learned well and by whom. As you analyze the causes of this success, you can make sure to use those ideas in the future. Public acknowledgement of the proficient performance in your classes creates a sense of collective responsibility, efficacy, moral purpose, and cultural proficiency—all crucial dispositions that will help your students in the future.

a. Purpose. Read Protocol Step 2 and explain its purposes. *For both the teacher and the group, it's important to acknowledge successes and to discover what prompted them.* Consult the examples below for clarity.

b. Observing Strengths. On your own Final Performance Grid, identify the most common areas of strength found in the Final Assessment results. You may use color-coding as you did in Phase II, or some other method.

c. Teacher T-Chart. Add the observed strengths to the right column of your own T-Chart (Figure 9.3).

d. Sharing Strengths. Teachers share their students' success by responding to questions such as, *What were the strengths (areas of proficient performance) on your final grid?*

e. Recording. The recorder writes each teacher's final performance strengths on the Recorder Sheet under "Our Students' Strengths."

f. Observing Progress, Initial to Final Assessment. Count the number of students reaching proficient in the Initial and Final Assessments. Include the progress made by your focus student. Record the findings on your T-Chart.

g. Sharing Progress. One at a time, respond to questions such as, *Comparing the Initial Assessment and Final Assessment results, how many of your students reached proficiency?*

h. Focus Student Progress. Share responses to this question, *What progress did your focus students make toward the TLA?*

i. Analyzing Reasons for Strengths. As a group, analyze possible causes for your successes by considering questions such as, *What did you do to facilitate the observed progress in your classes?* and *What did you learn about yourselves and your focus students that might have influenced their progress?*

j. Recording. The recorder writes the group's ideas under "Possible Reasons for Strengths" on the "Analyze" section of the Recorder Sheet.

Congratulate yourselves for your students' accomplishments.

BILL'S STUDY GROUP: PHASE IV STEP 2, OBSERVING AND ANALYZING PROFICIENT PERFORMANCE

Bill's Final Assessment Results: (As Entered on Teacher T-Chart)

Strengths

- Almost everyone in my class received a score of 3 or 4 for both the scientific aspects and the writing.
- The main areas of proficiency were in development of ideas, using scientific facts, and organization.

(Continued)

(Continued)

Final Student Performance Grid (partial list)

Student Name	Scores (Science/ Writing)		Areas of Strength Final	Areas For Improvement Final	Student Characteristics
Carlos	1/1	2/2	Clearly stated problem Used some scientific terms Used 3 resources	Few supporting facts or details for solution Organization: No concluding paragraph Mechanics errors make understanding difficult.	Hispanic Male Low-income Still learning English
Kendra	2/2	3/2	Accurate use of scientific terms Drew a picture to show the cause and effect	No logic to order of paragraphs Many sentence fragments Hard to read the explanation	Female African American Hates writing Family is breaking up Nonverbal
Susi	2/2	2/2	Writing includes some science terms Used correct format for paragraphs	No solution provided for the problem Confused causes with effects on environment Spelling errors (5) Sentence fragments (4)	Female Caucasian Shy Reading problems
*Janelle (Focus student)	1/2	3/3	Writing mostly correct Followed directions Science mostly correct	Solution needed a bit more support	African American Popular Needs help reading
Marco	2/2	2/2	Sentences complete	No support provided for the solution Science terms used incorrectly Disorganized argument	Caucasian Male Reading issues
Scoring: Science, Writing (1 is low and 4 is high) * Janelle is Bill's focus student.					

Number of Students Reaching Proficiency (Initial to Final Assessment)

- In their writing proficiency, all but othe four students listed on the grid improved their scores to reach a 3 or 4.
- In their science proficiency, all but the four students listed on the grid improved their scores to reach a 3 or 4.

Focus Student Performance and Reasons

- Janelle made great progress as seen in her two assessment scores: from 1 to 3 in science and from 2 to 3 in writing.
- I found a key to Janell's motivation when I incorporated more public presentations of students' work to her peers in a small group. She wanted to look good!

Study Group Recorder Sheet

Observe	Analyze
Our students' strengths	*Possible reasons for strengths*
• Used scientific facts correctly • Followed writing format and conventions	In every unit, we gave lots of modeling, practice, and specific feedback (e.g., self-assessment and peer assessment).

Protocol Step 3. Observing and Analyzing Non-Proficient Performance

Purpose: To understand patterns of non-proficient performance and influences on students' learning.

Now it is time to look at the outcomes many students did not achieve and what those students are like as learners and people. After observing and sharing the patterns found on your study group members' grids, you will select certain areas and student characteristics to analyze further. Finally, you will entertain multiple explanations for these students' lower performance. These ideas will guide your planned actions in the next step.

a. Purpose. Read Protocol Step 3 and explain the purpose. You may refer the group to Bill's study group example.

b. Final Performance Grid: Observing Areas for Improvement

- Color-Code. On your Final Grid's "Areas for Improvement" column, color-code common patterns. For example, highlight in yellow all the struggles that are the same; then use pink to highlight all the struggles of a different nature, and so on.

- Find Patterns. Place a star (*) next to the two or three most common color-coded areas (or circle them), as you did in Phase II.
- Teacher T-Chart. Write these common areas in the right column of your Teacher T-Chart in the row labelled "Areas Needing Improvement."

c. Final Performance Grid: Observing Characteristics of Students Not Reaching Proficient

- Find Patterns. On your Grid, circle the two or three most common characteristics among the students with lower performance.
- Teacher T-Chart. Write the characteristics on your own T-Chart.

d. Sharing and Recording Observations. One at a time, share the patterns found, using these questions:

- Areas for Improvement. Ask, *What* areas *are still in need of improvement on your Grid?* The recorder writes the areas on the "Observe" section of the sheet under the heading, "Our Students' Areas in Need of Improvement"
- Characteristics of Students. Ask, *Looking at your Grids, what are the students like who are struggling the most? How would you describe them as people and learners?* The recorder writes the information on the "Observe" section of the sheet under the heading, "Characteristics of Students Not Reaching Proficiency."

e. Analyzing Reasons for Observed Patterns. . Explain the difference between a possible explanation ("It could be . . . ") and a strategy ("Try this idea . . . "). Clarify that this step is for analyzing only; the suggestions and planning will take place in the next step. You might say, *By now, you are familiar with our recommendation to consider a wide variety of perspectives when seeking to understand the patterns you found. As you explore possible influences on students' learning, use the communication skills to check the explanatory power of each idea proposed.*

f. Analyzing Areas in Need of Improvement.

- Observing. As a group, look at the area labelled, "Our Students' Areas in Need of Improvement" on the "Observe" section of the recorder sheet.
- Analyzing. Consider possible causes by asking, *Why might these areas still be so difficult for students?*
- Recording. The recorder writes the possible reasons on the "Analyze" section of the Recorder Sheet.

g. Analyzing Students Not Reaching Proficiency.

- Observing. Look at the area labelled, "Characteristics of Students Not Reaching Proficiency" on the "Observe" section of the Recorder Sheet.
- Analyzing. Consider possible causes by asking, *What might have interfered with these specific students' learning?*
- When seeking possible explanations, consider:
  - Content (Outcomes, concepts, skills)
  - Student (Biography, culture, learning, and performance)
  - Pedagogy (Teaching strategies and resources)
  - Assessment (Fit with student and/or outcomes)
  - Context (Conditions in room, school, or community)
  - Teacher's Cultural Background and Filters
- Recording. The recorder writes the possible reasons on the "Analyze" section of the sheet.

h. Questions: *What questions does your group have about these students' learning?* Recorder writes these under "Questions" on the sheet.

FACILITATION TIPS

Sticking with the protocol

As you notice the patterns in your students' content challenges, you might be tempted to jump right past the next steps by sharing your favorite plans and ideas for teaching these areas. But we ask you to refrain—for now.

Multiple perspectives and causes

Don't stop before you discover the gold. By considering all aspects and perspectives, you may unearth a key to these students' success.

Avoiding the uncomfortable

It may be tempting to only scratch the surface of the problem. But don't forget your group's stated purpose: to relentlessly pursue ways to help your students succeed. The challenge for your study group is to use dialogue to dig deeply into possible reasons for some students not reaching the targets.

More information

Often during the work analysis the group finds that they can't come up with a reasonable explanation without gathering more information. The recorder writes these questions on the "Questions" area of the sheet for later consideration.

BILL'S STUDY GROUP'S RECORDER SHEET: PHASE IV, STEP 3 OBSERVING AND ANALYZING NON-PROFICIENT PERFORMANCE

Observe	Analyze
Our students' areas for improvement	**Possible reasons for areas for improvement**
• Trouble writing with correct development, organization, and mechanics • Didn't provide support for solutions, or failed to delineate the cause and effect of the scientific argument provided	• We didn't coordinate with English teachers on this assignment.
Characteristics of students not reaching proficiency	**Possible reasons for students not reaching proficiency**
• The struggling students are weak readers and are nonverbal. They speak little in class and often form partial answers and sentences when they respond.	• Reading and language difficulties; not able to read the material; can't write about what they can't read and understand.
Our Questions	
• What is the relationship between reading the content and writing about it?	

Protocol Step 4. Planning

Purpose: To identify next steps for improving the learning of those students not achieving proficient performance.

Now that you have some ideas about what might be hindering the progress of those students not reaching proficiency, it is time to devise approaches that best fit their strengths, needs, and cultural backgrounds. You will make a three-part plan: (1) developing strategies that are responsive to the students as learners and people, (2) making revisions to the assessment system used, and (3) finding ways to address the group's questions.

When the teacher or a group member puts a strategy on the table, it's important to check how well this approach might work, given what has been learned so far. This might include a paraphrase and then a probe asking what leads the person to think that this might be a useful strategy.

To engage the group in the Planning Step, use the following activities. The recorder writes the ideas on the sheet under "Plan."

a. Purpose. Examine Step 4 in the protocol and clarify purposes. Look at Bill's study group's example.

b. Outcomes to Learn Next. Dialogue about this question: *Based on what is known about the students not reaching proficiency, what do they most need to learn next?* The recorder writes these ideas under the "Plan" section on the sheet.

c. Responsive Approaches. As a group, consider the question, *Based on what is known about the students not reaching proficiency, what approaches might facilitate their learning, and why?* The recorder writes these ideas under the "Plan" section on the sheet.

d. Revision of Assessment. Also take time to consider the question, *What changes might you make to the Final Assessment for the next time you use it?* The recorder writes these ideas under the "Plan" section on the sheet.

e. Questions: Look at the questions written on the lower left corner of the Recorder Sheet. Ask, *What more might we want to learn about to effectively meet our students' learning needs?* The recorder adds new questions to the Sheet.

BILL'S STUDY GROUP'S RECORDER SHEET: PHASE IV, STEP 4 PLANNING

Important Outcomes for These Students to Learn Next

- We probably need to find out more about their language and reading skills before we know the appropriate next outcomes.

Responsive Approaches (and why they might help)

- For students with limited verbal skills and reading difficulties, we might
  a. Read aloud the directions for an assessment to the students (if students can't read it).
  b. Ask some students to talk about their learning before writing (generates ideas).

Final Assessment Revisions

- Our Final Assessment worked pretty well. It required students to apply what they had put in their research paper into a scientific argument in a real context.
- Next time, we might offer a rubric for a self-check before they turn in their assessment paper.

Our Questions and Interest in Further Professional Learning

- We need to talk to the reading and language specialists to learn:
  a. What are we doing to help our poor readers? What is the problem?
  b. How do our assessment methods impact weak readers?

Protocol Step 5. Reflecting

Purposes: To transfer learning from the study group to everyday practice, build collective responsibility, and improve group productivity.

We encourage you to reflect on three major areas: your own learning, your group's collaborative functioning, and what further professional learning you might pursue. Before sharing your thoughts with the group, take time to review your notes and jot down your thoughts.

Engage in the following activities to complete the reflections:

a. What Was Learned Today. Write about the following questions, and then share your responses, one at a time. *How does what you learned today differ from or confirm your earlier predictions and assumptions?* and *What did you learn about students and yourself today that might help promote your students' learning?*

b. Recording Reflections. Ask the recorder to add these ideas to the Study Group Log (p. 288).

c. Collaboration. Ask group to write about (and provide evidence of) how their use of the working agreements and communication skills influenced the group's ability to meet its purpose: *How consistently did we follow the agreements and communication skills today? What influence did the collaborative process have on our learning today?*

d. Professional Learning. Ask, *How might the group pursue further professional learning?* The recorder writes these ideas on the Study Group Log.

e. Study Group Log. Remind the recorder to copy the completed Study Group Log and distribute it to facilitator, all group members, and principal on next day.

BILL'S STUDY GROUP:
PHASE IV, STEP 5 REFLECTING

Predictions and Assumptions (Summary of Study Group Dialogue)

- We thought that more students might not reach proficiency. We were pleasantly surprised to see how many did so well.

What Was Learned About Our Students and Ourselves (Written on Study Group Log)

- We developed our students' writing success because we taught it and graded it consistently. The writing rubrics helped students self-assess and self-correct before we did any grading. That was powerful.
- When we shared the patterns in our Grids, we couldn't believe how many students were still struggling with supporting their recommendations with scientific evidence. As we talked, we realized that our textbook is lacking in this area and that we will have to supplement it.
- Finally, we are all a bit puzzled about the role of reading with those students who progressed very little. Our filtering systems definitely kept us from realizing how hard it would be to read a science text when your own language skills are still in development. We're all pretty educated, so we missed that. We need to explore the causes, and make some plans to address the underlying issues.

Collaboration: Working Agreements and Communication Skills (Summary of Study Group Dialogue)

- By now, we're pros at this CASL thing!

Professional Learning Needs (Written on Study Group Log)

- We know very little about helping struggling readers. As we focused on the writing, we realized how important reading comprehension is in science. We need to examine alternative approaches for helping students read our science content, perhaps other resources within the school. We will talk to our leadership about our need for professional learning in the teaching of reading comprehension.

Plans for CASL Celebration (Summary of Study Group Dialogue)

- We set aside an hour during a staff meeting for teachers to share their CASL Notebooks and learning. We examined the Phase V Celebration Protocol to prepare.

Protocol Step 6. Acting

To implement the plan and pursue additional professional learning if warranted. The teachers and group carry the plans out in the next few weeks.

a. Action. Selected group members (or the group as a whole) may pursue more information and further professional learning as needed.

b. Log. Copy completed CASL Study Group Log and on the next day distributes it to facilitator, all group members, and principal.

c. Preparation. Group members prepare for Phase V by reading the second half of this chapter.

CASL NOTEBOOK CONTENTS FROM PHASE IV

Study group members add the following items to their CASL notebook:

- Phase IV Protocol with notes on it
- Final Assessment Instrument
- Final Assessment Student Performance Grid
- Phase IV Teacher T-Chart
- Phase IV Study Group Log

PHASE IV ADAPTATIONS

Designing the Final Assessment

Don't wait until the end of the CASL months to develop the Final Assessment and its scoring criteria. The sooner these are designed, the better able teachers will be to aim their instruction toward the accomplishment of the outcomes tapped by the assessment.

Additional Professional Learning

Whatever direction the teachers desire to pursue, be sure to include the examination of student work samples, the gathering of evidence, and the definition of the desired learning targets. Also, capitalize on teachers' use of the collaborative inquiry cycle to analyze issues from multiple perspectives before choosing a plan of action.

Performance Grid Data and School Improvement Plans

The analysis of the data from the two Student Performance Grids can provide valuable insights for school improvement activities because the data are easily disaggregated by classroom, content, and student characteristics. You can use the data on the specific outcomes to revise curriculum. And you can use the information about struggling students to design interventions that may help those students catch up.

CASL PHASE V. INTEGRATING LEARNING INTO TEACHERS' PROFESSIONAL PRACTICE

Phase V begins with written reflections about the entire CASL experience. This is followed by an exhibit of both the teachers' and students' learning. Publicly sharing the evidence of one's own students' beginning and ending performance in a complex learning area makes teaching a transparent endeavor. It brings professional practice into concrete terms so that it can be examined and shared. Also, it goes a long way toward developing the shared values of cultural competency, collective responsibility, efficacy, and the moral stance that collaborative inquirers gain through the CASL process. As others witness the evidence of these dispositions and professional learning, they can't help but be intrigued and may wish to try it out themselves.

Teacher Learning Outcomes

The activities in Phase V develop in teachers the following capacities, described more fully in the framework presented in Chapter 2.

- Understand themselves and their students as people and learners so that they can provide culturally and linguistically responsive instruction, and thus increase their students' learning and success
- Engage in productive dialogue using working agreements and communication skills to inquire deeply into dilemmas of student learning
- Develop the professional knowledge base required for responsive teaching approaches
- Use the collaborative inquiry cycle to systematically study students' learning to discover approaches that foster each student's success
- Consider and restructure (as needed) the influence of personal filters (feelings, beliefs, values,) on their own practice
- Be guided by the dispositions of cultural competency, moral stance, efficacy, and collective responsibility

GUIDING A STUDY GROUP THROUGH PHASE V

The most important purpose for Phase V is to consolidate the teacher's learning by stepping back and reflecting upon the entire CASL experience. To this end, we ask teachers to examine their Notebook contents and to take an hour or so to write out their reflections. They will place these reflections in Section V of their CASL notebook. After this step, teachers often engage in a CASL Celebration where the notebooks and reflections are presented to other teachers.

Written Reflections on Professional Learning (Placed in Section V of CASL Notebook)

- Use the documentation in your CASL notebook and your personal notes to think about the following questions and write out your responses.

(1) *Given your Professional Learning Goal, what have you learned about how particular students learn in this TLA?*

(2) *What insights have you gained about teaching that can be used in the future to support the learning of your students?*

(3) *How did the CASL phases, the working agreements, and communication skills contribute to your own learning?*

(4) *What have you learned about yourself as a cultural being, and how does that influence your teaching of students whose backgrounds are different from your own?*

(5) *What professional learning needs do you now have, and how will this learning improve your practice?*

The CASL Celebration

The CASL Celebration works very well when study group members sit at small tables set up in the same large room and present their CASL projects to other teachers who were not in their group. Round tables work well, or a group can cluster around the end of an oblong table.

When only one or two study groups are presenting their CASL work, we have each study group teacher sit at a different station (table) and share with teachers who did not participate in CASL. The teacher takes about 15 minutes to follow the suggested format and then answers the other teachers' questions. Then the teacher remains at the table, and the others go to a different study group teacher's table.

When all or most teachers have participated in CASL study groups, they gain much by sharing with study group teachers from different grades or related content areas. If you have two or three study groups presenting, you can mix teachers from different groups at the same table. In this way, each teacher gets to learn about a few other teachers' CASL process.

To prepare for your CASL presentation, consult your CASL Notebook, and be ready to share with the group the following information:

1. Phase I. Target Learning Area

   - Describe your group's original target learning area and the reasons for selecting this area.
   - Explain how you refined or revised your understanding of this area of student learning and what prompted these insights.

2. Phase II. Initial Assessment and Student Performance Grid

   - Describe the task, directions, and scoring criteria you used.

- Show the patterns in your Performance Grid (content and student characteristics) that prompted you to select your focus student.
- Show your Professional Learning Goal.

3. Phase III. Cultural Autobiography

  - Describe your insights about your own cultural background during the months of CASL inquiry.
  - Explain how these aspects of your experience have influenced your teaching and learning.

4. Phase III. Focus Student Biography

  - Show your Focus Student's Biography and share which information helped you find responsive approaches for your student.

5. Early Phase III Work Sample

  - Show your focus student's first work sample to demonstrate where your student's learning began. Use the notes from your Phase III Protocol and the Study Group Recorder Sheet to describe your group's observations, analysis/interpretations, planned actions that you used with your focus student and why you used them, and any questions that surfaced.

6. Late Phase III Work Sample

  - Show your focus student's final work sample. Use the notes from your Phase III Protocol and the Study Group Recorder Sheet to explain:

    (1) How closely the final performance matched the intended outcomes (rubric).
    (2) Why you think the student did or did not reach the intended outcomes, emphasizing your role in this outcome.

7. Phase IV. Final Assessment

  - Show the Final Assessment Performance Grid and highlight progress made, students not reaching proficiency, possible influences on them, planned approaches for these students, and desired professional learning.

8. Written Reflections

  - Share your insights from your "Written Reflections on Professional Learning."

BILL'S STUDY GROUP:
PHASE V (BILL'S WRITTEN REFLECTIONS)

Given your Professional Learning Goal, what have you learned about how particular students learn in this TLA?

- When students have trouble reading, it is really hard to help them succeed in writing about science. When kids care to look good to others, and I have them share their skills with a small group, their motivation to do quality work often goes up.

What insights have you gained about teaching that can be used in the future to support the learning of your students?

- I learned from my study group that whatever I really emphasize, the students tend to learn. I gave lots of practice, taught them self-assessment, and used groups to give feedback.
- I really tried to understand where Jannell was coming from by listening into what she talked about with her friends. Then I used that to make small talk with her before and after class and when I saw her in the hall. As time went on, I learned that she really does value learning but did not want to look geeky to her peers. Based on this insight, I refrained from calling attention to her for her class work, and I called on her less, but I kept a close eye on her performance. The biggest difference came, however, with the writing when I had her read it to her small group, whom I had selected carefully. Suddenly she increased her effort because she cared about how her group members perceived her.

How did the CASL Phases, the working agreements, and the communication skills contribute to your own learning?

- I enjoyed my study group. We were structured and task oriented. It took a while for us to get the hang of the Phase III Protocol (we were guilty of interrupting and not exploring each idea put on the table), but as we met and practiced, we got better. It really helped us to slow down and inquire into multiple perspectives before deciding on the causes for what we observed. As we did this, we began to have some major breakthroughs as we tried more responsive approaches with our focus students. This was exciting.

What have you learned about yourself as a cultural being and how that influences your teaching of students whose backgrounds are different from your own?

- At first, I couldn't fathom why a student like Janell, who had everything, wouldn't take advantage of learning what I was offering her. I had always valued learning, and I was frustrated that she didn't. I also held her parents in contempt. As I came to understand her, I realized that she's a typical teenager who cares a lot about what others think—looking "smart" is not cool in her world. I finally owned my own biases toward her and began to have compassion for her need to be liked by others.

What professional learning needs do you now have, and how will this learning improve your practice?

- Students' lack of reading and verbal skills: We will consult with the county reading specialist and two other resources. Next year, we need to have proactive strategies for finding these students early on and addressing their needs.

SUMMARY

Phases IV and V put the final touches on the months of CASL inquiry. In Phase IV, it's important to analyze concrete evidence of the progress your students have made and to analyze your role in prompting your students' success—a nice contribution to your professional efficacy. Your analysis and planning for those students not yet meeting proficiency is the logical next step when you share collective responsibility for students' learning.

In Phase V, it's vital to reflect upon your own and the students' learning gains. The most powerful aspect of CASL—in fact, its whole purpose—is witnessed when you share and celebrate your months of relentlessly pursuing, discovering, and applying responsive equitable approaches for learning so that each and every student reaches excellence.

Figure 9.1 CASL Phase IV Protocol. Assessing Student Progress

To analyze student progress in the TLA, determine characteristics of struggling students, and pursue responsive approaches for those students.

- What progress have our students made toward the target learning area?
- What areas of learning have improved and for which students?
- How did we contribute to our students' success?
- What areas still need improvement and for which students? What might explain the lack of progress?
- How can we develop responsive approaches for these students?
- What additional professional learning might we need?

Teacher Learning Outcomes

Teachers develop the capacity to

- Understand themselves and their students as people and learners so that they can provide culturally and linguistically responsive instruction, and thus increase their students' learning and success.
- Engage in productive dialogue using working agreements and communication skills to inquire deeply into dilemmas of student learning.
- Develop the professional knowledge base required for responsive teaching approaches.
- Use the collaborative inquiry cycle to systematically study students' learning to discover approaches that foster each student's success.
- Consider and restructure (as needed) the influence of personal filters (feelings, beliefs, values) on their own practice.
- Be guided by the dispositions of cultural proficiency, moral stance, efficacy, and collective responsibility.
- Determine their needs for additional professional learning.

Materials

Group members bring:

- CASL Notebook and this book
- Class set of scored Final Assessments, with rubric

Facilitator brings:

- Phase IV Recorder Sheet (Figure 9.4)
- Blank chart paper (for recorder)
- Study Group Log (Figure 9.5)

Posted in meeting room:

- CASL Poster (Figure 3.1)
- Framework Poster (Figure 2.1)
- Parking Lot

Facilitator brings one blank copy for each teacher:

- Phase IV Protocol (Figure 9.1)
- Final Student Performance Grid (Figure 9.2)
- Teacher T-Chart (Figure 9.3)

Roles

Facilitator

- Teach, model, and monitor CASL working agreements and communication skills.
- Lead the group through Phase IV Protocol.
- Encourage multiple perspectives and interpretations.
- Paraphrase ideas offered and ask Recorder to write them on sheet.

Recorder

- Take notes—visible to all—during each step of the protocol.
- Complete and distribute Study Group Log.

Study Group Guide for CASL Phase IV Protocol
Assessing Student Progress

Opening the Session

- Greeting, Grounding, Framing the Session
- Review working agreements
- Review communication skills
- Distribute materials and assign roles

1. Sharing Background	
Purpose and Prompts	*Notes*
Data Context Purpose: To clarify the data sources • What were your prompts directions, procedures, and scoring criteria for the Initial and Final Assessments? **Predictions** Purpose: To raise awareness of teachers' predictions and assumptions • What predictions are you making about the Final Assessment results? • What leads you to these predictions? **Prepare Data** Purpose: To prepare data for analysis • On Teacher T-Chart, fill in column, "Initial Assessment" • Complete Final Student Performance Grid	*Predictions:* *Why I expect this:*

2. Observing	
Purpose and Prompts	*Notes*
Purpose: To identify patterns of success and discover influences on student learning • What were the strengths (areas of proficient learning) on your Final Grid? • Comparing the Initial to the Final Assessment results, how many students reached proficiency? • What did you do to facilitate the observed progress in your class? • What progress did your focus student make toward the TLA? • What did you learn about yourself and your focus student that might have influenced his or her progress?	*Teacher enters information on right side of T-Chart.* *Recorder writes each teacher's findings on sheet.*

(Continued)

(Continued)

3. Analyzing/Interpreting	
Purpose and Prompts	*Notes*
Purpose: To understand patterns of non-proficient performance and influences on students' learning. Based on your observations: • What areas are still in need of improvement on your Final Grid? Why? • What are students like who are struggling the most? How would you describe them as people and learners? • What might have interfered with these students' learning? • What questions does your group have about your students' learning?	*Teacher enters information on T-Chart.* *Recorder writes each teacher's ideas on Sheet.*

4. Planning	
Purpose and Prompts	*Notes*
Purpose: To identify next steps for improving the learning of those students not achieving proficient performance • Based on what is known about the students not reaching proficiency, what do they most need to learn next? • Based on what is known about the students not reaching proficiency, what approaches might facilitate their learning? • Why might those approaches be helpful? • What changes might you make to your Final Assessment the next time you use it? • How might the group address the questions that surfaced today?	

5. Reflecting	
Purpose and Prompts	*Notes*
Purpose: To transfer learning from the study group to everyday practice, build collective responsibility, and improve group productivity • How does what you learned today differ from or confirm your earlier predictions and assumptions? • What did you learn about students and yourself today that might help promote other students' learning? • How consistently did the group follow the working agreements and communication skills? • What influence did the collaborative process have on your learning today? • How might the group pursue further professional learning, if necessary?	

6. Acting	
Purpose and Prompts	*Notes*
Purpose: To implement the plan and pursue further professional learning • Recorder distributes Log to administrator and group members. • Group may pursue additional learning. Teachers read second half of Chapter 9, write their reflections, and prepare for the CASL celebration in Phase V.	

Figure 9.2 CASL Final Student Performance Grid

CASL FINAL STUDENT PERFORMANCE GRID

Directions. Sort your students' assessment products into three piles: lower scores, middle scores, and higher scores. Begin with the lower-scoring papers. Record the information below for each student's work. Be sure to look for evidence of strengths and needs *beyond those* described in the rubric.

Student Name	Initial Score	Final Score	Strengths	Areas for Improvement	Student Characteristics

Figure 9.3 Teacher T-Chart for Phase IV. Assessing Student Progress

Directions. Use this form to summarize information from each of your Student Performance Grids.

	Phase II: Initial Student Assessment Results	Phase IV: Final Student Assessment Results
Description of Assessment		
Strengths		
Number Reaching Proficiency		
Focus Student Performance and Reasons		
Areas Needing Improvement		
Number Not Reaching Proficiency		
Characteristics of Students Not Reaching Proficiency		
Questions I Have		

Figure 9.4 Recorder Sheet for CASL Phase IV. Assessing Student Progress

Directions. Use this format to write group's ideas on chart paper or electronic device so that all can see it.

Observe	Analyze
Our students' strengths	Possible reasons for strengths
Our students' areas in need of improvement	Possible reasons for areas in need of improvement
Characteristics of the students not reaching proficiency	Possible reasons for students not reaching proficiency
Questions and Further Professional Learning	**Plan**
	Important outcomes for these students to learn next
	Responsive approaches for these students. Why might these approaches help?
	Final Assessment revisions

Figure 9.5 Study Group Log

(Copy and Distribute to Administrator and Group Members after each Meeting)

Date: _____ Time Meeting Started: _____ and Ended: _____

Name of Group (Grade Level and/or Content):

Group Members:

Today's Facilitator: Today's Recorder:

Tasks Accomplished:

How Our New Learning Will Help Our Students (from Step 5. Reflections):

Inquiry Questions We Want to Pursue:

Resources, Professional Learning, or Assistance Needed by Our Study Group:

Conclusion

Of all the civil rights for which the world has struggled and fought for 5000 years, the right to learn is undoubtedly the most fundamental . . . We must insist upon this to give our children the fairness of a start which will equip them with such an array of facts and such an attitude toward truth that they can have a real chance to judge what the world is and what its greater minds have thought it might be. The freedom to learn . . . has been bought by bitter sacrifice. (W. E. B. Du Bois, *The Freedom to Learn* (1949), as quoted in Foner, 1970)

As the cultural and linguistic diversity of our nation's school-aged students grows at an unprecedented rate, we must rise to the present challenge by establishing new solutions to longstanding problems through collaborative exploration, discovery, and innovation. As demonstrated in the pages of this book, CASL is one powerful professional learning design that creates learning communities and tasks that transform teachers' practices and beliefs as they relentlessly persist in the discovery, development, and use of equitable approaches for learning so students successfully achieve learning excellence.

As Sue shared at the CASL celebration in Phase V,

The most important thing I have learned about my teaching through CASL is that I should not assume anything. All students are different, and, as their teacher, I'm responsible for tapping into their lives. CASL helped me focus in on all aspects of a student (including their personal lives and personality) when analyzing their work. As my study group and I reviewed everything that influenced Nika's work, we discovered that his heritage is precious to him. As I got to know Nika and his father, I could see and feel their commitment to their culture. In turn, I am more mindful of my own philosophy, theories, and beliefs because I had to verbalize and reflect on them. CASL helped me become a much more reflective and effective teacher.

We know that CASL can have similar effects with teachers in your school, district, or professional learning programs. We encourage you to adapt the system to your unique setting. We must mention, however, that all of the following distinct and essential features are crucial to the success of any adaption if you hope to increase cultural proficiency, teaching effectiveness, and results for all students.

- The Conceptual Framework: Teacher as Collaborative Inquirer
- Structured inquiry
- A focus on standards of excellence
- Case-study for equitable responsiveness
- Inquiry over time
- Productive and intentional collaboration
- Skilled facilitation and organizational support

We wish you success as you implement the CASL design. We hope that it provides many benefits to your students, teachers, and organization.

We invite you to contact us regarding your questions, concerns, suggestions, and insights. We learn so much from the experiences of others as they implement the CASL design. We will do our best to respond in a timely manner.

References

Ainsworth, L., & Viegut, D. (Eds.) (2006). *Common formative assessments: How to connect standards-based instruction and assessment.* Thousand Oaks, CA: Corwin.

Anderson, R. C. (1984). Some reflections on the acquisition of knowledge *Educational Researcher, 13*, 5–10.

Argyris, C. (1985). *Strategy, change, and defensive routines.* Boston, MA: Pitman.

Bacon, J. N., Totten, T. L., Bridges, T. L., III, & Jennings, M. E. (2010). *Examining teachers' beliefs about African American male students in a low-performing high school in an African American school district.* Teachers College Press. Retrieved from http://ddce.utexas.edu/aamri/2015/02/examining-teachers-beliefs-about-african-american-male-students-in-a-low-performing-high-school-in-an-african-american-school-district/

Ball, D. L., & Cohen, D. K. (1999). Developing practice, developing practitioners: Toward a practice-based theory of professional education. In G. Sykes & L. Darling-Hammond (Eds.), *Teaching as the learning profession: Handbook of policy and practice* (pp. 3–32). San Francisco: Jossey-Bass.

Bandura, A. (1997). *Self-efficacy: The exercise of control.* New York: W. H. Freeman.

Berliner, D. C. (1986). In pursuit of the expert. *Educational Researcher, 15*(7), 5–13.

Blank, R. K., & de las Alas, N. (2009). *Effects of teacher professional development on gains in student achievement: How meta-analysis provides scientific evidence useful to education leaders.* Washington, DC: Council of Chief State School Officers. Retrieved from http://www.ccsso.org/Documents/2009/Effects_of_Teacher_Professional_2009.pdf

Bloom, B. S. (1984). The two-sigma problem: The search for group methods as effective as one-to-one tutoring. *Educational Researcher, 13*(6), 4–16.

Blythe, T., Allen, D., & Powell, B. (1999). *Looking together at student work.* New York: Teachers College Press.

Bocchino, R. (1993). Are you planning the future or fixing the past? *Journal of Staff Development, 14*, 48–52.

Bohm, D. (1965). *The special theory of relativity.* New York: W. A. Benjamin.

Borko, H. (2004). Professional development and teacher learning: Mapping the terrain. *Educational Researcher, 33*(8). Retrieved from http://www.aera.net/uploadedFiles/Journals_and_Publications/Journals/Educational_Researcher/Volume_33_No_8/02_ERv33n8_Borko.pdf

Brinson, D., & Steiner, L. (October 2007). Building collective efficacy: How leaders inspire teachers to achieve. *Issue Brief.* The Center for Comprehensive School Reform and Improvement. Washington, DC: Learning Points Associates.

Retrieved from file:///Users/amycolton/Downloads/CenterIssueBriefOct07%
20(1).pdf.

Bryk, A. S., & Schneider, B. (2004). *Trust in schools: A core resource for improvement.*
New York: The Russell Sage Foundation.

Bryk, A., Sebring, P., Allensworth, E., Luppescu, S., & Easton, J. (2010). *Organizing schools for improvement: Lessons from Chicago.* Chicago, IL: University of Chicago.

Carini, P. (1979). *The art of seeing and the visibility of the person.* Grand Forks: University of North Dakota Press.

Chappuis, J., Stiggins, R., Chappuis, S., & Arter, J. (2011) *Classroom assessment for student learning: Doing it right—using it well* (2nd ed.). Boston, MA: Assessment Training Institute, Pearson Education.

Colton, A., & Langer, G. (2001). Unpublished program evaluation studies.

Colton, A., & Sparks-Langer, G. (1993). A conceptual framework to guide the development of teacher reflection and decision making. *Journal of Teacher Education, 44*(1), 45–54.

Colton, A., & Sparks-Langer, G. M. (1992). Restructuring student teaching experiences. In C. Glickman (Ed). *Supervision in transition.* Alexandria, VA: Association for Supervision and Curriculum Development.

Colton, A., & Sparks-Langer, G. M. (1993). A conceptual framework to guide the development of teacher reflection and decision making. *Journal of Teacher Education, 44*(1), 45–54.

Cooper, J. E., He, Y., & Levin, B. B. (2011). *Developing critical cultural competence: A guide for 21st century educators.* Thousand Oaks, CA: Corwin.

Costa, A. L., & Garmston, R. J. (1994). *Cognitive coaching: A foundation for Renaissance Schools.* Norwood, MA: Christopher-Gordon Publishers.

Costa, A. L., & Garmston, R. J. (2002). *Cognitive coaching: A foundation for Renaissance Schools* (2nd ed.). Norwood, MA: Christopher-Gordon Publishers.

Covey, S. R. (1989). *The seven habits of highly effective people.* New York: Simon & Schuster.

Croft, A., Coggshall, J. G., Dolan, M., & Powers, E. (2010). *Job-embedded professional development: What it is, who's responsible, and how to get it done well.* Washington, DC: National Comprehensive Center for Teacher Quality. Retrieved from http://files.eric.ed.gov/fulltext/ED520830.pdf

Dana, N. F., & Yendol-Hoppey, D. (2014). *The reflective educator's guide to classroom research* (3rd ed.). Thousand Oaks, CA: Corwin.

Danielson, C. (2011). *The framework for teaching evaluation instrument.* Princeton, NJ: The Danielson Group.

Darling-Hammond, L. (1998, February). Teacher learning that supports student learning. *Educational Leadership, 55*(5), 6–11.

Darling-Hammond, L. (2010). *Performance counts: Assessment systems that support high-quality learning.* Washington, DC: Council of Chief State School Officers.

Darling-Hammond, L., & Richardson, N. (2009). Teacher learning: What matters? *Educational Leadership, 66*(5), 46–53.

Darling-Hammond, L., Wei, R. C., Andree, A., Richardson, N., & Orphanos, S. (2009). *Professional learning in the learning profession: A status report on teacher development in the United States and abroad.* Dallas, TX: National Staff Development Council. Retrieved from http://learningforward.org/docs/pdf/nsdcstudy2009.pdf.

Deal, T. E., & Peterson, K. D. (1994). *The leadership paradox: Balancing logic and artistry in schools*. San Francisco: Jossey-Bass.

Desimone, L., Porter, A., Garet, M., Yoon, K., & Birman, B. (2002). Effects of professional development on teachers' instruction: Results from a three-year longitudinal study. *Educational Evaluation and Policy Analysis, 24*(2), 81–112.

Dewey, J. (1933). *How we think* (rev. ed.). Boston, MA: Heath.

DuFour, R. (2014). *The principal: Three keys to maximizing impact*. San Francisco: Jossey-Bass.

DuFour, R., & Berkey, T. (Fall, 1995). The principal as staff developer. *Journal of Staff Development, 16*(4), 2–6.

DuFour, R., & Mattos, M. (2013). How do principals really improve schools? *Educational Leadership, 70*(7), 34–40.

DuFour, R., Dufour, R., Eaker, R., & Many, T. (2010). *Learning by doing. Professional learning communities at work* (2nd ed.). Bloomington, IN: Solution Tree Press.

Ellinor, L., & Gerard, G. (1998). *Dialogue: Rediscovering the transforming power of conversation*. New York: John Wiley & Sons.

Flavell, J. H. (1963). *The developmental psychology of Jean Piaget*. Whitefish, MT: Literacy Licensing.

Floden, R. E., & Buchman, M. (1990). Philosophical inquiry in teacher education. In W. R. Houston (Ed.), *Handbook of research on teacher education* (pp. 42–58). New York: Macmillan.

Foner, P. S. (Ed.), *W.E.B. Du Bois Speaks* (1970) (pp. 230–231). New York: Pathfinder.

Fullan, M. (2001). *Leading in a culture of change*. San Francisco: Jossey-Bass.

Garet, M. S., Porter, A. C., Desimone, L., Birman, B. F., & Yoon, K. S. (2001). What makes professional development effective? Results from a national sample of teachers. *American Educational Research Journal, 38*(4), 915–945.

Garmston, R. J., & Wellman, B. M. (1999). *The adaptive school: A sourcebook for developing collaborative groups*. Norwood, MA: Christopher-Gordon Publishers.

Garmston, R. J., & Wellman, B. M. (2009). *The adaptive school: A sourcebook for developing collaborative groups* (2nd ed.). Norwood, MA: Christopher-Gordon Publishers.

Gearhart, M., & Osmundson, E. (2008). *Assessment portfolios as opportunities for teacher learning* (CRESST Report 736). Los Angeles: University of California, Center for Research on Evaluation, Standards, and Student Testing.

Gilligan, C. (1982). *In a different voice*. Cambridge, MA: Harvard University Press.

Glickman, C. (1981). *Developmental supervision: Alternative practices for helping teachers improve instruction*. Alexandria, VA: Association for Supervision and Curriculum Development.

Goddard, R. D., How, W. K., & Hoy, A. W. (2000). Collective teacher efficacy: Its meaning, measure, and impact on student achievement. *American Educational Journal, 37*(2), 479–507.

Goff, L. (1999) *Teacher and administrator perceptions concerning the use of teacher portfolios for professional development and evaluation*. Unpublished doctoral dissertation, The University of Southern Mississippi, Hattiesburg.

Goff, L., Langer, G. M., & Colton, A. (2000). Power of the portfolio. *Journal of Staff Development, 21*(4), 44–48.

Gray, S. (2009). *A study of teachers' professional learning and student outcomes*. Master's thesis for Grand Valley State University.

Great Lakes Area Regional Resource Center. (1998). Facilitation as a design process: Training manual. Columbus, Ohio: The Ohio State University. Developed under Cooperative Agreement Number H028A30004 with the U.S. Department of Education, Office of Special Education and Rehabilitation Services.

Guerra, P. L., & Nelson, S. W. (2009). Changing professional practice requires changing beliefs. *Phi Delta Kappan, 90*(05), 354–359.

Guskey, T. (2001). *High percentages are not the same as high standards.* Bloomington, IN: Phi Delta Kappan.

Hattie, J. (2012). *Visible learning for teachers: Maximizing impact on learning.* New York: Routledge.

Hawley, W. D., & Valli, L. (1999). The essentials of effective professional development: A new consensus. In L. Darling-Hammond & G. Sykes (Eds.), *Teaching as the learning profession: Handbook of policy and practice* (pp. 127–150). San Francisco: Jossey-Bass.

Heibert, J., Gallimore, R., & Stigler, J. W. (2002). A knowledge base for the teaching profession: What would it look like and how can we get one? *Educational Researcher, 31*(5), 3–15.

Herrera, S. (2010). *Biography-driven culturally responsive teaching.* New York: Teachers College Press.

Hoffman, L. (2011). Emotions affect cognitions. When emotions are strong our cognitive functions are profoundly affected. *Psychology Today.* Retrieved from https://www.psychologytoday.com/blog/beyond-freud/201110/emotions-affect-cognitions.

Hord, S., Roussin, J. L., & Sommers, W.A. (2009). *Guiding professional learning communities: Inspiration, challenge.* Retrieved from http://pages.solution-tree.com/rs/solutiontree/images/MarzanoTeacherEvaluationModel.pdf

Howard, G. R. (2015). *We can't lead where we won't go.* Thousand Oaks, CA: Corwin.

Hunter, R. (2004). *Madeline Hunter's mastery teaching.* Thousand Oaks, CA: Corwin.

Hunzicker, J. (2004). The beliefs-behavior connection: Leading teachers toward change. The key to changing teachers' behavior is to change their basic beliefs. *Principal, 84*(2), 44–46.

Joyce, B., & Showers, B. (2002). *Student achievement through staff development* (3rd ed.) Alexandria, VA: Association for Supervision and Curriculum Development.

Kee, K., Anderson, K., Dearing, V., Harris, E., & Shuster, F. (2010). *Coaching results: The new essential for school leaders.* Thousand Oaks, CA: Corwin.

Klinger, J. K., Artiles, A. J., Kozleski, E., Harry, B., Zion, S., Tate, W., Duran, G. Z., & Riley, D. (2005). Addressing the disproportionate representation of culturally and linguistically diverse students in special education through culturally responsive educational systems. *Education Policy Analysis Archives, 13,* 1–42.

Kolb, D. A. (1984). *Experiential learning: Experience as the source of learning and development.* Englewood Cliffs, NJ: Prentice Hall.

Kotter, J. (2008). *A sense of urgency.* Boston: Harvard Business Press.

Ladson-Billings, G. (1994). *The dreamkeepers.* San Francisco: Jossey-Bass.

Ladson-Billings, G., & Gomez, , M. L. (2001). Just showing up: Supporting early literacy through teachers' professional communities. *Phi Delta Kappan, 82*(9), 675–680.

Lambert, L., Walker, D., Zimmerman, J. E., Cooper, J. E., Lambert, M. D., Garner, M. E., & Slack, P. J. F. (1995). *The constructivist leader.* New York: Teachers College Press.

Langer, G. (1999, 2001). Unpublished program evaluation studies.

Langer, G. M., & Colton, A. B. (2005). Looking at student work. Growing schools' capacity for learning. *Educational Leadership, 62*(5), 22–27.

Langer, G., & Colton, A. (2006, 2007, 2008, 2011). Unpublished program evaluation studies.

Langer, G.M., Colton, A. B., & Goff, L. S. (2003). *Collaborative analysis of student work: Improving teaching and learning.* Alexandria, VA: Association for Supervision and Curriculum Development.

Langer, M., & Colton, A. B. (2005). Looking at student work. *Educational Leadership, 62*(5), 22–27.

Learning Forward. (2011). *Standards for professional learning.* Oxford, OH. Author.

Leithwood, K., Louis, K., Anderson, S., & Wahlstrom, K. (2004) *Learning for Leadership Project: Review of research, how leadership influences student learning.* New York, NY: The Wallace Foundation.

Lindsey, D. B., Martinez, R. S., & Lindsey, R. B. (2006). *Culturally proficient coaching: Supporting educators to create equitable schools.* Thousand Oaks, CA: Corwin.

Lindsey, R. B., Kikanza, J., Robins, K. N., & Terrell, R. D. (2009). *Cultural proficiency: A manual for school leaders.* Thousand Oaks, CA: Corwin.

Literacy and Numeracy Secretariat. (2010). *Capacity building series: Collaborative teacher inquiry.* Special edition #16. Retrieved from http://www.edu.gov.on.ca/eng/literacynumeracy/inspire/research/CBS_Collaborative_Teacher_Inquiry.pdf.

Little, J. W. (1993). *Teachers professional development in a climate of reform.* New York: National Center for Restructuring Education, Schools and Teaching.

Little, J. W. (1999). Organizing schools for teacher learning. In L. Darling-Hammond & G. Sykes (Eds.). *Teaching as the learning professional: Handbook of policy and practice* (pp. 233–262). San Francisco: Jossey-Bass.

Little, J. W., Gearhart, M., Curry, M., & Kafka, J. (1999). Looking at student work for teacher learning, teacher community, and school reform. *Phi Delta Kappan, 85*, 184–192.

Love, N. B., Stiles, K. E., Mundry, S. E., & DiRanna, K. (2008). *The data coach's guide to improving learning for all students: Unleashing the power of collaborative inquiry.* Thousand Oaks, CA: Corwin.

Loyd, J. W. (2006). *Collaborative learning communities: Influences on teacher and student learning.* Dissertation study, Wayne State University.

Lynn, M., Bacon, J. N., Totten, T. L., Bridges, T. L. III, & Jennings, M. E. (2010). Examining teachers' beliefs about African American male students in a low-performing high school in an African American school district. *Teachers College Record, 112*(1), 289–330.

Marchese, T. J. (1997). The new conversations about learning: Insights from neuroscience, and anthropology, cognitive science, and work-place studies. In *Assessing impact: Evidence and action* (pp.79–95). Washington, DC: American Association for Higher Education.

Marzano, R. (2011). The Marzano teacher evaluation model. Englewood, CO: Marzano Research Laboratory. Retrieved from http://www.marzanoevaluation.com/evaluation/causal_teacher_evaluation_model/

Marzano, R. (2011). *The Marzano teacher evaluation model.* Englewood, CO: Marzano Research Laboratory. Retrieved from http://pages.solution-tree.com/rs/solutiontree/images/MarzanoTeacherEvaluationModel.pdf

Marzano, R. J., Waters, T., & McNulty, B. A. (2005). *School leadership that works: From research to results.* Alexandria, VA: Association for Supervision and Curriculum Development.

McLaughlin, M. W., & Talbert, J. (1993). *Context that matters for teaching and learning.* Stanford, CA: Stanford University, Context Center on Secondary School Teaching.

Mezirow, J. (1995). Transformation theory of adult learning. In M. R. Welton (Ed.) *In defense of the lifeworld* (pp. 39–70). New York: SUNY Press.

Mezirow, J. (2000). *Learning as transformation: Critical perspectives on a theory in progress.* San Francisco: Jossey-Bass.

Miller, B., & Kantrov, I. (1998). *A guide to facilitating cases in education.* Portsmouth, NH: Heinemann.

National Board for Professional Teaching Standards. (1987). *The five core propositions.* Arlington, VA: Author. Retrieved from http://www.nbpts.org/five-core-propositions

Nelson, T. H., Slavit, D., Perkins, M., & Hathorn, T. (2008). The culture of collaborative inquiry: Learning to develop and support professional learning communities. *Teachers College Record, 11*(6), 1269–1303.

Nelson, T., & Slavit, D. (2008). Supported teacher collaborative inquiry. *Teacher Education Quarterly, 35*(1), 99–116.

Newmann, F., & Wehlage, G. (April 1993). Authentic learning: Five standards of authentic instruction. *Educational Leadership, 50*(7), 8–12.

Noddings, N. (1984). *Caring: A feminine approach to ethics and moral education.* Berkeley, CA: University of California Press.

Ott, J. S. (1989). *The organizational culture perspective.* Pacific Grove, CA: Brooks/Cole.

Perie, M., Moran, R., & Lutkus, A. D. (2005). *NAEP 2004 trends in academic progress: Three decades of student performance in reading and mathematics (NCES 2005–464).* U.S. Department of Education, Institute of Education Sciences, National Center for Education Statistics. Washington, DC: Government Printing Office.

Pohan, C. A. (1996). Preservice teachers' beliefs about diversity: Uncovering factors leading to multicultural responsiveness. *Equity & Excellence in Education, 29*(3), 62–69.

Pugach, M., & Johnson, C. (1990). Fostering the continued democratization of consultation through action research. *Teacher Education and Special Education, 13*(3–4), 240–245.

Putnam, R. T., & Borko, H. (2000, January/February). What do new views of knowledge and thinking have to say about research on teacher learning? *Educational Researcher, 29*(1), 4–15.

Reeves, D. (2002) Galileo's dilemma: The illusion of scientific certainty in educational research. *Education Week.* May 8, 2002.

Resnick, L. B., & Klopfer, L. E. (1989). Toward the thinking curriculum: An overview. In L. B. Resnick & L. E. Klopfer (Eds.). *Toward the thinking curriculum: Current cognitive research.* Alexandria, VA: Association for Supervision and Curriculum Development.

Rogoff, B. (1990). *Apprenticeship in thinking.* New York: Oxford University Press.

Rosenholz, J. (1989). *Teachers workplace.* New York: Longman.

Routman, R. (2014). *Read, write, lead: Breakthrough strategies for schoolwide literacy success.* Alexandria, VA: ASCD.

Schon, D. A. (1987). *Educating the reflective practitioner*. San Francisco: Jossey-Bass.

Senge, P. M. (1990). *The fifth discipline. The art and practice of the learning organization*. New York: Doubleday Currency.

Senge, P. M., Kleiner, A., Roberts, C., Ross, R. B., & Smith, B. J. (1994). *The fifth discipline fieldbook*. New York: Currency.

Shulman, L. S. (1986). Paradigms and research programs in the study of teaching: A contemporary perspective. In M. C. Wittrock (Ed.), *Handbook of research on teaching* (3rd ed., pp.3–36). New York: Macmillan Publishing.

Shulman, L. S. (1987). Knowledge and teaching: Foundations of the new reform. *Harvard Educational Review, 57*(1), 1–22.

Sinek, S. (2009). *Start with why: How great leaders inspire everyone to take action*. New York: Portfolio, Penguin Group.

Singleton, G. E., & Linton, C. W., (Eds.) (2005*). Courageous conversations about race: A field guide for achieving equity in schools*. Thousand Oaks, CA: Corwin.

Southwest Educational Development Laboratory. (2000). Launching professional learning communities: Beginning actions. *Issues About Change, 8*(1), 1–16. Retrieved from http://www.sedl.org/change/issues/issues81/issues-8.1.pdf.

Sparks, D. (2002). *Designing powerful professional development for teachers and principals*. Oxford, OH: National Staff Development Council.

Sparks, D. (2005). *Leading for results: Transforming teaching, learning, and relationships in school*. Thousand Oaks, CA: Corwin.

Sparks, G. M., Simmons, J. M., Pasch, M., Colton, A., & Starko, A. (1990). Reflective pedagogical thinking: How can we promote it and measure it? *Journal of Teacher Education, 41*(4), 23–32.

Thompson, C. L., & Zeuli, J. S. (1999). The frame and the tapestry: Standards-based reform and professional development. In L. Darling-Hammond & G. Sykes (Eds.), *Teaching and learning profession: Handbook of policy and practice*. San Francisco: Jossey-Bass.

Tschannen-Moran, M. (2004). *Trust matters: Leadership for successful schools*. San Francisco: Jossey-Bass.

Valencia, R. R. (Ed.) (1997). *The evolution of deficit thinking: Educational thought and practice*. The Stanford Series on Education and Public Policy. New York: Routledge Farmer.

Van Manen, M. (1977). Linking ways of knowing with ways of being practical. *Curriculum Inquiry, 6*, 205–228.

Vygotsky, L. S. (1978). *Mind in society: The development of higher psychological processes*. Cambridge, MA: Harvard University Press.

Wallace Foundation. (2013). *The school principal as leader: Guiding schools to better teaching and learning*. New York: Author.

Wasserman, S. (1994). *Introduction to case method teaching: A guide to the galaxy*. New York: Teachers College Press.

Wellman, B., & Lipton, L. (2004). *Data-driven dialogue: A facilitator's guide to collaborative inquiry*. Sherman, CT: MiraVia.

Wellman, B., & Lipton, L. (2009). *Data-driven dialogue: A facilitator's guide to collaborative inquiry*. Sherman, CT: MiraVia, LLC.

Wells, G. (1999). *Dialogic inquiry: Towards a sociocultural practice and theory of education*. Cambridge: Cambridge University Press.

Wolf, P., & Brandt, R. (1988). How the brain learns. *Educational Leadership, 56*(3), 8–1.

Wood, J. T. (1999). *Interpersonal communication: Everyday encounters* (2nd ed.). Belmont, CA: Wadsworth Publishing Company.

Yankelovich, D. (1999). *Interpersonal communication: Everyday encounters* (2nd ed.). New York: Touchstone Books.

Yero, J. L. (2002). *Teaching in mind: How teacher thinking shapes education.* Hamilton, MT: MindFlight Publishing.

Zand, D. E. (1997). *The leadership triad: Knowledge, trust, and power.* New York: Oxford University Press.

Zeichner, K. M. (2003). Teacher research as professional development for P-12 educators in the USA. *Educational Action Research, 11*(2), 301–325.

Zeichner, K. M., & Liston, D. P. (1987). Teaching student teachers to reflect. *Harvard Educational Review, 57*(10), 23–48.

Index

A SAGE Company

Helping educators make the greatest impact

CORWIN HAS ONE MISSION: to enhance education through intentional professional learning.

We build long-term relationships with our authors, educators, clients, and associations who partner with us to develop and continuously improve the best evidence-based practices that establish and support lifelong learning.

Advancing professional learning for student success

Learning Forward (formerly National Staff Development Council) is an international association of learning educators committed to one purpose in K–12 education: Every educator engages in effective professional learning every day so every student achieves.